[美] 傅强（Robert Foster）著　王培洁　译

迈向国际人

MODERN LEADERSHIP STRATEGIES FROM

中国古老智慧激发现代领导力策略

ANCIENT CHINESE WISDOM

洋博士与孙子、商鞅、诸葛亮等智者超时空接触
纵论现代领导力策略及领袖魅力装备

31 DAYS TO GREATER SUCCESS

北方文艺出版社

图书在版编目（CIP）数据

迈向国际人 /（美）傅强著；王培洁译 . — 哈尔滨：北方文艺出版社，2007.03（2012.5 重印）

ISBN 978-7-5317-1976-2

Ⅰ. ①迈… Ⅱ. ①傅… ②王… Ⅲ. ①领导学 Ⅳ. ① C933

中国版本图书馆 CIP 数据核字（2007）第 024661 号

迈向国际人——中国古老智慧激发现代领导力策略

作　　者 / [美] 傅强
责任编辑 / 徐秀梅　于祺盛
封面设计 / 门乃婷工作室
出版发行 / 北方文艺出版社
地　　址 / 哈尔滨市道里区经纬街 26 号
网　　址 / http://www.bfwy.com
邮　　编 / 150010
电子信箱 / bfwy@bfwy.com
经　　销 / 新华书店
印　　刷 / 环球印刷（北京）有限公司
开　　本 / 960×640　1/16
印　　张 / 19.25
字　　数 / 100 千
版　　次 / 2007 年 4 月第 1 版
印　　次 / 2012 年 5 月第 2 次印刷
定　　价 / 28.80 元
书　　号 / ISBN 978-7-5317-1976-2

Endorsements
名家推荐

I am a student of history, and I believe some of the best lessons we can learn are lessons from history. Rob Foster has done an excellent job drawing the very best lessons of Chinese wisdom from Chinese history. I believe this book on leadership success will help many people like me become better leaders.

—— Jon R. Wallace (President, Azusa Pacific University,DBA)

我喜欢从历史中学习，也一直认为历史是最好的老师。傅强博士从中国的历史中发掘出最好的智慧和训导。我相信，这本关于成功领导力的书籍可以帮助很多人，也包括我自己，成为更卓越的领袖。

——乔恩·R. 华莱士（阿苏撒太平洋大学校长，经营管理学博士）

The characteristics of a good leader remain a mystery to many people. A better understanding of leadership is especially important for China, as the nation and its people assume a greater role in the world of the twenty-first century. Rob Foster responds to this need in this very helpful book. Foster uses examples from China and around the world to explain how one can become a good leader, and the daily studies and questions encourage readers to see how they can become better leaders themselves. Anyone who reads this book will soon experience what real leadership is all about.

——John Copeland Nagle (John N. Matthews Professor of Law and Associate Dean for Faculty Research, University of Notre Dame)

好领袖的特征对于很多数人来说仍是一个迷。中国以及中国人在二十一世纪的世界中已经越来越重要，更好地理解领导力对这个国家来说尤为重要。傅强博士的这本书回应了这样的需要。本书的例子涵盖了中国的和世界的领导力典范，揭示了成为好领袖的秘诀。每天的学习和思考可以帮助读者懂得如何成为更好的领袖。任何阅读本书的读者将很快领悟到真正的领导力到底是怎么回事。

——约翰·卡布兰德·奈格博士（圣母大学法律教授，教研副主任）

Acknowledgements

First, I would like to thank my wife and my four children for their daily support and encouragement. I have learned through the years that dedicated friends are also an indispensable part of a successful life. Many friends supported the development of this book emotionally, financially, and logistically. I would like to thank, Nate Daeger, Rob Eberz, Doug Fike, Kenn Gulliksen, Tom Jennings, Rick Laymon, Paul Nelson, Dan Palmateer, John Robb, Sam and Patty Stallings, Graeme and Nicola Winthrop, and Sherry Young. Special thanks to my ever encouraging chief editor April Stier, Carol Berry for sacrificially offering her time as a copy editor, and Lucy Wang for translation. I would also like to express my appreciation to Rob Tucker and the entire staff at ZDL for editing and layout.

致　谢

首先，我想感谢妻子和四个孩子，谢谢他们每天的支持和鼓励。多年以来，我认识到好朋友是成功生活密不可分的组成部分。很多朋友在情感上、经济上和事务上支持这本书的出版。我想感谢内特·达格(Nate Daeger)、艾博(Rob Eberz)、汤姆·詹宁斯（Tom Jennings)、道格·凡克（Doug Fike)、肯·盖里格森（Kenn Gulliksen)、里克·莱曼(Rick Laymon)、保罗·纳尔逊（Paul Nelson)、但·帕尔玛提尔（Dan Palmateer)、约翰·罗布(John Robb)、萨姆·斯陶令和他的妻子派蒂(Sam and Patty Stallings)、文委汉、卫旎(Graeme and Nicola Winthrop)，以及杨雪莉(Sherry Young)。特别感谢主编埃普瑞尔·斯提尔(April Stier)，也谢谢卡罗尔·拜莉（Carol Berry）成为本书的编辑，为本书无私地奉献自己的才华。也感谢王培洁的翻译，以及 ZDL 的唐可（Rob Tucker）及其全体员工，谢谢你们的文字编辑和版式设计。

About the Author

Dr. Robert Foster currently lives in Beijing with his wife and four children. Dr. Foster holds a Bachelor degree in Elementary Education, a Master of Science and Administration from the University of Notre Dame, and a Doctorate in Educational Leadership and Administration from Azusa Pacific University. He previously taught at Beijing University in the department of International Studies, and now divides his time among directing study abroad programs (hosted in China, New Zealand, Australia, and the U.S.A), leadership consulting, writing, and speaking. His hobbies include running marathons, lifting weights, and acting. He regularly appears on Chinese television in advertisements for companies such as Bank of China, China Life, and others. Out of his great love for China and his home country, the U.S.A, he has developed a passion to help both countries learn from one another and benefit from their rich cultures and heritages.

For additional resources and training offered by Dr.Robert Foster visit :

http://www.summitu.com/

作者简介

傅强博士（Dr. Robert Foster）目前和妻子以及四个孩子住在北京。傅强博士曾获得圣母大学（University of Notre Dame）教育学士学位、科学与管理硕士学位，以及加州阿苏撒太平洋大学（Azusa Pacific University）教育领袖和管理博士学位。他曾经在北京大学国际关系学院任教，现在指导海外交流项目（在中国、新西兰、澳大利亚和美国举办），致力于领导力培训、写作和演讲。他爱好马拉松赛跑、举重和表演。他常常出现在中国的广告片中，曾经为中国银行、中国人寿保险等公司拍过广告。他深爱中国和自己祖国——美国，热心帮助两个国家的人民互相学习，彼此借鉴丰富的文化遗产。

要了解傅强博士提供的更多资料和培训信息，请访问：

http://www.summitu.com/

Introduction

Bookstore shelves around the world are stocked with titles dealing with success and leadership. Some focus on the life of a famous or wealthy individual like Donald Trump or Bill Gates. Others take a more academic or MBA approach. Still other books such as *The Art of War* or *The Analects of Confucius* have become classics by standing the test of time. The book you are now holding is unique in that it draws from all three of the above-mentioned sources. The world in which we currently live is moving faster and becoming more complex every day. To survive in the years to come, individuals in business, government, and the non-profit world will have to learn from the past, understand the present, and envision the future. You will need to think quicker, work smarter, dream wilder, and relate to each other in many different ways.[1]

Throughout the book I will allude to your team. By "team" I refer to the people around you that help you reach your goals. For many, your team will be coworkers or employees. Some of your teams may be your family or a small group in a social organization. Regardless of who constitutes your team, the principles enumerated in the following chapters will help you succeed in reaching goals and accomplishing more than you ever thought possible. The leadership principles offered in this book will draw out the leader within you and help you maximize the gifts and talents of your team for success.

前　言

在世界各地的书店中，成功学和领导力的书籍汗牛充栋。有的描述名人或有钱人的生活，如唐纳德·特朗普（Donald Trump）或比尔·盖茨；有的从学术或商业管理的角度入手；有的则经历了时间的考验，成为历久弥新的经典之作，如《孙子兵法》和《论语》。你手中这本书的独到之处在于它结合了以上三者。当今世界越来越复杂，人们前进的步伐越来越快。今天商界、政界和非赢利组织中的人们，要想在将来站稳脚跟，就必须要从历史中学习、了解当今世界并且能够预测未来走向，才能具备敏捷的思维和宽广的视野，在工作中更有头脑，以不同的方式与他人交往。[1]

我会在书中反复提到团队。我所指的“团队”是你周围的人，他们在帮助你共同完成你的目标。对很多人来说，你的团队就是同事或员工。团队的一个组成部分也可能是你的家人或社会机构中的小组。不论团队的组成人员如何，以后几章所列举的原则会帮助你成功达到目标，甚至超越你的极限。本书中的领袖原则可以发掘你内在的领导力，帮助你最大程度地发挥团队的恩赐，共同跨向卓越。

How to Read This Book

The 31 short chapters contained in this book have been written to inspire you to become a more successful person. I hope you enjoy each section and are personally challenged. My greatest desire, however, is for you to apply the principles set before you. If you fail to apply the principles in each chapter, you will regrettably miss the point for which this book was written. I believe the best way to approach this book is to read one chapter a day.

Each chapter presents a theme, starting with a gem or two of wisdom from China's rich history to illustrate the theme. Then I discuss the topic in a way I hope will inspire you to learn more about yourself and your style of leadership. I end with suggestions for application, questions to ponder, or principles to apply. The space provided at the end of each chapter is for you to make notes to yourself about areas for further investigation and growth. Each chapter can help you in your unique situations at work, home, or with friends. I also recommend that you invite one or more friends to join you in your journey of becoming more successful. The journey of self-improvement is like many other adventures — it is more enjoyable when shared! If you're a leader, I encourage you to take the next month and use this book as a training manual for improving your team.

Are you ready to release the leadership gifts within you? Are you ready to see your most important relationships improve by 50-100 percent? Are you ready to be more successful in your work and social circles? The only element required is your genuine willingness to learn and to put into practice what you read in the following chapters. Your life will change — not miraculously, not overnight — but one relationship at a time. If you are one of the adventurers ready to begin an exciting journey of self-improvement and success, I invite you to turn the page.

如何阅读本书

本书共包括31章，旨在激发你的灵感，帮助你更上一层楼。我盼望每一章的内容都能引起你的共鸣，享受阅读的乐趣。然而，我最大的愿望就是你能够把这些原则应用在自己的生活中。假如你没有应用每章的原则，就错失了本书写作的目的。我相信阅读本书的最佳方式就是一天一章。

每章都列出了一个主题，以中国历史中的一两句箴言开篇，说明主题。之后，我会就此主题展开讨论，希望能够启迪你，帮助你更多地了解自我以及你的领导风格。结尾处有建议性的应用材料、思考问题或应用原则，还提供空白处，供你做笔记，记录要探讨的问题和个人成长过程。不论你是上班、在家还是和朋友在一起，每章的内容都能够在特定的环境中帮助你。我也建议你找一两个或几个朋友加入你的行列，一起踏上成功之旅。改进自我的过程如同其他旅程，当你与他人共享时，快乐也加倍！如果你是一位领袖，我鼓励你下个月用这本书做培训资料，和你的团队一起改变！

你准备好要释放自己内在的领导力吗？你准备好迎接改变，以50%－100%的速度拓展重要的人际关系吗？你准备好在自己的工作领域和社交领域获得更大的成功吗？你唯一要做的就是发自内心地学习本书，然后将所学到的付诸行动。你的生活——并非奇迹般地在一夜之间——发生巨变，而是每次改变一个方面。如果你是一个敢于冒险的人，并且作好了准备，想要踏上自我改善与成功之旅，那么我邀请你翻开下一页。

Table of Contents

目　录

其身正，不令而行；其身不正，虽令不从。

——孔子[1]

If a man is righteous, people will follow him without being told; but if he is not, then no amount of orders will make them follow him.

——*Confucius*[1]

弹性策略

Resilient Strategies

第一天　程不识PK李广
——领袖的风格

Day 1:Leadership Style

花时间了解并培养你的领袖能力，会让你对周围的人产生很大的影响力。

By taking the time to recognize and develop your leadership abilities, you can have a great impact on those around you.

If a man is righteous, people will follow him without being told; but if he is not, then no amount of orders will make them follow him.

—— *Confucius* [1]

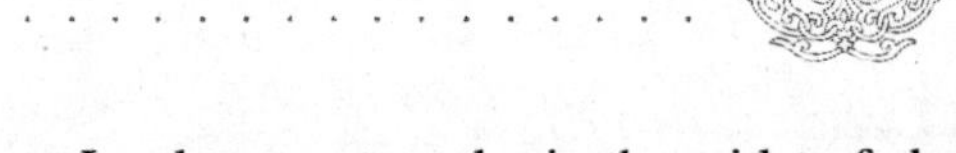

Leaders create order in the midst of chaos. They turn crisis situations into tales of victory. People naturally flock to leaders in times of uncertainty. These are the effects and results of leaders, but what does a leader look like? Would I know a truly great leader if I saw one? How can we find them among the many circles of people that make up our lives? How can I develop leadership skills in myself? The following chapter will answer these questions and offer several serious questions to ponder.

Most people have a fairly narrow view of leadership. They only view leaders as top business executives or government leaders such as presidents or prime ministers. Leaders in these positions do guide large numbers of people; however, leadership does not happen only at the head of an organization. People who manage small work teams, motivate coworkers to keep a positive attitude during stressful times, and keep their family relationships strong are also leaders. In one way or another, every person makes at least one leadership decision every day.

You have leadership abilities within you. Your world has a great need for dynamic leadership. Without leadership, the success of families, charity groups, religious organizations, sports teams, civic associations, and social clubs rests solely on chance. By taking the time to recognize and develop your leadership abilities, you can have a great impact on those around you.

Great companies all start with an idea and people willing to lead. Steve Jobs and Steven Wozniak, ages twenty-one and twenty-six, believed in and understood this concept. With almost no money and no real business experience, they entered an industry that barely existed. In 1976, only a few brainy techies had computers

其身正，不令而行；其身不正，虽令不从。

——孔子[1]

译文：上级行为端正，不发命令下级也会很好地完成；上级行为不正，即使下了命令下级也不会听从。

领袖在混乱中制造秩序。他们能够把危机转化成胜利。在外界环境不确定的情况下，人们会自然而然地聚拢在领袖身边。这就是领袖的作用和带来的效果。但是，领袖是什么样的？如果我见到一个真正的领袖，能够识别出来吗？我的生活圈子中有那么多人，怎样才能找到他们呢？我又该怎样培养自己的领袖才华呢？以下的内容会回答这些问题，同时也会提出另外一些严肃的问题，让我们一起来思考。

大部分人对领袖的观念相对狭隘。他们认为领袖就是商界的总裁或政府的领导，如总统或总理。这些位置上的领袖的确引领很多人，但是领袖不仅仅只是那些机构的高层人物。有的人在管理小型工作团队、在压力下激励自己的同事保持积极心态，他们就是领袖；那些维系稳固家庭关系的人也是领袖。每个人每天都以这样或那样的方式至少作出一个领导力上的决定。

你的内心拥有领袖的才华。你所生活的世界也需要充满活力的领导人才。领袖的缺失会让家庭、慈善组织、宗教机构、运动团体、公民协会以及社会俱乐部完全处在运气和机遇的控制中。花时间了解并培养你的领袖能力，会让你对周围的人产生很大的影响。

回顾所有大公司的成长过程，都是从一个想法开始，并拥有愿意带领的人。史蒂夫·乔布斯（Steve Jobs）和史蒂夫·沃兹尼克亚（Steven Wozniak），一个21岁，一个26岁，他们相信并明白这个理念。他们既没有钱，也没有

in their homes. However, Jobs and Wozniak pulled together thirteen hundred dollars by selling a van and a couple of calculators and launched Apple Computer, Inc. Their business started in Job's garage and didn't draw a lot of national publicity. But they announced a new message: "Computers are going to be the bicycle of the mind. Low-cost computers are for everyone."[2] They sought to popularize computers among all of society, not just among wealthy, "nerdy" types, and shared their vision with everyone who would listen. Jobs and Wozniak didn't experience immediate success, but they didn't give up. Six years later, people finally caught the vision, and Apple Computers sold 650,000 personal computers that year.

Jobs and Wozniak developed their own vision and leadership style in order to succeed. Leaders come in all shapes and sizes and no two people are the same. As an example, two great generals in the Qin Dynasty were Chen Bushi and Li Guang. Both served as governors of frontier provinces and fought many battles against the Huns. According to tradition, Li Guang's strategy was very basic, and he enforced very little discipline among his troops. He had few rules and let his men relax when they found restful places with food and water. He didn't even place sentries on duty. In spite of his relaxed leadership style, he made great advances into enemy lands and never lost a battle.

Chen Bushi's leadership style was just the opposite. He placed sentries on duty day and night. His men were very disciplined. He stressed military formations and enforced strict rules. His men also fought many battles against the Mongolian Huns without loss. General Chen Bushi once commented on the simplicity of Li Guang's strategy. "If suddenly attacked, he will be taken by surprise. Still, his troops are always fresh and in good spirits and would gladly die for him. Our army routine may be irksome and intricate, but the enemy will never catch us napping."[3] This general had the wisdom to see that more than one style of leadership could be successful. The key is for leaders to apply the style of leadership that is most effective for them.

Some wrongly argue that one style of leadership is better than the rest. If your world is small enough and your life-leadership experience limited to very few people or only those of a similar age and background, you may hold to the belief that there is one, and only one, way to lead. However, talented leaders are as varied as leadership situations are different.

If you plan to model your life after the most successful leader you know, your method will surely fail. The best you could ever hope to become is a poor imita-

真正的商业经历，却踏入了一个几乎无人涉足的领域。1976年，只有少数技术精英的家中才有电脑。然而，乔布斯和沃兹尼克亚卖掉了一辆车和两个计算处理器，好不容易筹集了1300美元，创办了苹果公司。他们的生意从乔布斯家的车库中起步，没有在国内引起任何关注。[2]但是他们发布了全新的信息："电脑将要成为有头脑的自行车。价格低廉的自行车是每个人都能够拥有的。"他们在社会各阶层推广计算机的普及，而不仅仅让它局限在富有的人群和知识分子之中，他们和每个愿意聆听的人分享自己的愿景。乔布斯和沃兹尼克亚没有马上品尝到成功的滋味，但并没有放弃。六年后，人们终于认同他们的远见，当年他们销售了65万台苹果电脑。

乔布斯和沃兹尼克亚拥有成功所需要的愿景和领袖风格。领袖风格因人而异，没有完全相同的两个人。同样，汉朝的程不识和李广两位将军就是这样的典范。他们都是驻守边疆对抗匈奴的大将军。李广的战术很简单，他很少在军队中强调纪律。当部队驻扎下来吃饭喝水的时候，他就让士兵放松，规矩很少，没有严格的军队编制和军队纪律。他甚至不设置岗哨。虽然他的领导风格随意，他却能节节深入敌军守地，从未在一场战役中失败过。

程不识的领导风格则和李广完全相反。他日夜设置岗哨。他的部队纪律严明。他注重军事架构和严格的军纪。他的部队也在许多对抗匈奴的战役中屡战屡胜。程不识将军曾经这样评价李广的简单战术："假如他们被偷袭，就会受到出其不意的攻击。当然，他的部队总是精力充沛、士气高涨，甘愿为他牺牲自己的性命。我们的常规程序看起来繁琐，令人感到厌烦，但是敌人永远都逮不到我们打盹的时候。"[3]程将军是个很有智慧的人，他知道成功的领袖风格不是只有一种。关键是领袖们要使用最适合自己、最有效的领袖风格。

有些人徒劳地争辩，以为一种风格要比另外一种更加优越。假如你的世界很小，你一生的领袖经历也只局限在少数几个人，或是相同年龄和相同背景的一些人身上，那么你可以认为世界上只有一种领导模式。然而，才华横溢的领袖们所具有的领袖风格各不相同，就如领导的环境缤纷各异一般。

tion of the one you are trying to model. Instead, you must begin the lifelong journey of discovery into your own unique self. As you begin to discover who you really are, you can thoughtfully find your personal leadership style.

Application

◆ What qualities do you already have that can have a positive influence on others?

◆ What type of leaders do you enjoy spending time with? (Leaders are often attracted to other leaders who use methods like their own.)

◆ What qualities do you admire about them?

Notation Area

Personal observations/Ideas for further exploration/Thoughts to remember

如果你打算以自己所认识的最出色的领袖为模板来效法他，那么你一定会失败。你所期待的最佳状态也只不过是那位领袖一个蹩脚的仿制品。相反，假如你开始自己生命的旅程，发掘自己，了解自己的独特性，那么当你开始认识到自己是谁的时候，你就可以通过深思熟虑找到自己的领袖风格。

应用

◆你所拥有的哪些品质可以积极地影响他人？

◆你喜欢和什么类型的领袖相处？（一般情况下，领袖会被和自己风格类似的领袖吸引。）

◆你钦佩他们身上的哪些品质？

笔记

个人体会／要进一步探讨的想法／要铭记在心的理念

燕雀焉知鸿鹄之志哉？

——陈胜

How can a swallow know the aspirations of a swan?

—— *Chen Sheng*

敢于梦想

Dare to Dream

第二天 燕雀焉知鸿鹄之志哉
——领袖的特质

Day 2:Traits of Leaders

成功的领袖清楚自己的弱点，但会最大程度发挥自己的优势。

Successful leaders are aware of their weaknesses but maximize their strengths.

How can a swallow know the aspirations of a swan?

—— Chen Sheng

Chen Sheng was a poor common laborer around 208 BC during the Qin Dynasty. He neither owned land nor had any reputation. What he did posses was leadership traits. One day while resting on his plow, he said to the men working beside him, "If any one of us becomes rich and famous in the future, let him not forget the others."[1] The men only laughed at him for thinking he could ever become rich or famous. Chen Sheng sighed, then stated, "Oh, how can a swallow know the aspirations of a swan?"[2] Years later Chen Sheng fulfilled his ambitions when he led a successful uprising against the Qin Dynasty and was named king. The saying "How can a swallow know the aspiration of a swan?" became a common idiom to show the gap between leaders with vision and those who settle for mediocrity. If you posses leadership traits, you will likely be misunderstood by those who do not.

Sherry Young, my aunt, is a great example of a woman who chose to exemplify leadership. For many years Sherry had a successful career as a commercial artist in the newspaper industry. Her artwork won her respect from coworkers and many awards. In her forties she decided to go back to university and pursue a masters degree in counseling. Upon completion of her degree, she quit her newspaper career and helped to create Bridge Builders Counseling. She partnered with a leading counselor and visionary in the city, Dan Lundblad. With Dan's visionary and administrative skills and Sherry's passion to serve, they began an organization that helps single mothers and children of poor families. They serve children who have been abandoned, abused, neglected, and impoverished. Through Bridge Builders, poor single families are counseled on how to overcome hurts in their

燕雀焉知鸿鹄之志哉？

——陈胜

陈胜是一个普普通通的劳动者，他很穷，生活在公元前208年的秦朝。他既没有土地，也没有任何名气。他所拥有的是领袖的特质。一天，在田地里休息的时候，他对身边的人说："苟富贵，勿相忘。"[1]其他人大笑，因为他竟然以为自己有一天会发财或出名。陈胜叹了口气说："燕雀焉知鸿鹄之志哉？"[2]数年后，陈胜起义反抗秦朝，被推举为王，完成了他的志向。"燕雀焉知鸿鹄之志"也变成了人们的常用语，说明具备远大理想的领袖和满足于平庸生活的普通人之间的差距。假如你具备领袖特质，很可能你会被那些没有的人所误解。

我的阿姨杨雪莉（Sherry Young）就是这样一个典范，她选择了在领导力方面作出表率。雪莉一直在报界工作，而且是个成功的艺术家，她的成就赢得了同事的敬重以及各种奖项。她在四十多岁的时候决定返回大学读书，攻读心理咨询专业硕士学位。完成学业后，她辞掉了自己在报界的职业，和丹·莱姆布兰查德（Dan Lumblad）共同创立了"建桥心理咨询中心"（Bridge Builders Counseling）。丹是本城中一个很有名的心理咨询师，也是一个梦想家。丹的愿景和管理才能加上雪莉服务他人的热诚和激情，使他们共同致力于服务单亲妈妈和贫穷家庭的孩子。他们主要服务被遗弃、被虐待、被忽略和穷困无助的儿童。贫穷的单亲妈妈在"建桥"获得辅导，学习怎样抚平自己生命中的伤痕。孩子们也在非指导游戏疗法中，表达自己成长过程中受到

lives. Through nondirective play therapy, children are able to express hurtful events in their lives that have been suppressed by fear and false guilt. Young boys without fathers at home are matched with role models and mentors who encourage them to become men of character. All these services are reaching out to the poorest, most needy areas in the city.

Her decision to lead this organization and leave her commercial art career at the newspaper has meant sacrifice. The single parents and children she serves understand the life-transforming difference she is making. Some of her peers and family, however, only see her as making less money and working longer hours to keep the doors open of a struggling organization located in the poor part of the city. Many months she doesn't know where the money will come from to pay her salary and those of the staff. In spite of the challenges and difficulties, Bridge Builders has been open more than twelve years now and has helped hundreds of lives. Sherry has endured the challenges and enjoyed the reward of serving the unique vision in her heart.

Many of you will have opportunities to use your unique leadership traits. I have no doubt that you have leadership skills, but what remains to be seen is whether you choose to step up, use your skills, and become a successful leader of a team. If you do, you will have the privilege of spending your life on meaningful work that springs from passions in your own heart.

Ask the average person on the street what comes to mind when they think of good leaders, and you are likely to hear a list of character qualities and behaviors. The list would likely include traits such as intelligence, charisma, enthusiasm, strength, bravery, integrity, honesty, or self-confidence. Isolating characteristics that differentiate leaders from nonleaders has been a focus of research for years. Researchers have attempted to discover traits that commonly appear in all leaders. Although no common list has yet emerged, they have identified a number of traits consistently associated with leaders. Individuals who have some of these traits are more likely to be successful leaders than those who do not possess them. Seven traits that have been constant in differentiating leaders from nonleaders are as follows:

1. Drive-Leaders approach tasks with energy. They desire to succeed and achieve positive results. They show initiative and persistence. They also tackle ambitious tasks.

伤害的事件，他们以前一直因为恐惧和错误的罪咎感在压抑自己，不敢告诉他人自己身上发生的事情。缺失父亲的男孩儿们也在这里找到自己的榜样和导师，这些成年人鼓励他们、帮助他们成为品格高尚的人。他们致力于扶助城里面最贫穷和最急需帮助的区域。

她离开了自己的报界生涯，创办这样的机构，这个决定本身就意味着牺牲。她所服务的母亲和孩子们明白她给他们的生命带来的改变。然而，她的一些同事和家人却只看到她挣钱比从前少多了，工作时间更长了，勉强支撑一个坐落在城市贫穷地区的机构，以使它不会关门大吉。她好几个月都不知道自己要从哪里筹钱支付自己和员工的工资。尽管面对重重困难的挑战，“建桥”迄今为止已经运营十年了，帮助了数百个生命。雪莉迎接着各样挑战，享受着梦想成真带来的乐趣和奖赏。你们中间很多人都有机会使用自己独特的领袖特质。我坚信你们具备领袖技能，但是我们需要看到的就是你是否选择跨出去，成为一个团队成功的领袖。如果你做到了，你就拥有一份特权，让自己的生命致力于有意义的工作，做自己内心所渴望的、让自己充满激情的事情。

如果你在大街上询问一个人，谈到好领袖的时候他心中想到了什么，你很可能会听到一长串儿的品格和行为。这份清单很可能会包括聪明、领袖魅力、热情、力量、勇敢、正直、诚实或自信等。人们多年来一直在研究，到底哪些特点把领袖和跟随者区分出来。研究者努力了解所有领袖都具有的特质。虽然没有列出一份放之四海而皆准的清单，但是他们发现了常常和领袖联系在一起的一些特质。拥有这些特质的人比没有的人更容易成为卓越的领袖。下面的七个特质常常可以把领袖和跟随者区分开来：

1. 动力——领袖做事时充满干劲。他们渴望成功，获得积极的结果。他们表现出主动性和韧性，也愿意处理具有挑战性的任务。
2. 领导的愿望——领袖希望自己能够影响他人和周围的环境。他们甘愿跨出去，承担带领的职责。他们甘愿冒险，不怕失败会影响自己的名誉。

2. Desire to Lead-Leaders want to influence people and situations. They willingly step up to lead. They are not afraid to put their name and reputation on the line.
3. Honesty-Leaders place a high premium on trust. They extend trust and build trust among others. They do this by being truthful in their words and actions. They do not slander others at any time, including when the people are not around.
4. Self-confidence-Leaders have a high level of self-confidence. This helps produce security in followers. Followers want to believe leaders know what they are doing.
5. Intelligence-Leaders need to possess a fairly high level of intelligence, especially in the areas of problem solving and vision casting. They need to process information from a variety of sources, synthesize it, interpret it, and make solid decisions based upon that information.
6. Good Communication-Leaders need to communicate clearly to followers. Communication is essential to cast vision, build trust, and encourage others in the midst of difficulty.
7. Job-relevant Knowledge-Leaders know their industry or area of influence. Knowledge and experience give leaders great perspective. Perspective allows leaders to make wise decisions with an understanding of future ramifications.[3]

You should seek to maximize strengths while shoring up weaknesses. One way to maximize strengths is to accept jobs that allow you to use them. You can build up weaknesses by developing a team with different giftings. You should also seek to improve your personal skills whenever possible.

3. 诚实——领袖看重彼此的信任。他们信任他人，也在人与人之间建立信任感。他们言行一致，为他人作出表率。他们在任何时候都不会诽谤他人，即使当事人不在场的时候也不会这样做。

4. 自信——领袖很自信。这有助于给跟随者带来安全感。跟随者希望看到一个事实，就是领袖知道自己在做什么。

5. 聪明——领袖需要有相当高程度的智慧，特别是在解决问题和规划愿景方面。他们需要处理各个方面的资讯，之后进行分析和诠释，最后根据资讯作出可靠的决定。

6. 良好的沟通——领袖需要和跟随者进行清楚的沟通。沟通是规划愿景、建立信任和在患难中鼓励他人的重要方法。

7. 与工作相关的知识——领袖了解自己所处的行业和具有影响力的领域。知识和经历带给领袖洞察力。洞察力帮助领袖了解未来的走向，作出明智的决定。[3]

你应该在弥补自己弱点的同时最大程度地发挥自己的优势。发挥自己优势的一种方法就是从事能够发挥自己优势的工作。你可以培养一个由拥有不同恩赐的人组成的团队，来弥补自己的弱点。你也要抓住每一个机会来改善自己的个人技巧。

Application

- ◆ Do a self-assessment using the above seven traits.
- ◆ How would you rate yourself from 1 to 5 on each trait?
- ◆ Which traits are your strengths?
- ◆ Are there any traits you need to improve?
- ◆ How would you list them in order of importance?
- ◆ Write down one way you can maximize your strengths or improve a weaker area today.

Notation Area

Personal observations/Ideas for further exploration/Thoughts to remember

应用

◆使用以上七个特质进行自我评估。

◆在1到5的计分栏中，你怎样评估自己的每项特质？

◆哪个特质是你的强项？

◆哪个特质是你需要改善的？

◆按照重要程度，你怎样给它们排序？

◆写下你今天以哪种方式可以最大程度地发挥自己的优势或改善自己的弱点。

笔记

个人体会／要进一步探讨的想法／要铭记在心的理念

因为我想过，强大的秦国不敢来侵犯赵国，就因为有我和廉将军两人在。要是秦国知道我们俩不和，就会趁机来侵犯赵国。两虎相争，必有一伤。我把国家的利益看得比私人的恩怨更重。

——蔺相如

It is my belief that, if not for General Lian Po's strength and my wisdom, the mighty king of Qin would invade Zhao. When two tigers fight, one must perish. I put the good of the country before private quarrels.

—— Lin Xiangru

将相和

Seeing the Truth

第三天 负荆请罪
——团队协作

Day 3:Teamwork

好领袖不会计较个人的名利。

Great leaders are not preoccupied with their own fame.

It is my belief that, if not for General Lian Po's strength and my wisdom, the mighty king of Qin would invade Zhao. When two tigers fight, one must perish. I put the good of the country before private quarrels.

——Lin Xiangru

Lin Xiangru served as minister for the king of Zhao. The king of Qin was looking for an opportunity to invade Zhao. On one occasion, Lin Xiangru entered into a battle of words with the ministers of Qin. His wisdom proved superior, thus averting war and saving the honor of the king of Zhao. As a reward, he was appointed chief minister of Zhao. His appointment angered Lian Po, a mighty general of Zhao. Lian Po felt he deserved the position and argued that Lin Xiangru's only asset was his ability to talk. He, on the other hand, had risked his life many times and conquered many cities for the kingdom. His jealousy consumed him, and he vowed to kill Lin Xiangru the next time they met. As a result, Lin Xiangru avoided him. Many of Lin Xiangru's protégés saw his actions as cowardly and began to leave him. Lin Xiangru asked his protégés, "Who is more powerful, General Lian Po or the king of Qin?" Without hesitation, they all answered, "The king of Qin." Lin Xiangru replied, "Then answer me this. If I, cowardly as I am in your eyes, am not afraid to lash out at the mighty king of Qin and his ministers in his court, why would I fear Lian Po?" He continued to explain: "It is my belief that, if not for General Lian Po's strength and my wisdom, the mighty king of Qin would invade Zhao. When two tigers fight, one must perish. I put the good of the country before private quarrels."[1] When Lian Po heard this, he came and bowed before Lin Xiangru with his back bare and a cane in his hand. After this, Lian Po and Lin Xiangru became close friends.

When personal pride and ambition control leaders' decisions, the organization will suffer. Great leaders are not preoccupied with their own fame. When you focus on your own needs or ambitions, you often overlook the team's greater purpose.

因为我想过，强大的秦国不敢来侵犯赵国，就因为有我和廉将军两人在。要是秦国知道我们俩不和，就会趁机来侵犯赵国。两虎相争，必有一伤。我把国家的利益看得比私人的恩怨更重。

——蔺相如

蔺相如是赵国的宰相。当时，秦王总想找机会入侵赵国。蔺相如曾经和秦王进行了一次舌战。他智慧超群，避免了一场恶战，同时也保住了赵王的尊严。他因此被拜为上卿。这惹恼了赵国的大将军廉颇。廉颇认为这个位置应该是自己的，认为蔺相如唯一的本领就是能言善道。他自己曾多次冒着生命危险，为国家攻占了许多城池。他陷入嫉妒之中，扬言下次见到蔺相如时要羞辱他。结果，蔺相如总是躲着他，绕道而行。蔺相如的门生认为他胆小如鼠，渐渐开始离开。蔺相如问自己的门生："廉将军跟秦王比，哪一个势力大？"他们毫不犹豫地回答："当然是秦王势力大。"蔺相如回答道："对呀！天下的诸侯都怕秦王。为了保卫赵国，我都敢当面责备他，怎么我见了廉将军反倒害怕了呢？"他这样解释："因为我想过，强大的秦国不敢来侵犯赵国，就因为有我和廉将军两人在。要是秦国知道我们俩不和，就会趁机来侵犯赵国。两虎相争，必有一伤。我把国家的利益看得比私人的恩怨更重。"[1] 廉颇听到后，就来见蔺相如。他裸着上身，背着荆条，跪在蔺相如面前。之后，廉颇和蔺相如成了最要好的朋友。

假如领袖被个人的骄傲或野心掌控，他带领的机构就会受到损伤。好领袖不会计较个人的名利。假如你注重自己的需要或野心，就会忽略团队的使命。

团队协作是如今最看重的才能之一。即使一个人才华横溢，但是和那些学会团队协作的人相比，他也很难在效果上超越对方。哈佛商学院做过一次有趣的实验，读研究生一年级的学生不再进行传统的期中考试，而是被随机

The ability to work well with others is one of the most sought-after skills in the global workplace. Individuals, however talented, can seldom produce better results than those who learn to work with a team. Harvard's business school conducted an experiment with its first-year graduate students. Instead of the traditional midterm exam, the class was randomly placed in teams of four. Each team was given a business problem to solve together. Their midterm grade would be based on the result of the team's final solution. Students argued that their individual grade could suffer because of a problematic or difficult team member. Professors simply told the students, "Welcome to the real world." The experiment concluded successfully, and a great amount of learning took place.

Persuading a group of individuals to work together as a team is not an easy task. Leaders of the future will need to learn how to effectively create and motivate teams. In some ways, leading a team parallels coaching a sports team. Here are some basic coaching techniques that you need to create a winning team:

- Create a common vision—A vision can be agreed on by the team or set by the leader. In either case, the leader is responsible for keeping the vision clearly before the group.
- Make team goals—Great achievements are often the result of successfully accomplishing many smaller goals. Setting attainable goals focused on the prize will keep your team encouraged and motivated. As the leader, encourage your team to celebrate even small victories.
- Recognize the individual—A winning team has many players. Acknowledging the contributions of some of the less-obvious members can create great unity and keep your team working together.
- Share glory, accept blame—As the leader the buck stops with you. When complimented for success, seek to share the spotlight with members of your team. When the team fails or makes mistakes, accept the criticism without pointing out individuals. You will have time to deal with those who made the mistake later. Praise in public, correct in private.
- Stay connected—It's important to know your team on a personal level. Seek to have at least one point of relational connection with team members. The connection point may be something totally unrelated to work, such as family background, hobbies, sports, or common experiences. Connecting with your team on a personal level can help build a strong team culture.

Some young boys were playing by railroad tracks when they decided to test

分成四组，每组要共同解决一个商业难题。学生的期中考试成绩根据团队最终解决问题的结果而定。有的学生发出了抗议，担心自己个人的成绩会因为某个有问题的或学业不好的团队成员受到影响。教授轻描淡写地说了一句："欢迎你们进入现实社会。"实验结果很成功，学生们也学到了很多。

说服一群人携手合作并不容易。未来的领袖需要学习怎样有效地创建并激励团队。带领团队在很多方面就像训练运动队一样。作为一名教练，假如你希望创建一个成功的队伍，就需要具备一些基本的训练技巧：

● 拥有共同的愿景

愿景可以经团队认同产生，也可以由领袖来确立。不论愿景以怎样的模式怎样产生，领袖都需要担当自己的责任，让团队清晰地看到愿景。

● 制定团队目标

只有成功地完成无数小目标，才能成就大目标。设定可完成的目标，注重奖励，这样就能不断鼓励并激励你的团队。你作为团队领袖，需要鼓励团队为每个小小的胜利而庆贺。

● 认可每个人

一个成功的团队拥有很多选手，有些队员似乎不那么容易受到大家的关注。领袖认同他们的贡献可以让团队更团结，帮助团队共同协作。

● 分享荣誉，承担责任

责任系在领袖的身上。当你因为成功接受掌声的时候，你要和团队成员共同分享荣誉。当团队失败或犯错误的时候，领袖要接受指责，不要指出其他人的问题——你以后还会有机会处理犯错误的人。要当众夸奖，私下指正。

● 保持联络

和团队建立私人关系很重要。和团队成员至少在一个方面要建立关系。这些联系的层面可能完全和工作无关，如家庭背景、爱好、运动或共同的经历。从个人层面和团队建立关系有助于创建稳固的团队文化。

有的小男孩儿喜欢在铁轨上玩耍，测试自己的平衡能力。他们伸开双臂平衡自己的身体，全部排成一列，在狭窄的铁轨上行走。有的孩子平衡能力比别人强

迈向国际人

their balance. With their arms spread out for balance, they all lined up and attempted to walk the narrow tracks. Certain boys were better than others, but even those with the best balance only walked four meters before falling. This went on for some time until two of the smaller boys came up with an idea. They went up to the biggest boy and bet him a candy bar that they could both walk fifty meters on the tracks without falling. Seeing an easy candy bar, the biggest boy agreed. With the bet made and witnessed by the group, the two younger boys hopped onto the tracks, reached out, and locked their arms. Together their balance was perfect, and they easily walked the fifty meters. What was impossible for them individually was easily achieved with a partner.[2] These boys learned the power of teamwork, and they enjoyed the sweet reward that followed. Working together as a team requires hard work and commitment to relationships. Successful leaders make teamwork a top priority and enjoy the benefits that follow.

Application

- Assess your relationships within your team.
- Seek to connect personally with each team member at some level.
- Is your team clear about its vision? Ask different members what they think the team vision is. If they are not clear or don't care, you have some work to do.
- Take time to celebrate a team victory this week.

中国古老智慧激发现代领导力策略

Notation Area

Personal observations/Ideas for further exploration/Thoughts to remember

一些，但是即使平衡能力最好的孩子，也最多只能走四码，之后就会从上面掉了下来。这种状态持续了一段时间，后来有两个小男孩儿想出了个好主意。他们和最大的男孩儿打赌，以一大块巧克力作为赌注，赌他们两个都能在铁轨上走50米，中间不掉下来。大男孩儿觉得自己轻而易举就能赚到一块巧克力，就击掌同意了。两个小男孩儿在众目睽睽之下跳上了铁轨，伸出手来，挽住了对方的胳膊。这样，他们很容易掌握平衡，轻松地走完了50米。在一个人做起来难上加难的一件事，竟然在同伴的帮助下轻松搞定。[2] 这些男孩儿认识了团队的力量，他们也享受了甜甜的回报。团队协作需要团队的努力，以及彼此在关系中的信任。成功的领袖把团队协作作为自己的第一优先，并且能够享受带来的成果。

应用

◆评估你在团队中的人际关系。

◆在某个层面上和每个团队成员建立个人关系。

◆你的团队清楚自己的愿景吗？请不同团队成员说出团队的愿景。假如他们不在意或不清楚的话，你就有事情要做了。

◆本周花点时间，庆祝一下团队的胜利。

笔记

个人体会／要进一步探讨的想法／要铭记在心的理念

仁言，不如仁声之入人深也。

——孟子

Kindly words do not enter so deeply into men as a reputation for kindness.

——Mencius

挑选士兵

Sorting the Troops

第四天 魏无忌的用人之道
——吸引人才，留住人才

Day 4:Attracting and Keeping Great Team Members

关系是吸引人才、留住人才的关键。

Relationships are key in recruiting and retaining talented team members.

Kindly words do not enter so deeply into men as a reputation for kindness.

——*Mencius*

Wei Wuji lived around 240 BC and was known for his wisdom and kindness. His father was King Zhao of Wei. His half brother, An Xi, became king after the death of King Zhao. Once An Xi became king, he appointed Wei Wuji lord of Xinling. His new responsibility involved taking command of a large army. His first task was to sort the army. He said, "If father and son are serving together, let the father go home. If there are brothers here, let the elder go home. And if any soldier is an only son, let him go home also to support his family."[1] As a result, he kept only those soldiers who would fight with an undivided heart. His reputation quickly spread, and he soon had three thousand protégés.

By 248 BC, the king placed him in charge of the entire army of Wei. It was said that his military strength shook the world. He recorded his stratagems in the book called *The Strategy of the Lord of Xinling*. After his death, he was most remembered for seeking men of valor and honor from all walks of life. His mighty men of valor came from mountain caves, fields, palaces, and city gutters.[2]

Today the task of finding and retaining quality people remains a challenge that faces most organizations. Some of the factors that affect retention in the U.S. are the same in countries such as China. In the U.S., for example, the economy is growing at a faster rate than the workforce. The development of fast-growing industries in the high-tech area has continued to outpace the workforce.

Cultural factors also directly influence keeping a strong team together. In older generations, companies treated employees like family and expected loyalty in return. It was not uncommon for a person to work for one company his entire life. However, the layoffs at the end of the last century, combined with economic recession at the beginning of this century, showed a shift in company mentality.

仁言，不如仁声之入人深也。

——孟子

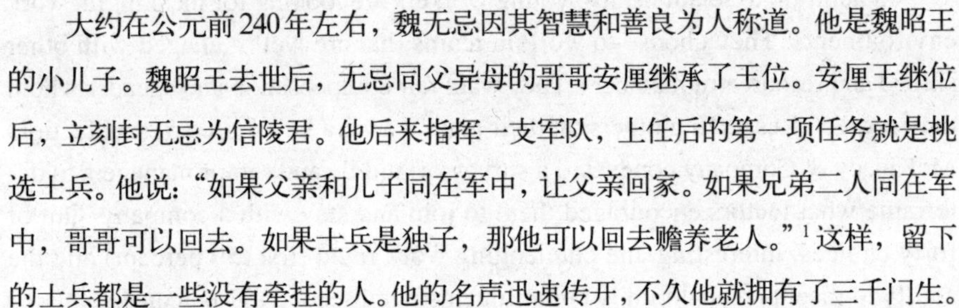

大约在公元前240年左右，魏无忌因其智慧和善良为人称道。他是魏昭王的小儿子。魏昭王去世后，无忌同父异母的哥哥安厘继承了王位。安厘王继位后，立刻封无忌为信陵君。他后来指挥一支军队，上任后的第一项任务就是挑选士兵。他说："如果父亲和儿子同在军中，让父亲回家。如果兄弟二人同在军中，哥哥可以回去。如果士兵是独子，那他可以回去赡养老人。"[1]这样，留下的士兵都是一些没有牵挂的人。他的名声迅速传开，不久他就拥有了三千门生。

公元前248年，国王任命他管理魏国的军队。据说，当时他的军备力量让世界震惊。他把自己的战略记录下来，写成了《魏公子兵法》。他去世后，仍然因为爱才而传名后世，他从各行各业中寻找德行和勇气兼备的人。他身边的一些勇士来自山野、田间、王宫和市井。[2]

时至今日，发掘并留住人才仍然是大部分机构面对的挑战。在留住人才方面影响美国的一些因素，也同样在影响着其他的国家，例如中国。美国的经济增长很快，其比率超过了劳动力增长的速度。高科技领域中快速发展的工业把劳动力增长的速度远远甩在了后面。

文化因素也要计算在内，它也影响着稳固团队的建立。从前，公司对待员工像对待家人一样，因此也期待对方回馈忠诚。你常常可以见到一个人一生都在一家公司工作。然而，上个世纪末大规模的解雇加上本世纪初的经济不景气，整个扭转了人们的雇佣心态。公司的忠诚不再像从前那样了。公司只对自己忠诚，而不是对员工忠诚。现在，生存是第一位的，结果员工也要

Companies became loyal only to themselves, not their employees. Company loyalty no longer exists as in former years. Now survival comes first, and as a result, workers take charge of planning their own careers. Staying marketable and positioned for future employment is a major priority. For some, this requires switching jobs every few years. In the U.S., most people will have as many as nine different jobs between the ages of 18 and 32.[3] In today's fast-moving, constantly changing work environment, the future is uncertain. Job-hopping is common as people search for the best possible work environment. As a result, most teams will be made up of young workers. Young workers have many benefits, such as freshness, high energy, and technical skills. On the negative side, they lack experience. Many young workers are interested in jobs that will further develop their skills. They are less likely to be loyal to a company and more likely to place loyalty on personal relationships.

In addition to relationships, young workers are looking for meaningful work environments. They choose to work in teams that are well managed with other skilled and resourceful members. They want fair compensation and a leader whom they respect. Respecting others on their team is also a key source of satisfaction. McKinsey & Company conducted a survey of middle and senior managers to determine what factors encouraged them to join and stay with a company. Out of forty choices, interesting and challenging work rated first (59 percent) and the ability to meet personal/family commitments rated second (51 percent).

Relationships are key in the retention process. Gallup researchers Marcus Buckingham and Curt Coffman say: "If your relationship with your manager is fractured, then no amount of in-chair massaging or company-sponsored dog walking will persuade you to stay and perform. It is better to work for a great manager in an old-fashioned company than for a terrible manager in a company offering an enlightened, company-focused culture."[4]

Southwest Airlines (SWA) has been recognized as a highly successful company for years. With thirty consecutive profitable years of business under their belt, SWA also has less than a 4 percent turnover rate—less than half the turnover rate of its competitors. Studies of SWA point to specific qualities of why SWA employees choose not to leave. They feel they have meaningful work, pride in the organization, fair compensation, and compatible supervisors.

People leave organizations for a variety of reasons. The following are some of the most prevalent reasons cited for employee departure:

- A leadership change. Either the relationship with the leader changes or the leader leaves.

规划自己的职业了，让自己适应市场并找到自己未来的定位，成了一个首要的优先次序。对于某些人来说，这就意味着每隔几年就换个工作。在美国，大部分人在18岁至32岁之间从事过九份工作。[3]在今天高速运转、常常改变的工作环境中，未来是不可预测的。跳槽也很普遍，因为人们在不断寻找最好的工作环境。结果，大部分团队由年轻人组成。年轻人具备很多优点，如初出茅庐、精力充沛，而且具备很强的专业技能。他们的不利因素是缺少经验。很多年轻人喜欢能够进一步培养自己职业技巧的工作。他们不太可能忠诚于一家公司，却会忠诚于彼此之间的个人关系。

除了关系之外，年轻人还注重有意义的工作环境。他们会选择在管理良好的团队中工作，和其他具备专业技能以及资源丰富的人员共同协作。他们希望获得公平的回报，也希望为自己钦佩的领袖效力。能够尊重团队中的其他人，也是一项重要的满意指标。麦肯锡（McKinsey&Company）对某些公司的中层和高层管理者进行了调查，了解是什么因素影响他们加盟并留在当前的公司。在40个选项中，有意思、富有挑战的工作高居榜首（59%），能够满足个人／家庭义务排在第二位（51%）。

关系是留住人才的关键。盖洛普的研究员马库斯·白金汉（Marcus Buckingham）和柯特·考夫曼（Curt Coffman）认为："假如你和经理之间的关系出现了裂痕，找个地方按摩来减压，或者公司掏钱让你去遛狗放松心情，这些办法都不管用，你不会留下来认真履行职责。与其在一家充满挑战、企业文化凝聚力很强的公司中天天面对一个糟糕的经理，不如在一家老式的公司中给一个好经理打工。"[4]

美国西南航空公司多年来一直被公认为是成功企业。他们的家底丰厚，已经连续30年赢利，而且员工的流动率不到4%——低于其竞争对手流动率的一半儿。对西南航空公司进行调查后，研究结果表明，一些具体的品质决定了为什么西南航空公司的员工会选择留下而不是离开。这些品质包括：他们感到自己的工作很有意义；为自己的公司感到骄傲；得到公平的回报；和主管的关系融洽。

人们离职的原因各不相同。以下是导致员工离职的一些主要因素：

- A conflict with a direct supervisor. The relationship becomes stressful or hostile without clear means for resolution.
- Close friends leave. One or more friends leave a company, causing a loss of meaningful relationships.
- Unfavorable change in job assignment. A person's daily tasks change so that work is no longer meaningful or becomes too stressful.[5]

Leaders need to constantly seek out people who can serve current needs as well as future projects. Effective orientations and adequate resources are essential to help them start strong and stay successful. Good people are hard to find and sometimes even harder to keep.

Application

◆ Assess the satisfaction and relational connections within your team.

◆ Schedule an event or structure a time for team members to develop closer relationships. Remember that most people like to have fun. Laughing together creates great memories.

Notation Area

Personal observations/Ideas for further exploration/Thoughts to remember

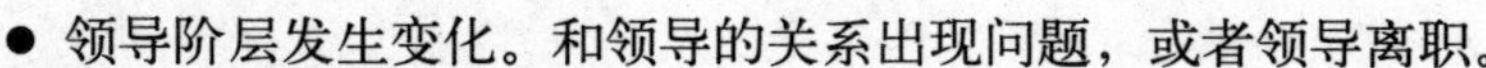

- 领导阶层发生变化。和领导的关系出现问题，或者领导离职。
- 和主管发生争执。彼此的关系中产生了压力或敌对情绪，没有妥当的解决方案。
- 好朋友离开。一个甚至数个朋友离开公司，导致自己缺少朋友和人际关系。
- 不喜欢分配给自己的工作职责。一个人每天要做的事情改变了，所以工作不再有意义，或带来太大的压力。[5]

领袖们需要找到能够满足当前需要以及今后项目发展需要的人才。准确的定位和充足的资源是帮助他们起步稳健和保持成功的关键。俗话说：良将难求。有的时候，留住人才更难。

应用

◆了解自己团队中的满意度以及彼此的关系。

◆设计一些事情或安排某个时间，让团队成员培养亲密关系。记住，大部分人喜欢游玩。在一起欢笑能创造美好的记忆。

笔记

个人体会／要进一步探讨的想法／要铭记在心的理念

胜者之战，若积决水于千仞之溪者，形也。

——孙子[1]

It is because of disposition that a victorious general is able to make his soldiers fight with the effect of pent-up waters which, suddenly released, plunge into a bottomless abyss.

——*Sun Tzu*[1]

努力向前

Breaking Forth

第五天 积决水于千仞之溪
——领袖魅力

Day 5:Charisma

把自己的战略记录下来，当人们振奋起来，关注自己的任务时，就能带来很好的效果。

When excited people are focused on a task, great results are produced.

It is because of disposition that a victorious general is able to make his soldiers fight with the effect of pent-up waters which, suddenly released, plunge into a bottomless abyss.

—— *Sun Tzu* [1]

Every journey begins with a first step. Every individual begins with God-given potential and tools for success. Tools that stand out in successful people include: charisma, initiative, enthusiasm, caring, and intelligence.

Your circumstances affect what happens to you. Your attitude affects what happens in you. Your charisma affects what happens through you. Charisma has been defined as "a personal magic of leadership arousing special popular loyalty or enthusiasm."[2] In addition to the seven qualities listed in Day 2, charisma is also important for successful leadership strength. Many are born with a charismatic personality, but many others develop this "magic" characteristic. Charismatic traits include concern for others, creativity, being a catalyst for positive change, and confidence.

Charismatic leaders are concerned about making others feel special and are less focused on improving their own image. Leaders who focus on helping others will feel better about who they are and will attract followers. People are naturally drawn to those who build up others.

Charismatic people make things happen in creative ways. When you are around charismatic people, life is exciting. They have an aversion to boring situations. In many cases, they can turn a seemingly boring situation into a great event or learning experience. They may be controversial, entertaining, or out of the ordinary, but never boring.

Charismatic leaders are catalysts for life and productivity. They are electrically charged with energy that brings new life to people and situations. I have a friend like this named Joe Jackson. When Joe Jackson walks into a room or party,

胜者之战，若积决水于千仞之溪者，形也。

——孙子[1]

译文：胜利者指挥作战，就像在八百丈高处掘开溪中积水一样，这就是军事实力的“形”。

万里之行始于足下。每个人在起步时都拥有成功所必需的上帝恩赐的潜力和资源。成功人士身上显著的特点包括：领袖魅力、主动性、激情、关心和智慧。

你的环境影响了什么事情会发生在你身上。你的态度决定你内心的状态。你的领袖魅力决定了因为你的存在会发生什么事情。领袖魅力具有如下定义：“领袖身上的个人影响力，很受人欢迎，让人产生特别的信任感或激情。”[2]除了在第二天列出的七种品质，领袖魅力对于成功的领导力也至关重要。很多人天生具备魅力人格，但是大部分人需要经过后天培养才能形成这种“魅力”人格。领袖魅力包括对他人的关心、创造力、成为积极改变的催化剂以及信心。

富有魅力的领袖关心他人，让别人觉得自己很特殊。他们不太注重改善自我形象。以他人为中心的领袖很自信，也会吸引更多的跟随者。人们自然而然地被吸引到让自己得到建造的人身边。

富有领袖魅力的人做事时具有创造性。如果你和他们一起做事，生活一点也不会枯燥。他们不喜欢一成不变的生活。很多时候，他们能够把看起来乏味的环境变成一件重大事件或一次值得学习的经历。他们可能有争议性、好玩有趣或与众不同，但是他们绝不会一成不变、令人生厌。

富有魅力的领袖是生活和效率的催化剂。他们像是充足了电一样，活力四射，给周围的人和环境带来生机。我有一位这样的朋友，他的名字叫乔·

life and fun just happen. Joe is hard to miss as a six-feet-tall (one-meter-eighty-two-centimeter), two-hundred-forty-pound (one-hundred-nine-kilogram) mass of muscle and positive energy. As a former U.S. National cheerleading champion, he continues to excite his team members just as he once led crowds at sporting events. On one occasion, Joe and some students were eating at a small restaurant in northern China. Some lively dance music came over the radio, and Joe just had to move. Within minutes, our ordinary meal turned into a dance party as the owners of the restaurant turned down the lights and turned up the music. We had a great time and made new friends with the restaurant employees. Charismatic leaders like Joe destroy lethargy and excite people. When energized people are focused on a task, they produce great results. Apathy and mediocrity are swallowed in positive energy.

Charismatic people are confident in who they are and in their abilities. Confidence allows them to work outside of their comfort zones, and in so doing, they challenge others out of theirs. They express hope and conviction of a successful outcome, even when obstacles are enormous. Confident leaders call people to rise to the challenge and make them feel successful just by joining the team. Confidence allows a charismatic person to give hope when all others have lost faith.

Charisma is a trait most of us need and desire. In order to develop charisma, leaders should seek to mature in the above characteristics. At the same time, they should avoid other destructive personality traits. The following traits hinder charismatic development:

Perfectionism. Perfectionists often produce excellence in what they do because of their commitment to distinction. However, perfectionists often find it difficult to affirm themselves, which in turn makes it difficult for them to affirm others. Their perfectionist standards stifle creativity and risk taking. People are not naturally drawn to perfectionists.

Pride. Pride is a common but very destructive human trait. A prideful person looks down on others. A team will not follow a prideful personality. Prideful leaders do not focus on the teams' success, but rather on status and position.

Insecurity. Insecurity breeds insecurity. If you want to see this in action, just spend time with adolescents. Insecure people avoid risk or potentially embarrassing situations. As a result, insecure individuals are likely to follow the crowd, lest they stand out and embarrass themselves. That is why we see such high levels of conformity at that age. The status quo is acceptable for them even if it bores others to death. Insecure leaders also are likely to shift blame to others when situations

杰克逊（Joe Jackson）。当他走入一个房间或一个晚会的时候，活力和笑声就出现了。乔有6英尺高（1.82米），240磅重（190公斤），他浑身都是肌肉，充满积极向上的力量，你很难对他视而不见。乔曾经是美国国家拉拉队冠军，所以他不断激励自己的团队成员，好像往日在运动场上带领大批人群一样。有一次，乔和一些学生在中国北部的一个小饭馆吃饭，收音机播出了一首非常欢快的曲子。乔再也控制不住自己了，他动了起来。几分钟内，这个普通的晚餐就变成了舞会。饭馆老板让灯光变暗，调大了音量。他们玩得开心极了，而且交到了新朋友，认识了饭馆的员工。像乔这样的领袖充满了魅力，他们能够改变冗长沉闷的生活，点燃人们的激情。当人们振奋起来，关注自己的任务时，他们就能带来很好的效果。冷漠和平庸被积极的力量所吞没。

富有领袖魅力的人对自己和自己的能力充满自信。自信让他们走出自己的安逸区域。当他们这么做的时候，也在挑战他人，使他们走出自己的安逸区。即使在困难重重的时候，他们仍旧充满盼望，确信结果会是最好的。自信的领袖号召人们起来面对挑战，即使他们只作出了加入团队的决定，也会让他们感到信心百倍。在所有人都失去信心的时候，自信让一个充满领袖魅力的人仍然充满盼望。

领袖魅力是我们大部分人需要并且渴望拥有的一个特质。领袖们应该在上述特质上力求成熟，培养自己的领袖魅力。同时，也应该避免其他破坏性的人格特征。以下特点会成为培养领袖魅力的障碍：

完美主义。因为完美主义者竭力让自己鹤立鸡群，所以常常带来优异的业绩。然而，完美主义者很难肯定自己，于是他们也不会肯定别人。他们完美的标准会扼杀人的创造性和冒险精神。人们不会自然而然地被完美主义者所吸引。

骄傲。骄傲是一种普遍特征，具有很大破坏性。骄傲的人瞧不起他人。一个团队不会跟随某个人骄傲的个性。骄傲的领袖并不注重团队的成功，而是注重个人的身份和地位。

不安全感。不安全感滋生更大的不安全感。假如你希望真实地见到这一幕，那么花些时间和青少年待一待吧。不安全的人逃避冒险或可能出现尴尬局面的

go wrong because they are not confident enough to admit mistakes.

Negativism. Negativism is the opposite of charisma. A negative leader can destroy most of the positive results caused by a charismatic leader with a few well-aimed critical comments. Negative personalities are depressing to be around. They tend to congregate with other negative people who focus on the glass being half empty. Negative thinking seldom finds solutions that lead to any productivity. People will flee from a negative leader.

Moodiness. Moody leaders do not develop close relationships with their teams. Their constantly fluctuating emotions make it difficult for them to be dependable, and team members may be hesitant to approach moody leaders. Moodiness inhibits solid leadership because others must continually stabilize a leader's mood before productivity can be accomplished.

Over-sensitivity. People who are overly sensitive continually nurse bruised emotions. They tend to be inwardly focused. While licking their own wounds, they seldom notice others' needs. People tiptoe away from overly sensitive leaders.[3] Individuals who possess traits that hinder charismatic development as mentioned above are self-conscious. Charismatic leaders think less of themselves and focus on making others feel important.

Developing charisma will have a positive effect on your success. Some leaders naturally possess charismatic qualities, while others must develop them by working on the positive character traits listed in this chapter. Begin today to enhance your charisma by asking yourself the following questions about positive ways to nurture charismatic traits:

- Do I regularly show concern for others?
- Have I introduced new or creative ideas and projects at work?
- In what areas am I confident?
- Am I a catalyst, meaning, do others feel energized when I am around?

Once you have honestly answered these questions, pick a couple of areas for improvement. At the same time, work at eliminating the actions that may cause others to perceive you as moody, perfectionistic, oversensitive, or negative.

环境。结果，没有安全感的人极可能会随大流，这样就不会与众不同，避免让自己感到尴尬。这也是为什么这个年龄段的年轻人都整齐划一，彼此一致。虽然可能会让旁观者感到沉闷，但他们非常满足于现状。在环境出现问题的时候，不安全的领袖可能也会归咎于他人，因为他们没有足够的勇气承认自己的错误。

消极。消极是领袖魅力的反面。消极的领袖只需几句挑剔的评论，只要正中目标，就可以把领袖魅力带来的所有积极效果全部打消。与具有消极个性的人相处令人感到压抑。这样的人喜欢和相同的人聚集在一起，他们只注重玻璃杯里空了的那一半。消极的思维很难产生有建设性的解决方案。人们会远离态度消极的领袖。

情绪化。情绪化的领袖不能和团队建立亲密的关系。他们的情绪波动很大，让人觉得不够可靠，团队中其他人也很犹豫，不愿意接近情绪化的领袖。情绪化破坏了稳定的领导力，因为其他人常常需要帮助领袖稳定情绪，之后才能完成自己的任务。

过分敏感。过分敏感的人常常需要照顾自己受伤的情感。他们过分注重自己的内心。他们在舔伤口的时候，很少注意到他人的需要。人们会踮着脚尖谨言慎行，避开过分敏感的领袖。[3]上述特点都阻碍了领袖魅力的形成，有这样特点的领袖清楚地知道自己的需要，而一个具备领袖魅力的人很少想到自己，更多关注他人的感受。

培养领袖魅力对你的成功具有积极的效果。一些领袖天生就有这样的魅力，另一些必须一点点培养，着重培养本章所列出的积极品格。从今天开始，强化你的领袖魅力，询问自己培养领袖魅力的相关问题：

- 我常常表现出对他人的关心吗？
- 我在工作的时候，提出了新的和有创造性的想法和计划吗？
- 我在哪个领域充满信心？
- 我是催化剂吗？当我出现的时候，大家觉得精神百倍吗？

诚实地回答这些问题，找出一两个需要改善的领域。同时，想想自己的哪些行为表现出情绪化、完美主义、过分敏感或消极，以后需要注意改变这些行为。

Application

This week ask a friend the following:

- When am I most likely to appear as moody? (The morning, end of the day, before a deadline, etc.)
- Am I oversensitive, and if so, in what areas?
- In what areas am I a perfectionist, and what negative effect does that have on others?
- In what situations have my negative comments or attitude hindered others?

Honest answers to these questions should give you more than enough to work on.

Notation Area

Personal observations/Ideas for further exploration/Thoughts to remember

应用

本周向一个朋友询问一下：

◆我在什么时候最情绪化？（早上、晚上、赶最后期限的时候，等等。）

◆我过度敏感吗？假如是的话，表现在哪些领域？

◆我在哪些领域是个完美主义者？带给别人什么消极后果？

◆我的消极言论或态度在哪些情况下对他人造成消极的影响？

诚实地回答这些问题，你可以发现：自己有很多需要改正的地方。

笔记

个人体会／要进一步探讨的想法／要铭记在心的理念

千里之行，始于足下。

——老子

A journey of a thousand miles begins with a single step.

——*Lao Zi*

忠信的功课

Lesson in Faithfulness

第六天 项梁婉拒“高才生”
——注重细节

Day 6:Do the Small Stuff

成功的领袖心中知道自己的愿景，每天都保证自己不忽略重要的细节。

Successful leaders keep the big picture in mind while daily ensuring that no important detail is overlooked.

A journey of a thousand miles begins with a single step.

——Lao Zi

Near the year 209 BC, Xiang Liang began preparations for war. He appointed men from local villages to positions of lieutenants, generals, sergeants, and scouts. One man of standing in a nearby village was not given an official position. He questioned Xiang Liang as to why he was overlooked. Xiang Liang referred to an earlier time when he had asked him to take care of small matters relating to a funeral. Xiang Liang remarked, "When I asked you to take on a simple task, you didn't do it well. Therefore you will not be given a position now."[1] The man's lack of faithfulness with small tasks in times of peace excluded him from a position of honor. The wisdom and leadership of Xiang Liang won him the respect of his followers.

Many people fall short of excellence when they overlook small details. The last 10 percent of a job is the difference between good work and excellent work. When I was a teenager, my father allowed my brother and me to go on landscaping jobs with him. Digging holes all day wasn't a lot of fun, but we learned how to work and the money was always a good incentive. After a long day's work, we were excited to finish. We were always tempted to leave when the bulk of the tools and materials were cleared. My dad, however, taught us to remove all the scraps, sweep hard-to-see places, and leave everything in perfect condition. No extra dirt or scraps of material were left lying anywhere. He often said the difference between professionals and amateurs is how they finish the job. In most jobs, the last details make a world of difference.

Years later, I was walking across my college campus when I saw the college president, Dr. Norman Bridges, walking in front of me. As he approached the

千里之行，始于足下。

——老子

公元前209年，项梁开始为起兵反秦作准备。他对当地村庄的一些人委以重任，一些人被任命为校尉、军侯和司马等职。附近一个村庄中，有一个声名显赫的人却没有被授予任何官职。他质问项梁，为什么会忽略自己。项梁提到从前发生过的事情，当时项梁请他在一个葬礼上办理一些小事。项梁说："我让你做小事的时候，你并没有认真完成，因此你现在也不能担任任何要职。"[1]一个人在和平时期对小事不忠心，后来让他失去了尊贵的地位。项梁的智慧和领导力赢得了跟随者的敬重。

很多人忽略细节，在很多事情上达不到卓越的标准。一项工作最后的10%常常是好工作和卓越工作之间的差异。在我还年少的时候，父亲让弟弟和我一起去做一些园艺工作。每天挖坑并不好玩，但是我们已经找到了工作的窍门，而且我们挣到的钱也是一个很好的激励。漫长的一天过去后，我们都很高兴能够快快结束工作，总想把一大堆工具和材料扔在原地。然而，爸爸却要我们把所有的废弃物都扫干净，甚至还要清扫不容易看到的地方，让一切都保持完美的状态，不可以留下任何垃圾或边角料。他常常说，职业人士和业余人士之间的差异就在于他们怎样完成自己的工作。在大部分工作中，最后的细节起到画龙点睛的妙处。

多年后的一天，我走在大学校园中，看到学校的校长诺曼·布里奇斯博士（Dr. Norman Bridges）走在我的前面。当他走到行政大楼的时候，注意

main administration building, he noticed a single piece of trash lying on the grass. Without hesitation he bent over, picked it up, and threw it in a trash can as he entered the building. That memory has stuck in my mind, and his example has served as a reminder that I am never above performing small, seemingly low-level tasks.

Great leaders learn to take care of the small everyday details. Every notable project has a thousand little details that must be completed before success will be reached. Successful leaders keep the big picture in mind while daily ensuring that no important detail is overlooked. Notable projects and personal character are much the same in this regard. A few seemingly small lapses in moral judgment or poor personal character choices can destroy a reputation that took a lifetime to establish. Daily diligence to do the right thing, however small it may seem, will reap great rewards. H. P. Liddon once said, "What we do on some great occasion will probably depend on what we already are; and what we are will be the result of previous years of self-discipline." Becoming a great leader can begin today as you complete the small tasks before you with excellence.

Application

- What small details are you putting off until tomorrow that you could finish today?

- Give extra attention to the projects on which you are currently working. Make sure the results will surpass the expectation of those you serve.

Notation Area

Personal observations/Ideas for further exploration/Thoughts to remember

到草地上有一片小小的碎屑。他想都没想就弯下腰，把它捡起来，扔进了垃圾桶，然后才进了楼。这个记忆深深地印入了我的脑海，他的榜样常常提醒我，去做一些看起来很卑微的小事。

伟大的领袖学会注重日常细节。每个大项目都包含无数细节，只有一点点完成，才能够获得成功。成功的领袖心中知道自己的愿景，但是每天都保证自己没有忽略重要的细节。在这点上，大项目和个人的品格非常相似。看起来是道德判断上的一点小失误或个人品格上错误的选择，都能够破坏需要一生的时间才能建立的声誉。每天认真提醒自己去做正确的事——虽然看起来都是小事，但能收获很大的回报。H.P.林顿（H.P.Liddon）曾经说："我们在重要场合中的所作所为取决于我们的品格，品格则出于多年来的自律。"当你开始卓越地完成摆在面前的小事，意味着你从今天开始一步一步地成为伟大的领袖。

应用

◆你把今天能完成的哪些小事拖到了明天？

◆对自己手中的项目多一份认真，让结果超出他人的期待。

笔记

个人体会／要进一步探讨的想法／要铭记在心的理念

领袖就要像刘备一样，即使在士气消沉的时候，也应该忍耐坚持。领袖需要超越当时自己周围的环境，从其他地方和源头汲取激情。

Leaders need to persevere even when morale and enthusiasm are lost. Great leaders draw their enthusiasm from sources beyond circumstances.

三顾茅庐

Three Visits

第七天 三顾茅庐
——成功的激情

Day 7:Enthusiasm to Succeed

带领中的激情是帮助团队既看到全局也做小事的关键。意味着你从今天开始一步一步地成为伟大的领袖。

Leading with enthusiasm is key to helping a team see the big picture while doing small details.

Leaders need to persevere even when morale and enthusiasm are lost. Great leaders draw their enthusiasm from sources beyond circumstances.

During the Three Kingdom Period around AD 190, Zhuge Liang (alias Kong Ming) was a famous statesman and military strategist. In AD 189, Liu Bian ascended the throne of the Eastern Han Dynasty at the age of fourteen following the death of his father. Because of his age, his mother, Empress Dowager, ruled the country with his uncle, General He Jin. Under their rule Eastern Han grew weaker and weaker. Within five years warlords had sprung up and were taking over cities across the country. Liu Bei represented one of the weaker warlords. His early battles were a series of continual defeats until he was left with only the small town of Xinye. One day he was told of a wise man by the name of Zhuge Liang who lived in Longzhong. Liu Bei decided to seek out and ask him to help recapture his kingdom. Upon arrival in Longzhong, Zhuge Liang intentionally avoided him on his first two visits in order to test his sincerity. On the third visit, Zhuge Liang agreed to see him and rewarded his diligence by becoming his adviser. Zhuge Liang developed a strategy for the country, and Liu Bei over time became the ruler of one of the Three Kingdoms.[1]

Just as Liu Bei persevered, leaders need to persevere even when morale and enthusiasm are lost. Leaders need to draw their enthusiasm from sources beyond circumstances. Walter Chrysler once said, "I feel sorry for the person who can't get genuinely excited about his work. Not only will he never be satisfied, but he will never achieve anything worthwhile."

Leading with enthusiasm is key to helping a team see the big picture while doing small details. Mature leaders have the ability to remain enthusiastic even when outward situations daunt team morale. Enthusiasm is contagious. When a

即使在士气消沉的时候，领袖也应该忍耐坚持。领袖需要超越当时自己周围的环境，从其他地方和源头汲取激情。

诸葛亮（又名孔明）是三国时期著名的政治家和军事战略指挥家。公元189年的时候，会灵帝去世，太子继位，太后临朝，和自己的哥哥（大将军何进）共同统治国家。在他们的掌握下，东汉变得越来越弱小。五年之中，各地诸侯纷纷起兵，攻占了许多城池。刘备的势力当时比较弱小。他吃了不少败仗，只剩下新野一座城池。一天，他听说在隆中住着一位智者，名叫诸葛亮。刘备决定求贤，夺回自己领土。在刘备到达隆中后，诸葛亮前两次故意避开他，测试他的真诚。第三次拜访的时候，诸葛亮同意见他，对他的孜孜不倦表示赞赏，成了他的谋士。诸葛亮为国家制定了一套战略，之后，刘备建立了蜀汉国，在历史上形成三国鼎立的局面。[1]

领袖就要像刘备一样，即使在士气消沉的时候，也应该忍耐坚持。领袖需要超越当时自己周围的环境，从其他地方和源头汲取激情。沃尔特·克莱斯勒（Walter Chrysler）曾说："有的人不能发自内心地热爱自己的工作，我为他们感到难过。这样的人不仅永远不会得到满足，而且永远也不能完成任何有价值的事情。"

充满激情的领导力非常关键，在团队忙于细节的时候，仍然需要帮助他们看到愿景和未来的规划。当外部环境让团队士气消沉的时候，成熟的领袖仍然能够保持自己的激情。激情富有感染力。当一个充满激情的人处在某个环境中的时候，他们不会选择一成不变的生活。你或者感到自己被他们提

passionate person enters a situation, neutrality is not an option. You will either grow spirited or be totally annoyed.

During my teens, I worked a short-term job in a paper factory. My responsibility was to blast the rust off old pieces of machinery — not very exciting. But I learned a valuable lesson from this opportunity. The learning came not from my job, which was mundane to say the least, but from my boss, Ron Stahl. Every morning Ron drove up in his big four-wheel drive, double-cab pickup truck. Climbing out of his truck and donning his hardhat, he walked over to our work area to greet us. Each morning he was upbeat as he explained the projects for the day. After hopping back into his truck to start his work, he would say to himself loud enough for us to hear, "I love this job." I couldn't say the same at the time, but I remember the positive effect that one statement made on the rest of my day. My boss's enthusiasm caused me to see some of the positive aspects of an otherwise depressing job. Regardless of the task, one of the best ways to stay motivated is to think about the positive aspects of the position. Speaking positively about your work and the situation will go a long way in creating a positive work environment.

My father was a great encourager and coach. As a physical education teacher, he had a great amount of coaching experience. In junior high, he taught me the principle of going the second mile. I was a pudgy little kid doing my best to be part of the school's football team. I remember very clearly the after-school practices and the excitement before a big game. I also remember the coaches' commitment to get us young boys in shape for the games. They pushed us hard during practice and — just to make sure we worked up enough sweat — they finished each practice with laps around the field. At first I always ran in the middle of the pack—not in front, but not in back. My father challenged me to put forth a little more effort and run with the boys in the front. He told me once my body was in condition, I could run just as easily in the front of the group as in the middle. He was right, and I soon ran in the front after every practice.

This same principle holds true for adults. A friend of mine in his mid-fifties who has run a marathon every year for the last ten years recently challenged me with the same second mile principle. After years of being in average physical condition, I decided to start running in order to improve my health and lose some weight. It was difficult to get started, but my friend encouraged me by saying I would soon run for three hours as easily as I could run for thirty minutes (my average run-time at that point). I took his challenge and found it to be true. Last

升、振奋不已，或者感到自己被干扰、心烦意乱。

我少年的时候，在一家造纸厂打工。我的工作是打磨生锈的旧机器——这份工作不太有意思。但是我从这个机会中学到很宝贵的一课。退一步说，我并没有从工作本身学到什么，而是从我的老板荣·斯塔尔（Ron Stahl）那里受益匪浅。荣开着一辆四轮驱动的双驾驶室大货车。每天早晨他开着车过来，钻出驾驶室，戴着安全帽，走到我们工作的地方和我们打招呼。他给我们分配一天的工作，每次都显得很乐观。之后，他会匆忙回到卡车中，自言自语地说（但声音却正好能够让我们听清楚）："我喜欢这份工作。"当时我无法说出同样的话语，但是我记住了一句话语给我的一天带来的积极效果。我老板的激情感染了我，让我看到一份沉闷的工作中的积极面。不论面对的任务是什么，让自己保持动力的最佳方式就是去思考其中的积极方面。积极面对自己的工作就可以采取主动，创建积极的工作氛围。

我的父亲是一名优秀的教练，他知道如何鼓励别人，具有丰富的教练经验。我初中的时候，他就教给我多走一里路的原则。我当时又矮又胖，却想成为学校橄榄球队的一员。放学后的训练和大赛前的兴奋至今仍然历历在目。我也还记得教练要让我们一群小男孩儿锻炼身体，为比赛作准备。在训练的时候，他要求很严格。为了让我们能多出点汗，每次训练结束的时候，我们都要沿着操场跑好多圈。一开始，我总是跑在队伍的中间——不是最前面，但是也不在后面。我的父亲挑战我，让我再多努力一点，和前面的男孩儿跑在一起。他告诉我，身体适应一下后，跑在前面就会像在中间一样轻松。他是对的。不久，每次训练后跑步的时候，我都能够跑在队伍的最前面。

同样的原则也适用于成人。我的一位朋友已经四十多岁了，在过去的十年中，每年都要跑马拉松，他同样用多走一里路的原则挑战我。多年来，我的体能只是处于一般状态。于是我决定开始跑步，改善健康，同时也能减轻体重。刚开始的时候很难，但是我的朋友鼓励我，告诉我坚持一段时间后，跑三个小时就会像跑30分钟一样轻松（这是我当时跑步的平均时间）。我接受了他的挑战，发现事实的确如此。去年春天，我已经39岁了，在中国的长城

spring at the age of thirty-nine, I ran a half marathon on the Great Wall of China and felt about as tired as I used to feel after a half-hour run. Today as I write, most of my body is sore as a result of running my first full marathon. I never thought I could run a marathon, but with consistent training I actually finished the race.

Many physical, economic, or career goals seem impossible, but with additional effort they can become reality. You can choose to run in the middle of the pack, or you can run with the leaders. Do you strive to do excellent work, or are you content to do only what is asked of you? Do you go the second mile and make sure your work surpasses the expectation of your boss or clients? If you want to be a leader and part of a winning team, additional work will be required. The same principle applies in relationships. If you want an excellent home life, do you schedule quality time and energy to build your relationship with your spouse and/or children? Can you think of ways to please others without expecting something in return?

Application

◆ Think of at least one situation at work and at home where you can go the second mile.

◆ Focus on enthusiastically finishing the last 10 percent of your current project.

◆ Identify some enthusiastic people in your life and seek out opportunities to be with them and learn from them.

Notation Area

Personal observations/Ideas for further exploration/Thoughts to remember

上跑完了马拉松全程的一半，感到就像从前跑完30分钟的疲劳程度一样。今天，我写作的时候，由于第一次跑完了马拉松全程，身体很酸痛。我从来没有想到自己能够跑完马拉松，但是坚持训练，我竟然能够跑完比赛。

很多体能上、经济上或其他的职业目标看起来不可能，但是再努力一下，就能够成为现实。你可以选择跑在人群的中间，也可以选择和领袖们一起跑。你是努力成就卓越，还是满足于别人要求你做的事情？你会多走一里路，让你的工作超过老板和客户的期待吗？假如你希望成为领袖和胜利团队的一分子，就需要更努力一些。同样的原则也适用于人际关系。如果你希望拥有美好的家庭生活，那么你是否为配偶和孩子安排高品质的时光，建立你和他们的关系？你是否想出一些方法让别人感到快乐，同时又不期待任何回报呢？

应用

◆思考一下，在工作场合中和家庭中至少想出一个情景，让自己多走一里路。

◆充满热情，出色地完成手中任务的最后10%。

◆在你的生活中发现充满激情的人，找机会和他们在一起，向他们学习。

笔记

个人体会／要进一步探讨的想法／要铭记在心的理念

卓越的团队领袖会提拔比自己更有才华的人，也会挑选让自己变得更强大的人。

Great team leaders promote others more skilled than themselves and seek out those who will make them stronger.

好宰相

A Better Minister

第八天 樊姬的智慧
——栽培他人

Day 8:Enlargers

带领团队的时候，在团队开始信任你之前，你需要先信任他们。

When leading a team, you will need to believe in your team before they believe in you.

Great team leaders promote others more skilled than themselves and seek out those who will make them stronger.

King Zhuang of Chu had a prime minister named Yu Qiuzi. On one occasion Lady Fan, King Zhuang's wife, called into question Prime Minister Yu's loyalty to the king. She said to her husband, "I have been your wife for eleven years, and in that time I have never heard Yu Qiuzi dismiss incompetent officials or promote good officials. If he ignores corruption or fails to promote wise officials, he is not doing his job."

King Zhuang listened to his wife and challenged Yu. Yu did not have a good answer for his behavior and thus resigned. He was replaced by Sun Shu'ao. Under Shu'ao, the country enjoyed unprecedented prosperity.[1] Because of Lady Fan's security in her position, she felt free to challenge others, and this confidence ultimately led to greater prosperity for all.

Qi Huangyang serves as another example of a secure leader. He served as minister for Duke Ping, ruler of Jin. On one occasion Duke Ping sought his advice on whom to appoint as ruler of Nanyang. Qi Huangyang recommended Xie Hu, in spite of the fact that he was his adversary. Xie Hu was appointed and proved to be a good ruler over Nanyang. Later when Duke Ping asked advice on appointing a new judge for the court, Qi Huangyang recommended his son Qi Wu. Qi Wu was appointed and proved to be a fair and honest judge. Confucius praised Qi Huangyang when he said: "Qi Huangyang made recommendations without prejudice and without fear of being accused of nepotism. He is truly unbiased. In serving his country, he never let personal interest interfere with his work."[2] Great team leaders promote others more skilled than themselves and seek out those who will make them stronger. In this way, leaders grow in their own lives while building up the team

卓越的团队领袖会提拔比自己更有才华的人，也会挑选让自己变得更强大的人。

楚庄王的宰相名叫虞邱子。一次楚庄王询问妻子樊姬，宰相虞邱子是否对国王忠诚。她对丈夫说："我做你的妻子11年，在我跟随你的这段时间里，从未听说他罢黜不称职的官员或提拔能干的官员。假如他对腐败视而不见，或者没有提升博学的官员，那么他就不称职。"

楚庄王听到妻子的话，询问虞邱子。他无言以对，无法解释自己的行为，于是请辞。孙叔敖继任担任宰相。在孙叔敖的管理下，国家获得了空前的繁荣昌盛。[1]樊姬对自己的地位很有安全感，所以也会很果敢，不断提拔别人。

祁黄羊也是个值得学习的榜样，让我们看到了一个有安全感的领袖。他当时是晋悼公的中军尉。祁黄羊以年老为由，辞退中军尉的职务。晋悼公问谁可以继任他的职务。祁黄羊回答，解狐可以胜任。晋悼公反问："解狐不是你的仇人吗？"祁黄羊回答说："你问我谁能任此职，不是问我的仇人是谁。"晋悼公称赞说："好的。"于是就任用解狐继任这个职位。过了些时候，晋悼公又问祁黄羊："国家缺个尉官，谁可以胜任呢？"祁黄羊回答说："祁午可以担任。"晋悼公反问："祁午不是你的儿子吗？"祁黄羊回答说："你是问我谁可以担任尉官，不是问我的儿子是谁。"晋悼公称赞说："好的。"于是就任用祁午为尉官。解狐和祁午任职以后，忠于职守，政绩显著，受到赞扬。孔子听说这件事后，称赞说："祁黄羊的主张好啊！'外举不避仇，内举不避亲，祁黄羊可谓公矣。'"[2]

they are called to serve. A person that builds up another is what I will refer to as an "enlarger."

I have people in my life I love to spend time with. When I am with them, I feel as if I grow in some way. They make me feel good and add to who I am. This type of person is an enlarger. A principle common in all of life is that it takes the greater person to initiate the giving. When leading a team, you will need to believe in your team before they believe in you. You will have to extend trust before they prove trustworthy. You shouldn't hold back compliments or other forms of encouragement if you want to develop your team. Look for ways to give genuine commendations. Two thousand years ago, Publius Syrus, the Roman playwright, wrote, "We are interested in others when they are interested in us."[3]

We all love the person who helps us go to another level. Teachers, leaders, or team members can enlarge others when they take time to learn about the people around them. Listening to what others talk about, how they spend their money, and their future plans will help you make contributions to their lives. A leader really cares and finds ways to help others improve their abilities and talents. By providing opportunities and resources to improve their skills, you will keep your team fresh. This type of leader will have low turnover and a list of others waiting to join the team.

Respecting others is one way of enlarging them. The greatest leadership techniques will be outdone every time by the simple act of truly respecting those on your team. The opposite is also true. Team members, regardless of your praise for their performance, will always feel minimized if inwardly they think you don't respect them. Everything in relationships begins with respect. Human relations author Less Giblin states, "You can't make the other fellow feel important in your presence if you secretly feel that he is a nobody."[4] Showing respect will have a positive effect on every member of your team.

Noticing specific contributions of team members is another way to be an enlarger. Whenever possible, give credit to members of the team publicly, especially when they are not around. Feelings get hurt when someone criticizes us behind our backs. The opposite is also true — saying positive things about others behind their backs encourages and uplifts. This also applies within the family. If I compliment my wife privately, I might gain one positive point in her emotional bank (if we were keeping score). If I compliment her in front of friends, I could score two points. But for her to hear that I was complimenting her when she wasn't

卓越的团队领袖会提拔比自己更有才华的人，也会挑选让自己变得更强大的人。这样，领袖们不仅自己在生命中变得更成熟，而且能够建造自己所服务的团队。他们是建造他人的栽培者。

我喜欢和自己周围的一些人待在一起。当我和他们在一起的时候，我觉得自己在某些方面成长了。他们让我有良好的感觉，让我的生命成长。他们就是栽培者。生命中的一个普遍原则说明，只有伟大的人才能主动给予。带领团队的时候，在团队开始信任你之前，你需要先信任他们。在他人证实自己的可靠之前，你需要先信任他人。如果你希望建立自己的团队，就不应该吝啬而不肯赞美他人，或给予他人其他形式的鼓励。寻找机会，给予他人真诚的赞美。两千年前，罗马的剧作家帕布利乌斯·塞鲁斯（Publius Syrus）写到："当他人对我们表现出兴趣和关注的时候，我们也能对他人产生同样的兴趣。"[3]

我们都喜欢帮助自己更上一层楼的人。当老师、领袖或团队成员花时间了解自己周围的人时，都能够栽培他人。聆听他人的话语，并且了解他们怎样用钱、他们对未来的规划，可以帮助你知道怎样在他们的生命中投资。一个领袖要关心他人，愿意寻找适当的方式帮助他人增加和改善他们的能力和才华。当你提供机会和资源改善他们的能力，你就能够保持团队的新鲜和活力。这样，领袖带领的团队中流动性就会很小，而且还有长长的一队人在等着加入团队。

尊重他人是栽培团队的另一种方式。真诚地尊重团队中的每个人是制胜的法则，胜于最好的领导技巧。反之亦然。不论你怎样赞美团队中成员的表现，假如他们的内心感到你并不尊重他们，仍会觉得自己被小瞧。人际关系中的一切从尊重开始。人际关系大师莱斯·吉布林（Less Giblin）说："假如你心中觉得他人一文不值，就很难让别人在你面前感到自己的重要性。"[4]表现出对他人的尊重会对团队的每个成员产生积极的效果。

关注团队成员的特殊贡献是另外一种栽培的方式。假如可能，要公开赞美团队中的成员，尤其他们不在的时候更应如此。如果别人在背后批评我

around, I am sure to score three to five positive emotional points. I call it passing around good gossip. Try it for a couple of days. Give genuine compliments to team members when they are not around. In no time you will notice the positive effect.

Application

- Make a list of compliments that each member of your team deserves. Start sharing these with them.

- Whenever possible, share these compliments with others who know them. (Be a good gossiper.)

Notation Area

Personal observations/Ideas for further exploration/Thoughts to remember

们，会让我们感到受伤。——在别人背后讲积极的事情，则能鼓励和提升士气。这样的方法也适用于家庭。假如我私下里赞美太太，就在她的情感银行中存入积极的一分（假如我们计分来算的话）。如果我在朋友面前赞美她，就能得两分。如果太太得知，她不在场的时候，我曾在他人面前赞美她，就能够得三到五分。我把这称作"美好的闲话"。尝试两天看看。在团队成员不在的时候，给予他们真诚的赞美。不久，你就会注意到积极的效果。

应用

◆列出每个团队成员所配得的赞美。开始和他们分享你的赞美。

◆一有机会就和认识他们的人分享这些赞誉（闲言碎语也有好的）。

笔记

个人体会／要进一步探讨的想法／要铭记在心的理念

君子欲讷于言，而敏于行。

——孔子

The superior man is modest in his speech, but exceeds in his actions.

——Confucius

李广传奇

Li Guang's Legacy

第九天　有福同享的李广
——以他人为中心

Day 9: Other-Centeredness

人们一定会回应那些真诚对待自己的人。

People can't help but respond to others who are genuinely interested in them.

The superior man is modest in his speech, but exceeds in his actions.

——*Confucius*

Li Guang was a great general during the Qin Dynasty. Whenever Li Guang received a reward, he divided it among his men. He did the same with food supplies. If his troops were short of food or water, he would not eat or drink until his men had their fill. Because of his generosity and consideration, he earned both the respect and loyalty of his men. Upon his death one historian stated, "I found him as unassuming as an ordinary citizen, with no conversational gifts. Yet when he died, his sincerity and honesty had so impressed men that, whether they knew him or not, all mourned for him."[1]

Most people are not interested in you or me. From morning to night their number one interest is themselves. They are constantly thinking about who is nice to them, who appreciates them, who cares for them. Lynn Povich worked at *Newsweek* for twenty-five years. Starting as a secretary, she worked her way up the corporate ladder to senior editor and found herself supervising many of her former supervisors. Many of her colleagues were excited about her promotion. One section editor, however, grew jealous. He felt she was not qualified and only received the position because she was a woman. Povich ignored his comments and worked hard at her job. In the first few months she demonstrated a genuine interest in each section she supervised by listening and talking to the writers.

After six months her big critic walked into her office, sat down across from her, and told her what he thought. "I have to tell you something," he said. "I was totally against this move. I thought you were too young. I thought you didn't have the experience. I thought you got the promotion only because you were a woman." In spite of his original judgment, Lynn's selflessness won him over. He watched her

君子欲讷于言，而敏于行。

——孔子

译文：君子必须要能谨慎地说话，而勤勉地做事。

李广是汉朝的著名将军。每次李广得到赏赐时，就和军中将士分享。对于食物供应也是如此。如果军队缺少粮草和水，他也会和士兵一起忍饥挨饿，直到军队的粮草充足。由于他的慷慨和体恤，获得了士兵的尊重和忠诚。在他去世后，一位历史学家这样评论说："余睹李将军悛悛如鄙人，口不能道辞。及死之日，天下知与不知，皆为尽哀。"（译文：我所见过的李将军老实得像个质朴的乡下人，不善言谈。死后，天下无论是否认识他的人，都很哀恸。）[1]

大部分人对他人并没有浓厚的兴趣。从早到晚，他们的第一兴趣就是自己。他们常常在想谁对他们好，谁欣赏他们，谁关心他们。林恩·鲍维奇（Lynn Povich）在《新闻周刊》（*Newsweek*）工作近二十五年。她从秘书做起，在集团中努力工作，一帆风顺，后来成了高级编辑，很多原先的老上级都归她主管。很多同事对她获得提升都感到很兴奋。然而，一个专栏主编却很嫉妒她，觉得她并不胜任这项工作，之所以被任命只是因为她是女人。鲍维奇没有理睬他的评论，工作非常努力。在头几个月中，她对其他作者认真聆听，和他们谈话，表现出对自己所主管的每个部门的真诚和兴趣。

六个月后，那个一直持批评态度的专栏主编走进办公室，坐在她的对面，说出了自己的想法："我得告诉你一些事情。"他说，"我当时完全反对提升你，觉得你太年轻了，以为你没有经验。我觉得你之所以被任命，就是

show genuine interest in the success of the other writers and editors. At last he commented, "I've had four guys who were senior editors before you. None of them genuinely cared. It's absolutely clear that you really are interested, and you show that interest to everyone."[2]

Povich moved on to become editor-in-chief of *Working Woman* magazine because she genuinely cared for her team. In discussing her management style, Povich comments, "First of all, you can't be remote. You have to touch base with them on a regular basis. . . . I'm interested in their work, and I'm interested in them as people."[3]

People can't help but respond to others who are genuinely interested in them. It's a basic fact of human beings. We are flattered by attention from others. It makes us feel important and valuable as people. A leader who shows interest in others will have a team interested in him or her. Great leaders regularly show authentic interest in others.

We can learn to show interest in others every day. Learning how to care is crucial for a leader. It is especially important to show interest in people that others overlook. Secretaries, assistants, receptionists, messengers, and building guards are all significant. These are people who help our lives run a little more smoothly every day. Little things like learning their names and asking questions about their families or holiday plans show that we care. Gestures of kindness make even a dull job more interesting. This type of behavior is something that can be learned with just a little bit of practice. Once you realize the importance of caring, you will have no trouble making it a part of your life. Soon you will find yourself expressing interest in others and genuinely caring about the people around you.

You can make more friends in two months by becoming genuinely interested in other people than you can in two years by trying to get others interested in you.

——Dale Carnegie

因为你是个女人。"虽然他起初判断失误，但是林恩的无私赢得了他的信任。他看到她对其他作者和编辑表现出真诚和兴趣。最后，他这样评论："在你之前，我还经历过另外四个高级编辑。他们没有一个人真正关心作者和编辑。我可以看出来你真正感兴趣，你向每个人表示你的关心。"[2]

因为鲍维奇真正关心自己的团队，她不断被提拔，后来成了《职业女性》（*Working Woman*）杂志社的主编。当鲍维奇讨论自己的管理风格时，她这样评论："首先，你不能遥不可及。你需要常常和他们保持联络……我对他们的工作感兴趣，我对他们个人本身也很关心。"[3]

人们忍不住要回应那些真诚对待自己的人，这是人类的本性。我们会因为他人的关注而感到受宠若惊。这让我们感到自己做人的重要性和价值。一个领袖如果对团队成员表现出关心和兴趣，才能够建立一个关心自己的团队。卓越的领袖常常这样做。

我们每天都可以学习怎样表现出对他人的关心。学习如何关心是一个领袖的关键，关心被人忽略的人尤为重要。秘书、助理、接待员、送信的人以及门卫都很重要。这些人让我们每天的生活变得更顺利一点。记住他们的名字、询问他们的家人的状况以及度假的计划，都能表现出我们的关心。充满善意的手势会让一份沉闷乏味的工作变得更有意思。这样的行为需要一点点练习就可以学会。一旦你意识到关心的重要性，就会轻而易举地把它变成自己生活的一部分，慢慢学会表达对周围人的真诚和关心。

如果你表达出对他人的真诚和关心，会在两个月中交到很多朋友。你可能一直希望获得他人的关心，但是这样做两年中交到的朋友，可能还没有那两个月中交到的朋友多。

——戴尔·卡内基

Application

◆ Choose one or two people whom you have overlooked and show them genuine kindness this week.

Notation Area

Personal observations/Ideas for further exploration/Thoughts to remember

应用

◆选择一两个你从前忽略的人，在本周向他们表达真诚的善意。

笔记

个人体会／要进一步探讨的想法／要铭记在心的理念

故进不求名，退不避罪，唯人是保，而利合于主，国之宝也。

——孙子[1]

The general who in advancing does not seek personal fame and in retreating is not concerned with disgrace, but whose only purpose is to protect the country and promote the best interest of his sovereign, is the precious jewel of the state.

——Sun Tzu[1]

服侍的心

A Heart of Service

第十天 孙子的国之宝
——超越期望值

Day 10:Exceed Expectations

成功领袖的关键在于迈出小我，注意到他人的需要。

The key to successful leading requires stepping outside yourself and discovering what others need.

The general who in advancing does not seek personal fame and in retreating is not concerned with disgrace, but whose only purpose is to protect the country and promote the best interest of his sovereign, is the precious jewel of the state.

——*Sun Tzu* [1]

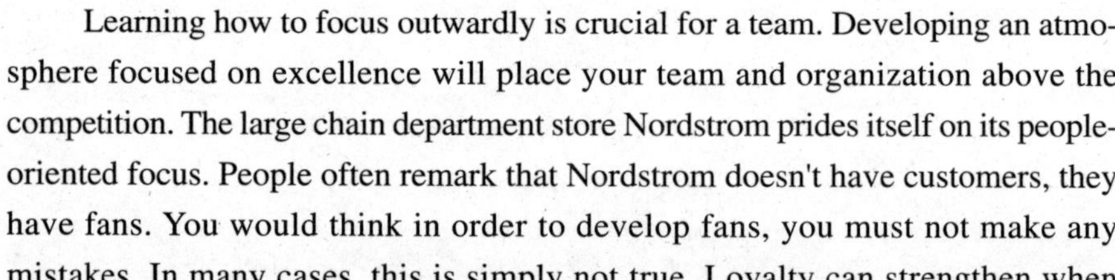

Learning how to focus outwardly is crucial for a team. Developing an atmosphere focused on excellence will place your team and organization above the competition. The large chain department store Nordstrom prides itself on its people-oriented focus. People often remark that Nordstrom doesn't have customers, they have fans. You would think in order to develop fans, you must not make any mistakes. In many cases, this is simply not true. Loyalty can strengthen when people with complaints have their problems solved in a way that exceeds their expectations.

In just the last two weeks, one company lost my loyalty and another one gained it. The first company was a coffee shop that has spread across our city. The company is American-owned and has prospered in Beijing. A recent summer promotional campaign promised a T-shirt or mug if you ordered some of their summertime specialty drinks. I am a creature of habit and always order the same thing, but my wife started buying the specialty drinks and collecting stickers in order to receive the T-shirt. As I ordered the last drink needed to win a T-shirt, the cashier told me that all the shirts were gone. A little disappointed but still hopeful, I asked if there was a replacement item, like the mug. I assumed that because they were an American company, they would replace the item with something of equal or higher value in order to keep customers satisfied. She went on to tell me that I could have a mug, but I needed to order five more specialty drinks. In other words, no substitution was being offered in place of the T-shirt. She also informed me if I really wanted a T-shirt, I could buy one. They still had shirts to sell, but none left to give away. A bit upset, I sat down and looked over the promotional material, and it did

故进不求名，退不避罪，唯人是保，而利合于主，国之宝也。

——孙子[1]

译文：进不求功名，退不避罪责，只求保全民众有利于国君，这样的将帅，才是国家的珍宝。

学习一致对外，这对于一个团队来说至关重要。培养出追求卓越的团队，这会让你的团队和机构遥遥领先。大型连锁店诺斯丹（Nordstrom）为自己以人为本的着眼点而感到骄傲。人们常常这样评论，诺斯丹没有"顾客"，有的只是"粉丝"（fans，追捧者）。你可能以为要想培养"粉丝"，就不能犯一点错误。但是在很多情况下，事实并非如此。如果人们的抱怨和问题得到妥善解决，甚至超越了自己的期望值，就能够赢得人们的忠实。

在过去的两周中，一家公司失去了我这位忠实的顾客，而另一家则赢得了我的信任。头一家是美国公司，拥有遍布各个城市的咖啡店，在北京也很受欢迎。最近他们有夏季促销活动，如果你点夏天的促销饮品，积攒到一定数量，就能够得到一件T恤或一个杯子。我有自己的习惯，每次点的东西都一样，但我的妻子开始点夏季促销饮品，把获得的贴纸攒起来，希望能够赢得一件T恤。我点了兑换一件T恤所需要的最后一杯饮料，但是收银员却告诉我T恤已经全部送光了。我稍稍有点失望，但是还是满怀希望。我询问是否可以有其他替代的礼物，像杯子之类的东西。我想因为他们是家美国公司，可能会用等价的甚至是价值更高一点的东西代替，好让自己的顾客感到满意。收银员则告诉我再点五杯饮品才可以拿到一个杯子。换句话说，T恤没有了，也没有什么替代品。她还告诉我，假如喜欢T恤的话，可以买一件。他们还有用于销售的T恤，但是赠送的却一件也没有了。我稍稍感到不舒服，

state "while supplies last." Although the company didn't offer service less than what they promised, they fell short of my expectations built from experiencing similar businesses in the United States. They lost my loyalty.

On the opposite end of customer service, the Haier appliance company has always impressed me with their service. When our washing machine malfunctioned, we gave them a call. They promptly came over, and although they were unable to fix the problem the first time, they worked hard not to inconvenience our family's schedule. We also received a polite call in the evening, checking to see if the service we received that day solved our problem. In the end, part of the problem turned out to be our drains and not the machine. However, my confidence in the company improved because of their service after my initial purchase.

A study conducted by the Technical Assistance Research Program (TARP) based in Washington D.C. showed that most customers don't complain to management about a problem. They found that, depending on the severity of the problem, a customer will tell nine to sixteen friends and acquaintances about their negative experience. The study also found that 13 percent of customers will tell more than twenty people, and two-thirds of customers with bad experiences will never buy from that store again. Remember, this all transpires without the manager ever hearing the complaint.

TARP also found that 95 percent of dissatisfied customers would buy from the store again if their problem were solved quickly. They also will tell an average of eight people about the positive resolution to their problem. Showing concern for others' problems has a direct effect on the success of every organization. Great leaders show concern for their teams and help them show concern for others. That is to say, exceeding expectations is one way that you improve on or develop your level of concern.

In order to feel genuine concern for others, it is important to see things from their viewpoint. Looking at situations from another person's point of view is fundamental in any healthy relationship. The retail industry has caught onto this principle. Most people are familiar with the Golden Rule: Do to others as you would have them do to you. Companies now have what they call the Platinum Rule: Treat others as they would want you to treat them. Regardless of the country where you live, you probably have entered stores where clerks are huddled together talking; it is clear that customer service is far from their top priority. When someone finally breaks away to assist you, they almost make you feel apologetic

坐下来认真看了一下促销的材料，上面的确写着“送完为止”。虽然公司所提供的服务并没有食言，但是我根据美国同类商业惯例所产生的期待却没有得到满足。他们失去了我的忠诚。

在客户服务方面，海尔电器公司则恰恰相反，他们的服务一直给我留下了深刻的印象。我们的洗衣机出现故障的时候，打一个电话，售后服务人员就立刻赶过来。虽然没能在第一次解决问题，但是他们克服困难，不给我们家庭本来的计划带来一点点不便。晚上我们还接到了一个很有礼貌的电话，了解我们是否得到了恰当的服务，是否解决了我们的问题。最后我们发现，是下水出了问题，而不是机器的故障。然而，我们享受到的优质服务增加了我们对这家公司的信心。

华盛顿的技术援助研究项目（Technical Assistance Research Program）做了一项调查，统计结果显示，大部分顾客不会向公司的管理阶层反映问题。他们发现，根据问题的严重程度，一位顾客可能会把自己的消极经历告诉9到16位顾客。研究也发现，13%的顾客会告诉超过20个人。有过消极经历的顾客中，三分之二的人以后不再购买这家商店的东西。记住，这一切都是在经理们毫不知情的情况下发生的，他们根本就没有听到任何抱怨。

技术援助项目也发现，如果问题被迅速解决，95%的顾客会再次购买那家商店的物品。他们也会把问题得到积极解决的经历和大约8个人分享。对他人的问题表现出关注，这一点可以产生直接效果，在机构中带来成功。卓越的领袖对自己的团队表现出关心，也帮助团队的成员表现出对他人的关心。也就是说，超越他人的期待也是你改变或培养自己对他人的关心程度的一种方式。

要想表示对他人真正的关心，重要一点就是从他人的角度看待问题，这是任何健康关系的基础。零售业就遵守了这个原则。大部分人都熟悉黄金法则：你希望别人怎样对待你，也要怎样对待别人。现在的公司遵行他们所称的白金法则：他人希望你怎样对待自己，你就要用这样的方法对待他们。不论在哪个国家，你都能够看到店员们挤在一处聊天。显然，顾客服务根本不

for interrupting their social hour. In the U.S. and China, customer service has become a priority. Sam Walton said, "Exceed your customers' expectations. If you do, they'll come back over and over. Give them what they want and a little more."[2] One way that Walton applied this principle was by placing full-time greeters at the entrances of his Wal-Mart stores. Their sole responsibility was to welcome customers and help them find what they were looking for. Walton figured customers would appreciate a store that provided such a service.[3]

A leader needs to help his team think about what the customer wants. They should assess how their customers view them. Scandinavian Airlines (SAS) president Jan Carlzon said, "Last year, each of our ten million customers came in contact with approximately five SAS employees. This contact lasted an average of fifteen seconds. These fifty million moments of truth are moments that ultimately determine whether SAS will succeed."[4]

The key to successful leading requires stepping outside yourself and discovering what others need. Your team can model the same service to others that they have seen you model for them. Noticing the needs of your team is a great way to begin this modeling process. Seek to provide your team with the emotional and physical resources they need to grow and succeed. Model this type of personal service with the team and with clients for the next month. I promise you, your team will notice, and in no time at all they will start to do the same.

在他们的首要优先权范围中。当你一再招呼店员，终于有人转身帮助你时，简直让你觉得自己打扰了他们的社交时光，好像应该感到愧疚似的。现在，无论是在美国还是在中国，客户服务已经变成了第一优先。萨姆·沃尔顿（Sam Walton）说："超越顾客的期望值。假如你做到了这一点，他们会一次次回来。给他们想要的东西，而且再多一点点。"[2]沃尔顿在实践中应用了这个原则，让迎宾员一直站在沃尔玛商店的门口。他们只有一个责任，就是迎接顾客，帮助他们找到自己想要的东西。沃尔顿发现顾客喜欢提供这类服务的商店。[3]

领袖需要帮助团队想到顾客的需要。他们需要评估顾客怎样看待自己。北欧航空公司（Scandinavian Airlines）的总裁简·卡尔宗（Jan Carlzon）说："去年，我们的一千万位顾客大约每位接触到五名北欧航空公司的员工。每次这样的接触平均下来大约持续15秒钟。这五千万个真实的时刻最终决定了北欧航空公司的成败。"[4]

成功领袖的关键在于迈出小我，注意到他人的需要。你的团队会把你作为榜样，你怎样为他人提供服务，他们也会同样服务于人。注意到团队的需要是一个良好的开始，这会让你开始成为团队的榜样。领袖要为自己的团队提供情感和身体上的需要，帮助他们成长和成功。下个月，你就为顾客提供个性化的服务，为团队做个好榜样吧。我敢保证，你的团队会注意到这些变化，不久，他们也会这样做。

Application

- Identify some of the emotional and physical needs of your team. Start meeting the easiest needs and keep working on the rest. For example, take note of who is emotionally down or struggling, ask them about it, and find ways you can help.

- Make an effort to specifically train your team on customer priority thinking (by role playing, contests, "secret shoppers" who report back on the customer service they received, and competitions). These principles are just as appropriate in the home as in the workplace.

Notation Area

Personal observations/Ideas for further exploration/Thoughts to remember

应用

◆发现团队的情感和身体需要。开始时，先满足最简单的需要，然后不断致力于其他需要。例如，询问一下谁在因为情感需要而挣扎，找到可以帮助他的方法。

◆致力于团队培训，进行具体的顾客至上的思维培训（可以通过角色扮演、竞赛和“秘密顾客”的方法，让他们报告自己所享受到的顾客服务）。这些原则不仅适用于商场，也同样适用于家庭。

笔记

个人体会／要进一步探讨的想法／要铭记在心的理念

当你变革的时候，不能期待大家都喜欢你，很多人会墨守成规。士大夫会被自己所学到的东西捆绑住手脚。他们是良好的管理者，因为他们能够推行法律，但是他们不敢改变现状。睿智的人起草法律，普通人则受到法律的管理。

——商鞅

You cannot expect to be popular when bringing about change. The average person clings to what they know. The learned are handicapped by their learning. They make good administrators because they can enforce laws, but they are not daring enough to change the status quo. Wise men create the laws while the simple are governed by them.

——*Shang Yang*

商鞅变法

Shang Yang's reforms

第十一天 商鞅变法
——变化中的领袖角色

Day 11:The Leader's Role in Change

在变化的过程中，卓越的领袖改变的不仅仅是系统和程序，他们改变人和对人、对事的态度。

During the change process, great leaders change more than systems and procedures. They change people and attitudes.

You cannot expect to be popular when bringing about change. The average person clings to what they know. The learned are handicapped by their learning. They make good administrators because they can enforce laws, but they are not daring enough to change the status quo. Wise men create the laws while the simple are governed by them.

——*Shang Yang*

In the middle of the fifth century BC, China entered into the Warring States period. Small states were swallowed up by bigger states until seven states gained dominance. Qin, located in northwest China, was the most backward state and was considered barbarian by the others. In order to rectify this backward reputation, the Qin rulers sought to recruit men of great abilities from the other six states. One of these men was Shang Yang. In the course of time, Shang Yang instituted unprecedented reform policies. His reforms rewarded men based on their military merits and contribution of grain, thus doing away with the hereditary aristocracy. Peasants were given the right to own land. Laws were strict, and people were expected to report crimes lest they also receive punishment.

The king of Qin was concerned that such drastic reforms were causing too much discontent. Shang Yang encouraged him to keep going and warned him that if he stopped now, the reforms would have no effect. "Your Majesty," he said, "You cannot expect to be popular when bringing about change. The average person clings to what they know. The learned are handicapped by their learning. They make good administrators because they can enforce laws, but they are not daring enough to change the status quo. Wise men create the laws while the simple are governed by them. Even if the reforms are not fully supported, we must move ahead for the future good of the state." Shang Yang's reforms brought prosperity and order to the state. Qin soon became both strong and prosperous.[1]

Leading during a time of change will test your ability to learn from situations and people. Few leaders live their lives avoiding change. Most leaders are agents of change. When describing future leaders, authors of *The Leader in You*, Stuart

当你变革的时候，不能期待大家都喜欢你，很多人会墨守成规。士大夫会被自己所学到的东西捆绑住手脚。他们是良好的管理者，因为他们能够推行法律，但是他们不敢改变现状。睿智的人起草法律，普通人则受到法律的管理。

——商鞅

在公元前五世纪中叶，中国进入了战国时期。小国家被大国吞并，最后只有七个国家仍旧占据统治地位。秦国位于中国的西北部，是当时最落后的国家，被其他国家当成野蛮民族。秦王为了改善自己落后的名声，从其他六国招募一些人才，其中一个就是商鞅。后来，商鞅提出并实施了一系列史无前例的改革政策。这些措施根据人的军事才华和捐粮的数量进行奖赏，因此就废除了世袭的贵族制度。农民有权利拥有土地。法律非常严明，人们要报告身边的犯罪事件，否则就会受到惩罚。

秦王担心这样激烈的改革措施会带来不满情绪。商鞅鼓励他继续坚持下去，并且警告他：假如现在就停止，改革就不会带来丝毫益处。“大王，”他说，“当你变革的时候，不能期待大家都喜欢你，很多人会墨守成规。士大夫会被自己所学到的东西捆绑住手脚。他们是良好的管理者，因为他们能够推行法律，但是他们不敢改变现状。睿智的人起草法律，普通人则受到法律的管理。即使改革不被完全支持，我们要考虑到国家的利益，必须继续推行下去。”商鞅的改革给国家带来了繁荣和秩序，秦国很快变得强大和富足。[1]

在变革中做领袖能够测试你的能力，帮助你从环境和周围的人身上学习。很少有领袖能在有生之年避免改变。大部分领袖都处于变化的风云中。《你心中潜在的领袖》（*The Leader in You*）的作者斯图亚特·莱文（Stuart Levine）和迈克尔·克罗姆（Michael Crom）这样描述未来的领袖：“他们需

Levine and Michael Crom, state, "They will have to keep their wits about them through conditions of near-constant change."[2]

One of the most challenging and potentially rewarding projects for a leader involves guiding an organization through a major change. Leading toward change is often harder than starting an entirely new organization. It is true that charisma, vision, and strong leadership are needed in both. Leaders often attract others who believe in their vision when launching a new campaign. Those who don't buy the vision simply go their own way. But during a process of change, people already have a vested interest in the status quo. Just the rumor of change can cause a fight or flight reaction.

A reporter interviewed a man on his one-hundredth birthday. The reporter said, "I bet you've seen a lot of changes in your life!" "Yes," the man said, "and I've been against every one of them."[3]

This man's response too often echoes the common mind-set of workers today. People experience pain over any new idea. If you suggest trying something a new way, you may actually see the resistance. Their bodies tense up. They shoot you dirty looks. They might even experience physical pain in the form of stress, headaches, or ulcers. On the opposite end of the spectrum, there are those with an entrepreneurial spirit who will say, "Let's give it a go. Even if it flops, we will learn from it and can do better next time." Leaders need to be prepared for varied responses when changes are introduced.

During the change process, great leaders change more than systems and procedures. They change people and attitudes. They help people shift from managing to leading. As you learn to move from directing to guiding, your team can move from competing to collaborating, suspicion to trust, from withholding information to sharing. Under the right conditions, people shift from passive mode to that of risk-taking. When a team truly feels valued as people, and not just assets, they can change from apathy to involvement, from resentment to contentment, from failure to success.[4] Leaders may be rewarded at times by seeing outward changes in systems and structure build inward character among team members.

Napoleon Bonaparte stands out as one of history's most successful military strategists. One of his most formidable opponents, the Duke of Wellington, once said, "I consider Napoleon's presence in the field to equal forty thousand men in the balance."[5] Napoleon once told a defeated opponent the mistake that cost him the battle: "You draw up your plans the day before battle, when you do not yet

要保持警觉，帮助团队平安度过未来不断发生的变化。”[2]

对于领袖来说，一个最具挑战，同时也最具潜力的任务，就是在大变化中为一个机构导航。在变化中带领和导航，要比创办一个全新的机构更难。当然，在这两种情况下都需要领袖魅力、愿景和很强的领导力。在创办新项目的时候，领袖们常常会吸引相信自己愿景的人。对这样的愿景不感兴趣的人可以走自己的路。但是在改变中，人们已经在当前的状况下有了一些既得利益，仅仅是改变的谣言就足以带来人们对抗或逃跑的效应。

记者采访一位百岁老人。记者问道："我相信您一生中一定见过很多改变。"老人回答道："的确如此，而且我也和每个改变对抗过。"[3]

这位老人的回答和今天人们的普遍心态类似。人们面对任何一个新想法都会感到痛苦。假如你建议尝试全新的方法，就会看到他人的抵制：他们的身体变得僵硬紧张，摆出一张苦瓜脸，甚至可能因为压力产生身体上的不舒适、头痛或溃疡。然而还有另一种极端的人，这些具备企业家激情的人会说："我们尝试一下。即使失败了，也可以从中学习，下次能够做得更好。"在变化中，领袖需要预备自己，面对各样的挑战。

在变化的过程中，卓越的领袖改变的不仅仅是系统和程序，也会改变你对人、对事的态度。他们帮助他人改变，不再是管理而是带领。当你学习从指示变成指导的时候，你的团队也会从竞争变为合作，从怀疑变为信任，从隐瞒资讯到分享资讯。在特定的条件下，人们会从消极的模式转变为勇于冒险。一个团队真正感受到自己被作为人而珍视，而不是隶属的财产，他们就从冷漠变成参与，从仇恨变成满足，从失败走向成功。[4]领袖此时也会获得自己的奖赏，因为他能够看到系统外在的改变和团队成员内心中品格的建立。

拿破仑·波拿巴(Napoleon Bonaparte)才华横溢，是历史上最成功的军事战略家之一。他最强劲的对手惠灵顿公爵(Duke of Wellington)曾说过："拿破仑出现在战场上，抵得上四万名士兵。"[5]面对自己的手下败将，拿破仑曾经这样评论对方战场失利的主要因素："你在战役之前定下自己的作战计划，但是那个时候，你还不知道自己对手的行动呢。"[6]战役打响前五分钟，他没

know your adversary's movements."[6] The inability to change battle plans at the last minute was a weakness Napoleon capitalized on in order to win the victory. Lack of adaptability is a weakness you can't afford in your team.

If leaders want to be effective change agents, they need to possess the following characteristics to some degree:

- An innovative spirit. Do you see areas where improvement is needed? Where could new ideas or processes greatly improve results? Develop those ideas and share them with the team.
- Values based on principle. Personal character and fortitude create stability. Many voices will challenge a leader's direction. Others will attack your character in order to undermine your authority. Your passion for principle and personal character will help you weather the attacks.
- A low need for affirmation and the ability to take criticism lightly. Leaders must learn to draw their affirmation from sources external to the project. Those within the project are likely to give affirmation only when decisions are personally favorable. This type of affirmation is very fickle and should not affect the leader's decisions.
- A curious mind. Curious leaders are open to learning new things. Such leaders ask genuine questions and listen for wise answers from multiple sources.
- A persevering attitude. Small setbacks are bound to happen in any change process. Great leaders learn from each failure in order to achieve even greater success in the future.[7]

有对自己的作战计划进行改动。于是，拿破仑利用对方的弱点赢得了胜利。缺少适应性也是团队中的一个大问题，后果不堪设想。

假如领袖希望自己成为能带来改变的力量，他们就需要拥有以下品格：

- 创新精神。你看到需要改善的地方了吗？新的想法和方法可以在哪些地方大大改善可能出现的结果？领袖要有新的想法，和团队分享自己的意见。
- 基于原则建立的价值观。个人的品格和不屈不挠的精神能够建立稳定性。众说纷纭会改变领袖的方向，还有人会攻击你的品格，削弱你的权柄。你对原则的追求和个人的品格能够帮助你经受住攻击。
- 不太需要他人的肯定，轻松对待批评。领袖们必须学会从工作以外的地方获得肯定。只有在你的决定迎合了他人的喜好时，你才有可能从工作场合获得肯定。这类肯定转瞬即逝，不应该影响领袖的决定。
- 保持求知欲。求知欲很强的领袖愿意学习新知识。这样的领袖会提出真诚的问题，多方听取建议。
- 不屈不挠的态度。在任何改变的过程中都会出现小小的挫折。卓越的领袖能够从失败中学习，在未来赢得更大的成功。[7]

Application

- Do you need to initiate change within your team? If you do, ensure that you have emotional support and affirmative individuals outside of your team.

- Which of the above traits do you already possess?

- What inward character traits surfaced last time you were faced with a change at work?

- Pick a trait or two that you would like to improve.

Notation Area

Personal observations/Ideas for further exploration/Thoughts to remember

应用

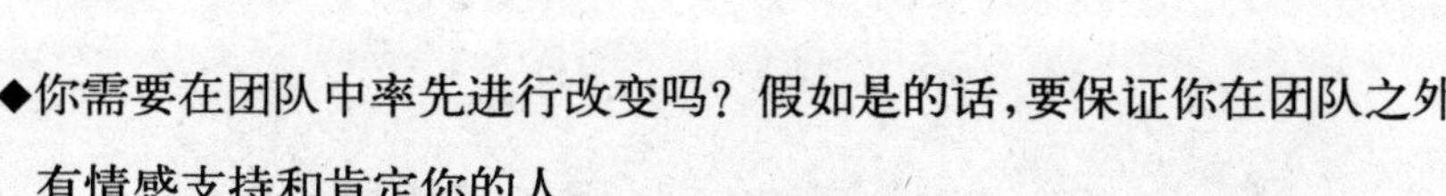

◆你需要在团队中率先进行改变吗？假如是的话，要保证你在团队之外有情感支持和肯定你的人。

◆你已经拥有以上哪些特征？

◆你从前在工作中面对挑战的时候，哪些内在的性格特征浮现出来？

◆挑选一两个你希望改善的特征。

笔记

个人体会／要进一步探讨的想法／要铭记在心的理念

知人者智，自知者明。胜人者有力，自胜者强。

——《道德经》

Knowing others is intelligence; knowing yourself is true wisdom. Mastering others is strength; mastering yourself is true power.

——*Tao Te Ching*

假想的恐惧

Imaginary Fears

第十二天 草木皆兵
——变化中的挑战

Day 12:The Challenges of Change

领袖应该成为改变中的要素，他们的价值观要基于原则。

Leaders need to be change agents whose values are based on principle.

Knowing others is intelligence; knowing yourself is true wisdom. Mastering others is strength; mastering yourself is true power.

——*Tao Te Ching*

King Fu Jian led a large army attack on Eastern Han around AD 383. His first assault was not successful. As he prepared for his second assault on the city wall, he was shaken by the battle array of the Eastern Han army as it spread out before the city wall. Fu Jian then looked at the mountains around the city and mistook the many trees on the hillside for enemy soldiers. His courage sapped as he led his troops into battle, King Fu Jian lost the battle that day. The saying "every bush and tree looks like an enemy" originated from this battle. The proverb warns of how one can be defeated by imagined difficulties.[1]

The process of change creates many imagined fears. Just as fear caused a military defeat for Fu Jian, imagined fears among your team will hinder a change process. Leaders face the challenge of overcoming all the barriers that cause people to resist change. One barrier that consistently hinders change is fear. People fear the loss of control and the loss of desirable benefits. When people are not in control of the change process, they feel helpless and unstable. Team members are naturally concerned about losing such things as status, money, and friendships.

One way to help people overcome their fear is to make some aspects of the change negotiable. Allow people to decide, to some extent, how the change will be implemented. People also resist change when the proposed reward does not outweigh the perceived losses. Many of us become complacent and just don't like change, living by the quote, "If it ain't broke, don't fix it." Sometimes, however, we see problems but are unwilling to fix them. Leaders working with a new group of people or organization are likely to hear the response, "But that's not the way we do it around here."

知人者智，自知者明。胜人者有力，自胜者强。

——《道德经》

译文：能了解、认识别人叫做聪明，能认识、了解自己才算智慧。能战胜别人是有力的，能克制自己的弱点才算刚强。

公元383年，前秦国王符坚率大军攻打东晋。他的第一次攻击并未奏效。当他站在城墙上，准备第二次攻击的时候，他看到东晋军队的阵容排列整齐，感到非常震撼。符坚看到远处的山脉，把山上的许多树木也错认为敌军。他的勇气已经消耗殆尽。“草木皆兵”这个成语由此而来。这个成语让我们看到符坚疑神疑鬼，会被自己想象的东西吓倒。[1]

改变的过程会带来很多假想的恐惧。正如恐惧导致了符坚在军事上的失败，同样，团队中假想的恐惧也会阻碍改变的进程。领袖必须面对挑战和克服障碍，因为一般情况下，障碍的出现会让人们拒绝改变。阻碍改变的一个障碍常常就是恐惧。人们惧怕失去控制，失去自己想要获得的东西。当自己不再能够控制改变的进程时，人们会感到无助和不稳定。团队成员自然害怕会失去地位、金钱和友谊之类的东西。

帮助人们克服恐惧的一种方式就是协商改变的某些方面，可以在某种程度上让人们决定该怎样推行改变的进程。当改变可能让人们失去相应的利益时，人们也会抵制改变。很多人满足于现状，不喜欢生活中出现的任何改变。他们的座右铭就是：“假如没坏，就不需要修理。”然而，有时候，我们看到了问题，却不愿意去修正。领袖们来到新的人群中或机构里的时候，常常会听到这样的说法：“我们这儿以前不是这样做事的。”

过渡改变期间的领袖至关重要。假如领袖没有获得人们的尊重和信任，

Leadership is crucial during any transitional change, but if a leader is not trusted, change will be almost impossible. When the leader isn't respected or trusted, even a desirable change can be resisted. Distrust in leadership will create a negative atmosphere that will make the process very painful for all involved.

The common barriers of fear, complacency, routine, and distrust exist to some extent in most organizations. It is the leader's responsibility to help people move beyond them. There are two ways to help people overcome these barriers.

First, education and communication during a time of change is crucial. A leader can almost never give too much information. Inform your team as specifically as possible the what's, why's, and how's of the change. Show genuine concern for their fears and teach new skills when they are needed. This will facilitate people's trust as they observe you aiding and equipping them to survive in the new system. Second, be open to questions both publicly and privately. Encourage participation: if people feel they have valued input they are less likely to resist. Allowing them to contribute ideas returns a sense of control they may feel they've lost.

As mentioned earlier, leaders need to be change agents whose values are based on principle-they know what they are doing is the right thing to do. Leaders have little need for affirmation and have the ability to take criticism-they move forward with confidence even though many try to discredit them. Along with these qualities, a leader should assess how well he is doing the following:

- Honor present and past commitments. By recognizing early contributors, you build bridges from the past to the future. Great leaders look to the future without forgetting the present. Always build bridges from the present to the future.
- Be humble and optimistic. You don't always have to be right. It's okay if you don't have all the answers. Let your team contribute.
- Learn from everyone. Listen to the concerns and ideas of your team. Listening to others should not be viewed as a weakness.
- Budget for the unexpected. Many a great project has failed for lack of funding. Don't let it happen to you. Realize there will be surprise expenses, and budget accordingly.
- Read the signs of change in advance. Those prepared can take positive advantage of changing situations. It is easier to create the future than it is

改变几乎不太可能，即使是可取的改变也会遭到抵制。对领袖的不信任会引起消极的氛围，整个过程让所有参与的人都感到苦不堪言。

大多数机构中，在某种程度上都有惧怕、自以为是、惯例和不信任这些普遍的障碍。领袖的责任是帮助人们超越这一切。有两种方法可以帮助人们克服这些障碍。

首先，改变期间的培训和沟通很关键。领袖告知大家多少信息都不为过，如改变中会发生什么事情，为什么发生，怎样发生。要真诚地关心他们表现出来的惧怕。假如需要的话，可以教导他们新的技巧。当人们看到你帮助和装备他们面对新环境时，也会增加对你的信任。第二，以开放的心态面对公开提出的和私下流传的问题，应该鼓励大家参与。如果人们觉得自己提出了宝贵的意见，他们就不太可能抵制改变。提供意见会让他们拥有自己在支配的感受，这样就可以弥补他们在改变中可能出现的失控感。

正如前文所提到的，领袖应该成为改变的要素，他们的价值观要基于原则——他们知道自己的行为是正确的。领袖不太需要他人的肯定，能够轻松面对批评——虽然有很多人怀疑他们的可信度，但是他们仍然靠着信心前进。除了具备这些品质，领袖还需要评估一下以下各点：

- 遵守自己现在和过去的承诺。承认他人从前的帮助，就在过去和未来之间建起了一座桥梁。卓越的领袖展望未来的时候并没有忘记现在，而是把现在和未来联系起来。
- 谦逊乐观。你不必成为不犯错误的人。假如你不知道所有问题的答案也没有关系，这正好可以让你的团队贡献自己的力量。
- 从每个人身上学习。聆听团队关注的问题和想法，特别要聆听“弱者”的想法。
- 预备不时之需。很多大项目都因为缺少资金而失败。不要让这样的事情发生在自己身上。要将意料之外的花销计入预算中。
- 提前发现变化的兆头。提前预备的人能够采取积极的措施，面对改

to rewrite the past.

- View change as positive and a natural result of growth. Things do change, so you can either grumble through it or embrace it.
- Celebrate the unique differences of your team. Embrace the variety of gifts represented by your people. You will need all kinds of talent and creative points of view if you are going to achieve success.
- Be decisive and don't allow your vision to die in a committee. Set a course and invite others to get on board. Committed members can help redirect and fine-tune your vision, but don't let them stop you.
- Show the appropriate appreciation to your team. Successful changes require the support of many individuals. Take the time to let people know that you see and appreciate their investments in the vision.[2]

The first time you lead your team into change will likely be a great learning experience. The perspective you gain from successes and failures will prove invaluable for your future success. I have heard it said that good leaders possess good perspective, better leaders have better perspective, and great leaders enjoy great perspective. Leaders should soberly embark in change processes with a great expectation for learning.

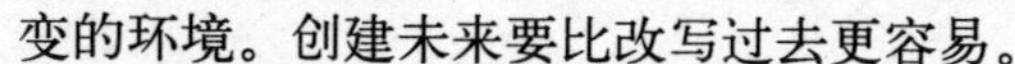

变的环境。创建未来要比改写过去更容易。

- 把改变看作成长所带来的、积极且自然的结果。事情的确会发生改变，所以你可以选择抱怨不休，也可以选择面对改变。
- 接纳团队的独特性。接纳团队成员表现出来的不同恩赐。假如你希望取得成功，就需要人们具有各种各样的才华，提出各种有创造性的观点。
- 认定自己的目标，不要让你的愿景在委员会审议中猝死。确定路线，邀请他人加入董事会。其他成员可以引导你、帮助你调整自己的愿景，但是不要让他们拦住你的脚步。
- 向团队表达适当的感激。成功的改变需要很多的人参与。花些时间让大家知道，你看到并且感激他们对愿景的投入。[2]

第一次带领团队面对改变可能是个很大的学习经历。你从成功和失败中学到的看法和观点，会给你未来的成功带来无法估量的潜力。我听过这样的说法：好领袖拥有好的视角，更好的领袖具备更好的视角，卓越的领袖拥有卓越的视角。领袖应该冷静面对改变的过程，并且知道自己会从中学到很多。

Application

◆ Which of the above leadership traits can you develop in order to better serve your team?

◆ Think of past or present situations when you succeeded or failed to exhibit the above leadership traits. What was the outcome in the situation and how might it have been different?

Notation Area

Personal observations/Ideas for further exploration/Thoughts to remember

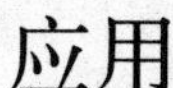

应用

◆ 在以上的领袖特征中，你可以培养哪些特点来服务自己的团队？

◆ 想出过去或现在发生的一个例子，说明自己成功地表现了以上的品格，或是自己由于失败而没有表现出这些品格。当时的结果如何？结果本可以成为什么样子？

笔记

个人体会／要进一步探讨的想法／要铭记在心的理念

为政以德，譬如北辰，居其所而众星共之。

——孔子

He who exercises government by means of his virtue may be compared to the north polar star, which keeps its place and all the stars turn towards it.

——*Confucius*

周亚夫将军大营

The Camp of General Zhou Yafa

第十三天 军纪严明
——变化中的环境

Day 13: The Changing Environment

卓越的领袖不会被改变的环境中所出现的暴风雨吓倒。尽管面对重重挑战，他们会引导团队走在正确的道路上。

Great leaders are not overwhelmed by the storm of constantly changing circumstances. They guide their team on a straight course of success in spite of challenges.

He who exercises government by means of his virtue may be compared to the north polar star, which keeps its place and all the stars turn towards it.

—— *Confucius*

In 158 BC the Hun army invaded China's northern border. Emperor Wen of the Han dynasty appointed three generals, Liu Li, Xu Li, and Zhou Yafu, to protect the northern territory. On one occasion the emperor traveled to the northern border and made a personal visit to these three generals. The emperor's party was able to enter straight into the camp and barracks of General Liu Li and General Xu Li. However when they arrived at the camp of General Zhou, they were stopped. The guards on duty were informed that this was the royal entourage and the emperor himself was in the party. The soldier responded that he could take orders only from General Zhou and the party would have to wait. Only after the emperor sent a message to General Zhou with royal credentials was the gate opened. General Zhou received the emperor in front of his barracks in full uniform.

When the emperor finished his inspection, he commended Zhou for his well-disciplined army. In speaking to his officials, Emperor Wen remarked that the other two generals' camps could easily be captured by a surprise attack. General Zhou's camp was safe, and his men did not bend the rules for anyone.

Sometimes when you bend the rules, you lose more than you gain.[1] Constancy of discipline earned the praise of the emperor. Enemies will always change tactics to catch you off guard. Change is crucial for success, but some things should remain the same.

We are living in a time of accelerated change. China is experiencing unprecedented change in its major cities. In the U.S., about 20 percent of the population migrates to a new primary residence every year. This demonstrates a clear transformation from the past when a person lived and worked in the same place for

为政以德，譬如北辰，居其所而众星共之。

——孔子

译文：以道德教化来治理政事，就会像北极星那样，自己居于一定的方位，而群星都会环绕在它的周围。

公元前158年，匈奴部队入侵中国北部边陲。汉文帝任命刘礼、徐厉和周亚夫为大将军，去保护北部领土。有一次，皇帝驾临北部边境，亲自拜访三位将军。皇帝的随行人员长驱直入，来到刘礼将军和徐厉将军的大营。但是，当他们来到周将军的大营时被拦了下来。值班的守卫被告知这是皇家随行人员，而且皇帝本人也在其中。士兵回答说他只听从周将军的将令，所以随行人员必须在此等候。后来汉文帝给周将军下了圣旨，通知他亲自迎接，这才打开营门。周将军全副铠甲，在营门口迎接皇帝。

皇帝视察之后，夸奖周将军的部队军纪严明。汉文帝和自己的官员提起这件事，认为其他两位将军的大营在奇袭之下很容易被占领。但是周将军的大营却十分安全，他的士兵不会为任何人在规章制度上作出妥协。

有时候，当你在规章制度上作出妥协的时候，你所失去的比获得的更多。[1]前后一致的军纪赢得了皇帝的赞誉。敌人可以改变战略，让你的守卫防不胜防。虽然改变是成功的关键，但是有的事情应该坚守原则。

我们生活在一个加速改变的时代中。中国的大城市正在经历史无前例的改变。美国每年也有大约20%的人口移居到新的居住地。这清楚地表明，整个世界都在经历改变，人们不会像从前那样，在同一个地方工作生活40到50年。有数据显示，如今，人们一生平均换五次工作。这还不包括大学时在

forty to fifty years. Statistics show that, on average, modern workers change jobs five times in their lifetime. This does not include working at fast food restaurants during college, but major career changes. With the world becoming a global village, even previously untouched parts of society are experiencing unprecedented change.

Oftentimes when one change is completed, another follows closely on its heels. A classic model illustrating organizational change was developed by Kurt Lewin and is shown in Figure 13.1. It involves unfreezing the status quo, changing to a new culture, and refreezing to a new permanent culture. This model illustrates the fact that change is a process and it takes time.

Figure 13.1:Kurt Lewin's Three-step Change Process [2]

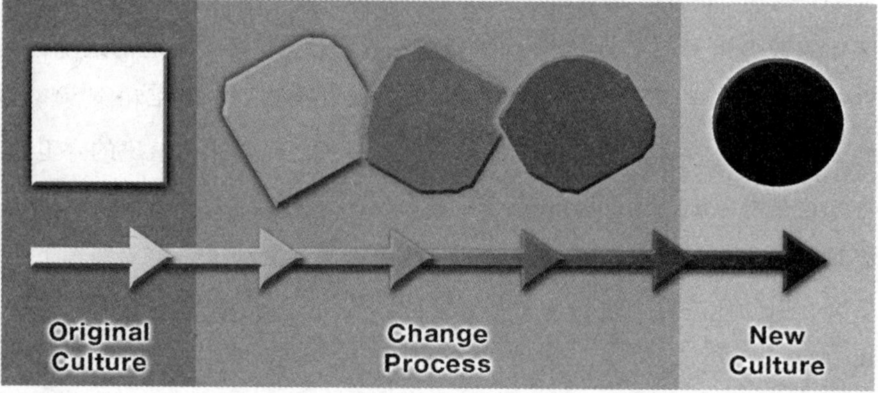

The model works well in relatively stable environments where changes are infrequent. However, the ability to make fast and frequent changes is becoming a basic survival strategy for organizations. The model that more appropriately fits our times is one where only the core values of an organization remain constant. The external is able to adapt quickly to the needs and demands of the market. This new model is illustrated in Figure 13.2.

This improved model involves the same process of unfreezing the culture and taking it through the change process, but refreezing only a core of the culture. The core represents those artifacts, values, and characteristics that are central to the organization. The outside remains flexible, in a state of constant improvement and change. This type of change requires your team to establish core principles resistant to changing environments. A team culture built on principles of integrity,

快餐店打工，而是主要的职业变化。世界已经变成一个地球村，即使从前没有被触及的社会层面也经历着空前的改变。

一般情况下，一个改变完成后，另一个会接踵而至。库尔特·勒温（Kurt Lewin）绘制了机构变化的经典图表，如图表 13.1 所示。其中包括：打破现状、改变成新文化和塑造长期的新文化。这个模式说明了一个事实：改变是一个进程，而且需要时间。

图表 13.1：库尔特·勒温的三步改变进程[2]

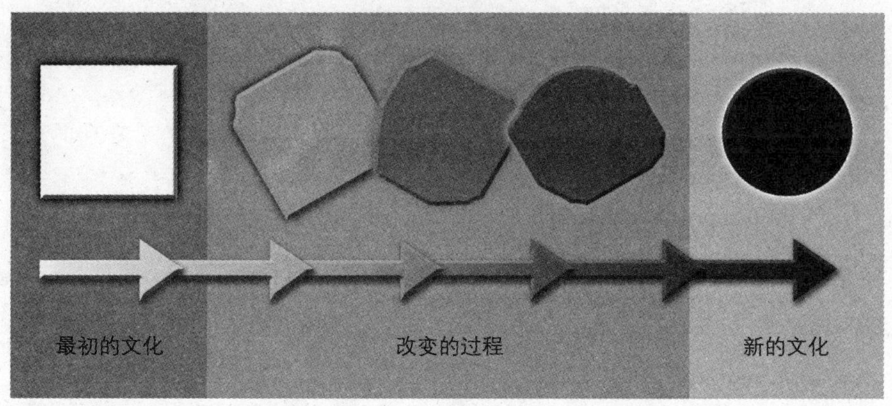

这个模式适用于相对稳定，很少发生变化的环境。然而，迅速和频繁改变的能力，已经成为机构的基本生存策略。更适合今天时代的模式是机构的核心价值保持不变，而外部环境则要适应市场迅速改变的需要和要求。这个新的模式如图表 13.2 所示。

经过改良的模式也包括打破文化和经历变化的过程，但是重塑的只是文化的某个核心。核心代表机构重要的传统、价值观和独有的特征。外在仍然保持其灵活性，处于不断改善和变化中。这种改变要求你的团队建立核心原则，抵制不断改变的环境。不论外部环境如何改变，基于正直、诚

Core Cultural Change

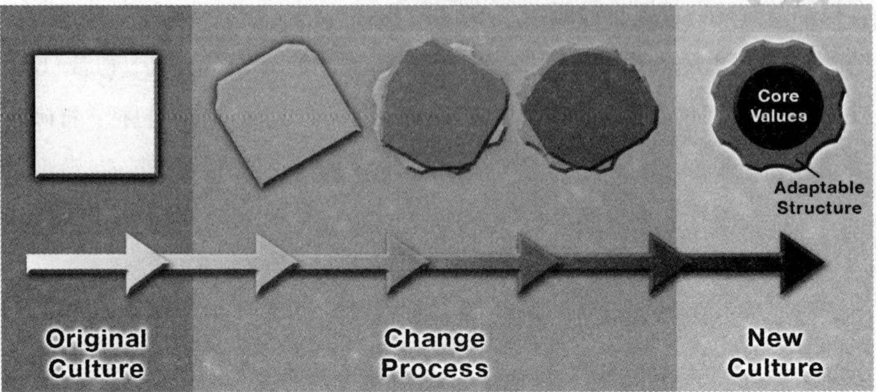

honesty, fairness, respect, and excellence will consistently succeed, in spite of changing conditions. The motto is true:

Methods are many,
Principles are few.
Methods may change,
But principles never do.[3]

Wise leaders guide their team through strategic changes, positioning them for future success. Changing external structures while clarifying core principles represents stability and flexibility. Flexibility and stability are crucial for individual as well as corporate survival. Strong leadership has never been more needed than it is today. The world needs leaders who not only create change, but who guide their team to the desired end. People follow leaders who understand the following:

- Motivation: People need compelling reasons to stay committed through the hard times.
- Vision: Teams need to hear, understand, and believe in a common vision.
- Character: People follow leaders they can trust.
- Sharing Rewards: This shows team members they are valued.
- Communication: People want information and they want to be listened to. Great leaders maintain open communication with their teams.[4]

Leaders need to help their teams identify core values. The few principles that

核心文化的改变

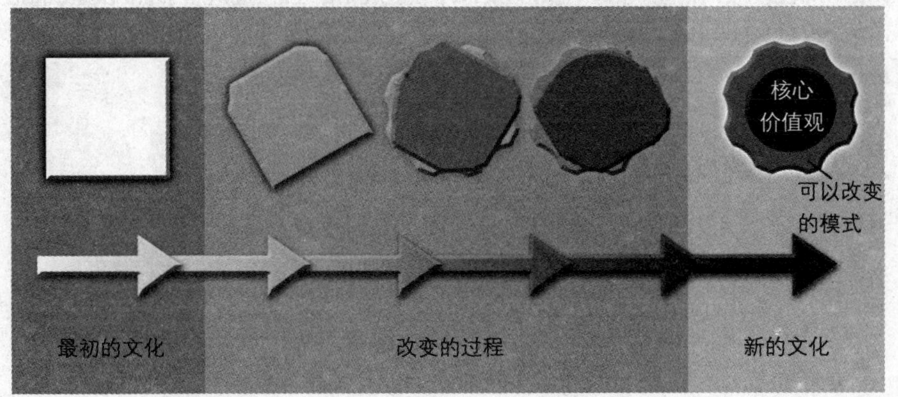

实、公平、尊重和卓越之上的团队文化必然能够百战百胜。有这样一个座右铭：

方法有很多，原则却不多。方法会改变，原则永不变。[3]

智慧的领袖在战略改变中引导团队，把他们放在恰当的位置上，能够在将来获得更大的成功。在强调核心原则的时候改变外部的结构，集稳定和弹性于一身。弹性和稳定性不仅对个人，而且对机构的生存都至关重要。历史上任何时候都没有像今天这样呼唤卓越的领导力。世界需要领袖，他们不仅能够作出改变，而且带领团队到达目的地。人们跟随这样的领袖，能够享受下面的一切：

- 激励：在艰苦的时刻，人们需要坚持的理由。
- 愿景：团队需要听到、理解和相信共同的美好前景。
- 品格：人们跟随可信赖的领袖。
- 分享胜利果实：让团队的成员知道自己被重视。
- 沟通：人们需要信息，他们希望有人能够聆听自己讲话。卓越的领袖和团队保持公开交流。[4]

领袖需要帮助团队认识核心价值。不应该改变代表团队信念的核心原

represent the core of the team's beliefs should not change. It remains the leader's role to keep the values and vision clearly before the team. Great leaders are not overwhelmed by the storm of constantly changing circumstances. They guide their team on a straight course of success in spite of challenges.

Application

- ◆ Identify core principles with your team.
- ◆ How will you help your team understand and own the values they choose?
- ◆ Do the identified principles support your future vision?
- ◆ Identify everything that is not a part of the core and may undergo changes in the near future.
- ◆ Prepare your team mentally for critical changes that need to be made.
- ◆ Teach your team how to evaluate each step as it relates back to the core principles.

Notation Area

Personal observations/Ideas for further exploration/Thoughts to remember

则。领袖的角色就是让价值观和愿景清晰地摆在团队的面前。卓越的领袖不会被改变的环境中所出现的暴风雨吓倒。尽管面对重重挑战，他们会引导团队勇往直前。

应用

◆确认团队中的核心原则。

◆你怎样帮助团队了解并活出自己选择的价值观？

◆现行的原则支持你未来的愿景吗？

◆分辨不属于核心价值的东西，它们在不久的将来可能会经历变化。

◆在心理上预备团队，面对关键的变化。

◆教导团队了解怎样评估每个步骤，看看是否与核心原则一致。

笔记

个人体会／要进一步探讨的想法／要铭记在心的理念

学而不思则罔，思而不学则殆。

——孔子

If one learns from others but does not think, one will be bewildered. If, on the other hand, one thinks but does not learn from others, one will be in peril.

——*Confucius*

学习与思考

Think and Learn

第十四天 学而不思则罔
——变化的原因

Day 14:Sources of Change

领袖担当改变不是因为这一切轻而易举，而是因为这是正确的事情。

Leaders don't enforce change because it's easy, but because it's the right thing to do.

If one learns from others but does not think, one will be bewildered. If, on the other hand, one thinks but does not learn from others, one will be in peril.

—— *Confucius*

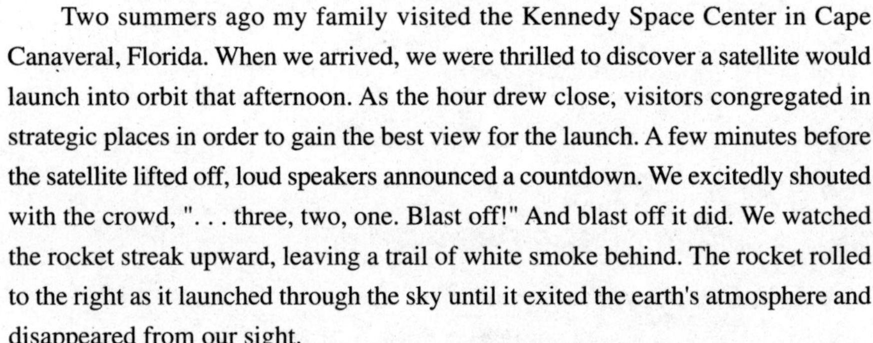

Two summers ago my family visited the Kennedy Space Center in Cape Canaveral, Florida. When we arrived, we were thrilled to discover a satellite would launch into orbit that afternoon. As the hour drew close, visitors congregated in strategic places in order to gain the best view for the launch. A few minutes before the satellite lifted off, loud speakers announced a countdown. We excitedly shouted with the crowd, ". . . three, two, one. Blast off!" And blast off it did. We watched the rocket streak upward, leaving a trail of white smoke behind. The rocket rolled to the right as it launched through the sky until it exited the earth's atmosphere and disappeared from our sight.

While at the space center, I learned a great deal about the U.S. space shuttle. I learned that in order to lift the shuttle off the launch pad, it uses two solid rocket boosters (SRB), three main engines of the orbiter, and one external fuel tank. The sheer size and power of the rockets were amazing. When the shuttle is resting on the launch pad fully fueled, it weighs about two million kilograms (4.5 million pounds). The final launch procedure begins about a half minute before lift off. If you were in the shuttle, you would experience the following:

- T minus 31 seconds: The onboard computers take over the launch sequence.
- T minus 6.6 seconds: The shuttle's main engines are ignited one at a time (0.12 seconds apart).The engines build up to more than 90 percent of their maximum thrust.
- T minus 0 seconds: The SRBs are ignited and the shuttle lifts off the pad.
- T plus 60 seconds: The shuttle rolls right (180 degree roll, 78 degree pitch).
- T plus 2 minutes: SRBs separate from the orbiter and fuel tank at an

学而不思则罔，思而不学则殆。

——孔子

译文：只读书学习，而不思考问题，就会罔然无知，没有收获；只是空想，而不读书学习，就会疑惑迷茫。

两年前的夏天，我和家人一起去了佛罗里达州卡纳维拉尔角的肯尼迪航天中心。我们到达的当天下午，正好有一颗卫星要进入轨道。我们激动极了。那一时刻快要到来的时候，为了能够有最好的视角可以看到卫星发射，参观的人群聚集在最佳方位。人造卫星升空前几分钟，扩音器里开始倒数计时。我们和人群一起兴奋地喊着："……三、二、一，点火！"点火升空了。我们看着火箭加速向上，后面拖着一条白色的烟尾巴。火箭沿着正确的轨道，升入天空，离开了大气层，从我们的视线中消失。

在航天中心，我对航天飞机有了初步的了解。为了把火箭从发射台推入太空，航天飞机需要一对大型固体推进剂捆绑式助推火箭，三台人造卫星的主发动机，一个外挂燃料箱。火箭那子弹头式的巨大外形和强大的动力都让人感到惊诧。航天飞机装满了燃料，安装在发射台的时候，整个系统的起飞重量达2000吨(450万磅)。火箭发射的最后一个程序始于起飞前半分钟。假如你在航天飞机中，会经历下面过程：

- 起飞前31秒：计算机开始接管发射程序。
- 起飞前6.6秒：两台火箭助推器和三台液体火箭基本同时点火（三台主发动机点火时间间隔0.12秒，然后是固体火箭点火）。主机积累了超过90%的动力。
- 起飞：固体燃料推进的火箭加速器被点燃，航天飞机垂直上升离开发

altitude of 45 kilometers (28 miles). Two million kilograms of ship just went from sitting on the launch pad to blasting up 45 kilometers in two minutes. That's moving!

- T plus 7.7 minutes: The main engines throttle down to keep acceleration below 3 Gs so that the shuttle does not break apart.
- T plus 45 minutes:Engines fire to place the shuttle in circular orbit (about 400 kilometers or 250 miles). The orbiter has now successfully reached outer space. [1]

Just as space shuttle engineers launch the space shuttle into outer space, leaders need to create their own blast-off sequence in order to propel their team into a change process. Before launching into change, leaders must effectively assess the situation and know why change is needed. Several sources exist that create the need for change. These sources can be both internal and external. External sources include the marketplace, government laws and regulations, technology, labor, and economic change. Internal sources include declining productivity, losing a competitive edge, shifts in worker-management relations, and internal strife in team attitudes. These, and many other factors, can cause a leader to change the team in the areas of structure, technology, or people. Figure 14.1 illustrates these three categories of change.

Figure 14. 1 [2]

Three Categories of Change

Structure	Technology	People
Formalization Centralization Job Redesign	Work processes Methods Equipment	Attitudes Expectations Perceptions Behavior

Every MBA graduate eagerly desires to institute change. In most cases, their attempts produce their first experience of failure in the real world. While formulas and programs look great on paper, actually implementing them can become in-

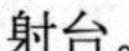

射台。

- 起飞后60秒：航天飞机向右摆动调整飞行姿态（180度摆动，78度斜度）。起飞后两分钟：航天飞机达到45公里高度（8英里），助推器燃料耗尽，自动熄火并同航天飞机分离，主发动机继续工作，航天飞机持续上升。两分钟内，重达2000吨的航天飞机从在发射台上一动不动到冲入云霄45公里。太壮观了！
- 起飞后7.7分钟：三台主发动机减低速度，让加速度保持在3Gs以下，保证航天飞机不至于断裂。
- 起飞后45分钟：发动机点火，让航天飞机围绕预定轨道在大约400公里（250英里）的高度飞行，现在卫星已经成功到达外太空。[1]

和航天飞机工程师发射火箭进入外太空一样，领袖们需要创建自己的启动程序，来推动自己的团队进入改变的进程。在启动改变的时候，领袖必须有效地评估环境，知道为什么需要改变。有几种内在的和外在的原因引发改变。外在的原因包括市场、政府的法律和规则、技术、劳工和经济的改变。内在的原因包括生产能力衰退、竞争力缺失、管理层和劳工关系的改变，以及团队中出现的内在冲突。这些因素以及很多其他的因素，能够让领袖在架构、技术或人事领域进行改变。图表14.1列举了这三个领域的改变。

图表14.1[2]

改变的三个范畴

架构	技术	人事
形式化	工作程序	态度
集中化	方法	期待
工作重组	装备	看法
		行为

comprehensibly complicated when people are involved. Long ago Machiavelli, the father of the study of organizational behavior, noted: "There is no more delicate matter than to introduce change. For he who innovates will have for his enemies all those who are well-off under the existing order of things, and only lukewarm supporters in those who might be better off under the new."[3] So how can we know when to introduce change? I like Michael Beers's formula because it's simple to understand, yet it encompasses many factors. His formula for predicting the time to introduce change is: $C = (D \times S \times P) > X$ where:

C = change

D = dissatisfaction with the current state of affairs

S = an identifiable and desired end state

P = a practical plan for achieving the desired end state

X = cost of change to the organization[4]

This formula shows that the dissatisfaction in a current state, an identifiable goal, and a plan for achieving that goal must outweigh the cost of the change. The cost can be measured in a number of ways, including disruption in team relationships, retraining, new equipment, increased stress, and so on. Note that leaders play a major role in helping others see why they should be dissatisfied. Leaders can do this by showing the team that change is necessary for survival. The leader must have factual information in order to convince the team that the status quo will result in disaster. Another possibility is to paint a tantalizing picture of the desired end results. The details of the plan will still need attention, but you can instill a dream of better things to come. For the leader who sees the need for change, using Beers's formula can help determine the timing of when the team is ready for change.

However, knowing a change is needed and deciphering when to launch a new initiative does not help the leader determine how to make a change successful. The following list identifies some elements that can help ensure a successful cultural change:

1. Present your team with the facts. Demonstrate how your future success is dependent on positive change.
2. Identify and empower new leaders with new vision.
3. Change the way you assimilate new team members.
4. Change the social and monetary reward systems.[5]

每个工商管理硕士都急切地迎接改变。大部分情况下，他们实际上是在真实的世界中体验自己第一次的失败经历。虽然公式和程序在纸上看起来很棒，但其中涉及人的时候，实际操作的吃力程度令人费解。很久以前，组织行为研究之父——马基雅弗利（Machiavelli）注意到："没有什么事情比改变更棘手。因为改革者面对的敌人是在现行制度下富足的人，而他仅有的一小群支持者也犹豫不决，无所适从。他们之所以会拥护改变，是因为自己可能在新的制度下获得更大的利益。"[3]所以，我们怎么才知道何时引入改变呢？我喜欢迈克尔·比尔斯（Michael Beers）的公式，因为它容易理解，而且还包括很多因素。他的公式预测了引入改变的时间：$C=(D\times S\times P)>X$，其中：

C 代表"改变"

D 代表"对当前状况产生不满"

S 代表"清楚地知道想要的结果是什么"

P 代表"拥有具体的计划，知道如何达成所要的结果"

X 代表"机构为改变而付出的代价"[4]

这个公式说明：对当前状况产生不满、清楚地知道想要的结果是什么、有具体的计划而且知道如何达成所要的结果，这一切加起来，需要超过机构为改变而付出的代价。可以从多方面衡量代价，包括团队中彼此关系的破裂、重新培训、新的设备、压力增加，等等。请注意一点，领袖的角色很重要，他们需要帮助他人看到为什么自己不能满足于现状。领袖可以让团队看到，改变是生存的必要条件。领袖必须拿出事实资料，让团队看到现状存在着隐患，或者阐明另外一种可能性，也就是给团队描述一幅画面，让大家看到最后想要的结果以及其中的紧迫感。计划的细节仍然需要关注，但是你能够帮助团队看到这样的梦想，知道更美好的事情必将到来。对于看到有进行改变的需要的领袖们，比尔斯的公式可以帮助他们确定时机，明白团队何时预备好面对改变。

然而，知道改变的必要性，并且能够诠释，知道何时采取主动权开始改变，这一切并不能够帮助领袖知道怎样带来成功的改变。以下列出的清单说

Leaders can apply one or more of the above suggestions. Choosing the right approach at the right time will also prove to be crucial in keeping your team secure and moving ahead with the change.

This chapter hasn't painted a very comfortable picture for the leader who needs to be a change agent, so to end on a positive note, I would like to share a parable about twins.

At the moment of conception, a set of twins began communicating with one another-not with words, but they understood one another just as if they could speak. Together they explored their new world in the womb of their mother. They enjoyed spinning and swimming in the warm fluid. One rambunctious day, they learned to bungee jump with their umbilical cord and throw each other against the soft walls of the uterus. Their world in the womb was safe, secure. It was all they knew. As months passed, they began to change and their world became more and more crowded. One day after their ears developed, they even heard the voice of their mother softly singing a lullaby. They sensed a big change was coming. One of the twins became excited about the change while the other was full of fears and apprehension.

"What do you think will happen to us?" the fearful twin asked.

"We will soon leave this world and go to be with our mother in the world outside of the womb," the other answered.

"But I like the womb and don't want to leave! Who knows what it will be like out there?"

The courageous twin answered, "We know our mother is there, and she loves us. The world outside the womb can't be that bad."

But the fearful twin argued, "How do we even know there is a mother? We might have made her up to make ourselves feel better."

"That's crazy. Of course there is a mother! How else did we get here?"

"Have you ever seen her? Has anyone ever come from out there into our world to prove that she or the other world really exists? No, we are doomed! If life in the womb ends in birth, I wish I had never been conceived."

Unable to be comforted, the fearful twin fell into despair and spent the last days in the womb fretting over the changes he must soon endure. But when the day actually arrived and they both passed from the only world they knew into the other, they cried for joy, for the love they felt from the tender arms that held them and the face that smiled upon them surpassed their greatest desires.

明哪些要素可以带来成功的文化改变：

1.给团队列出事实。让大家看到未来的成功取决于积极的改变。

2.用新的愿景发现新的领袖，并且给他们授权。

3.改变你吸纳新团队成员的方式。

4.改变社会和酬劳奖励系统。[5]

领袖可以采纳以上的一个或者更多的建议。在恰当的时候选择正确的方法也是一个关键，这决定你的团队是否安全，可以在改变中继续前进。

领袖是改变中的重要因素，这章并没有为他们描绘出一幅宁静的画面。所以，为了在结尾的时候带来一个积极的音符，我想分享一个双胞胎的比喻。

怀孕的时候，两个双胞胎开始彼此交流——没有语言，但是他们却像是会说话一样彼此了解。他们一起在母亲的子宫中探索新世界，享受在温暖的液体中旋转和游泳。在一个躁动不休的日子里，他们学会了蹦极，用脐带跳来跳去，在子宫柔软的壁上彼此冲来撞去。他们在子宫中的世界安全，稳定。这是他们熟悉的一切。随着日子一天天过去，他们开始改变，他们的世界也变得越来越拥挤了。一天，他们长出了耳朵，甚至听到了妈妈唱摇篮曲轻柔的声音。他们感到马上要出现巨大的改变了。其中一个孪生子对于未来的改变感到非常激动，另外一个却充满了恐惧和担忧。

“你觉得会发生什么？”那个惧怕的孪生子问。

“我们马上要离开这个世界，在子宫外边的世界和妈妈在一起。”另一个回答。

“但是我喜欢子宫，不愿意离开！谁知道外边是什么样子！”

勇敢的孪生子回答说：“我们有妈妈，而且她爱我们。子宫外边的世界不会太糟糕的。”

但是惧怕的孪生子争辩道：“我们怎么能知道存在一个妈妈呢？有可能是我们自己制造了个妈妈，让自己感觉舒服一些。”

The twins in this parable went through a variety of emotions. One handled the changes with optimism, while the other was consumed with fear. In the same way, you should expect people on your team to go through a variety of emotions during a change process. Your role is to support and keep them moving so that you also can "cry with joy" when they reach new levels of excellence as a result of the change.

Those who introduce change will have more scars from the battle than most. However, leaders called to bring about change will find the end victory well worth the cost. Leaders don't enforce change because it's easy, but because it's the right thing to do.

“你简直疯了。当然有妈妈！否则我们怎么才能到达另外一个世界？”

“你见过她吗？她难道来到我们的世界，证实过她和另外一个世界的存在吗？没有，这一切早已命中注定！假如子宫里的生活以出生结束的话，我真希望自己永远都没有受孕成形。”

惧怕的那个孪生子落入了绝望中，根本无法获得任何安慰，在子宫中最后的日子里，他对于未来要承担的改变焦虑担忧。但是，当那一天来到的时候，他们都离开了自己唯一知道的那个世界，进入了另一个世界。他们喜极而泣。他们被拥抱在温暖的双臂中，感受到了浓浓的爱意，对着他们欢笑的那张脸，超过了他们所能想象到的最大的渴望。

这个比喻中的孪生子经历了各样的情感。一个以乐观的心态面对改变，另一个则被恐惧所吞噬。同样，面对改变的时候，团队中的成员会经历各种各样的情感。你的角色就是支持他们，帮助他们继续前行。这样，当他们由于改变到达更卓越的层面时，你们可以一起“喜极而泣”。

带来改变的人身上的伤疤会比大多数人更多一些，因为他们经历了更多的恶战。然而，被呼召带来改变的领袖会发现，最后的胜利远远超过了自己所付出的一些代价。领袖担当改变不是因为这一切轻而易举，而因为这是正确的事情。

Application

◆ Assess your team's level of commitment to the status quo. What would it take for them to see the need for change?

◆ Using Beers's formula, assess your team's need for change.

◆ If change is needed, choose one thing to change in the area of structure, technology, or people.

◆ Take note of which team members adapt well to change and those who need extra support.

Notation Area

Personal observations/Ideas for further exploration/Thoughts to remember

应用

◆根据现状，评估团队的委身程度。他们怎样才能看到现状需要被改变？

◆使用比尔斯的公式，评估你的团队是否需要改变。

◆假如需要改变的话，在架构、技术或人事方面选择一件事进行改变。

◆注意团队中哪个成员能够很好地适应改变，哪个成员需要特别的支持。

笔记

个人体会／要进一步探讨的想法／要铭记在心的理念

故兵闻拙速，未睹巧之久也。夫兵久而国利者，未之有也。

——孙子[1]

Thus, while mistakes have been made as a result of hasty decisions in war, we have yet to observe a well planned operation carry on year after year. Long, drawn-out war has never benefited the country.

——*Sun Tzu*[1]

令人疲惫的战争

Battle Weary

第十五天 速决与持久
——冲突为领袖所用

Day 15: Conflict as a Tool

冲突是成长中的团队或机构的自然组成部分。冲突不见得一定是消极的，它可以被引导，成为积极的力量，能够改善整个团队。

Conflict is a natural part of a growing team or organization. It doesn't have to be negative and can be directed to become a positive force that will improve the overall team.

Thus, while mistakes have been made as a result of hasty decisions in war, we have yet to observe a well planned operation carry on year after year. Long, drawn-out war has never benefited the country.

—— *Sun Tzu* [1]

Just as prolonged war has never benefited a country, extended states of intense conflict have never benefited a team. If death and taxes compose two guaranteed elements of this life, then conflict is the third. The ability to effectively handle conflict separates leaders (winners) from nonleaders.

One that proved this was Edwin Moses. Moses won the gold medal in the 1976 Montreal Olympics and for more than ten years never lost. Many could run faster, but none could jump the hurdles faster. Edwin Moses won because he learned how to manage the obstacles (hurdles in his case) better than the rest.[2] Just as the hurdles gave Edwin Moses the ability to surpass the competition, conflict helps separate good leaders from great leaders. The importance of conflict management is reinforced by a survey of topics that managers consider most important in development programs. The survey revealed conflict management as having a higher importance than decision-making, leadership, and communications skills. In further support of this claim, a research study involving managers studied twenty-five skill and personality factors. The study sought to determine which, if any, were related to managerial success. The definition of "success" included positive evaluations from the boss as well as promotions and salary increases. Of the twenty-five measures, only one-the ability to handle conflict-was positively related to managerial success.[3]

So what is "conflict"? A simple definition would be "mental struggle resulting from incompatible or opposing needs, drives, wishes, or external or internal demands."[4] Conflict has traditionally been viewed as a bad struggle. Most people avoid conflict. Few enjoy the conflict resulting from confronting, rebuking, and

故兵闻拙速，未睹巧之久也。夫兵久而国利者，未之有也。

——孙子[1]

译文：所以，用兵作战，只听说指挥虽拙但求速胜，而没有见过战争求持久的。战争久拖不决对国家有利的情形是没有的。

长期战争不会给国家带来任何利益，同样，假如紧张冲突延续时间过长，也不会给团队带来任何好处。有效处理冲突的能力就把领袖（获胜者）和跟随者分别出来。

埃德温·摩西（Edwin Moses）就是个明证。摩西在1976年蒙特利尔奥林匹克运动会上赢得了金牌，他连续十年从未输过一场比赛。很多人跑得比他更快，但是没有一个人在跨栏时能够超越他。埃德温·摩西之所以赢得比赛，是因为他学会了如何更好地处理“障碍”（对于他来说是“跨栏”）。[2]栏杆给了埃德温·摩西机会和能力，让他能够在竞争中不断超越。同样，冲突也让好领袖和卓越的领袖之间的差异凸现出来。很多调查报告都重点强调处理冲突的重要性，经理们也认为这是项目发展过程中最重要的一个环节。调查显示，处理冲突比决定、领导力和沟通技巧都更重要。为了进一步支持这样的说法，有人就25种技巧和个性因素对经理们进行了调查。调查旨在发现什么因素可以决定管理成败。“成功”包括来自老板的积极评估以及提升和增加工资。在25个评估条件中，只有“处理冲突的能力”这一条和管理的成败有正相关。[3]

什么是“冲突”？一个简单的定义就是：“冲突是由于彼此不协调或相互矛盾的愿望、动力或外在及内在的需求而产生的内心挣扎。”[4]冲突在传统意义上被看作是问题。大部分情况下人们会避免冲突。很少有人享受由对

arguing. However, one cannot go through life avoiding everything that causes conflict. Standing up for what is right will produce conflict. Believing in something will put you in conflict with those who hold opposite opinions. Conflict is a part of life that will not go away, and the sooner you become good at it, the more successful you will be.[5]

Most people, when faced with conflict or interpersonal differences, avoid the individuals causing the difficulty. Unfortunately, avoidance seldom removes the problem and instead gives it time to fester. The longer we take to confront a situation, the more the situation drains personal and emotional energy. As time passes, we more easily assign negative motives and actions to others. Have you ever fabricated arguments with others (boss, spouse, coworker) in your head? I know I have. I manage to work up my emotions by picturing in great detail the person I am in conflict with. In my daydream, I amazingly win all the hypothetical arguments. My own mental debate, my point of view is so wise and justified and the other's is hilariously stupid. However, when I actually confront and deal with the situation, the discussion seldom goes the way I had imagined. Over the years, I have learned the sooner I can bring clarity to a situation, the better. I like to practice "keeping short accounts." This means when conflict or differences arise, I seek the earliest appropriate opportunity to deal with it. Some groups apply the twenty-four hour rule. If a difficulty arises with a team member, don't allow more than twenty-four hours to pass before you resolve it.

As a leader you will need to seek ways to build relationships with team members. Relationships will often be the key to resolving a conflict. Because of this, it is especially important to build relationships with team members prone to conflict.

When conflict arises between team members, leaders are often the first to initiate a resolution. Some situations call for correction; others simply need clarification due to misunderstandings. In either case, those involved in the conflict are likely to be on the defensive. By establishing a positive relationship with team members before conflict arises, they are more likely to trust you to speak into the situation. When team members truly believe that you have their best interest in mind, they are able to let down their defenses and work toward resolution. People in general are more concerned with how much you care rather than how much you know. They often don't care about what you know until they know you care.

The negative view of conflict does not come from people's imaginations-

抗、责备和争辩所产生的冲突。然而，一个人一生中不可能避免所有导致冲突的事情。坚持正确的事情也会带来冲突。对某些事情的信念也会让你和持相反意见的人产生冲突。冲突是生活的组成部分，挥之不去。你适应得越快，就能够越成功。[5]

大部分人在面对冲突或人与人之间的差异时，会逃避那些引发问题的人。不幸的是，逃避并不能让问题消失，而是会给它滋生蔓延的机会。我们公开对抗的时间拖得越久，局面就会变得越糟，消耗彼此之间的情感和精力。随着时间的流逝，我们渐渐会认为对方有消极的动机和行为。你是否曾经在头脑中虚构自己和他人（老板、配偶或同事）之间的争论？我自己曾经这样做过。我在头脑中栩栩如生地描绘和我产生冲突之人的画面，用这样的方法来整理自己的情绪。在白日梦中，我奇妙地赢得了所有假想的争论。在我的头脑中，自己的辩论和观点都无懈可击，有理有节，而另一个人却愚不可及。然而，当我实际面对和处理问题的时候，双方的讨论很少按照我想象中的方法进行。随着时间的推移，我学会一点：越早澄清事实越好。当冲突或差异产生的时候，我会在第一时间，利用最恰当的机会处理清楚。有的团队使用"24小时原则"：假如团队成员之间出现问题，必须在24小时内解决。

作为领袖，你需要和团队成员建立关系。关系是解决冲突的关键，和可能出现冲突的团队成员建立关系尤其重要。

当团队里出现了冲突，一般由领袖率先解决问题。有些情况下需要纠正，有些可能只是出现了误解，澄清问题就可以了。有些时候，冲突中的人很容易具有很强的防御性。在冲突发生之前和团队成员建立积极的关系，使他们更容易信任你，听取你的建议。当团队成员相信你把他们的利益放在心中，就能够放下自己的防御性，努力找出解决问题的方法。人们一般在意的是你的关心程度，而不是你拥有的知识有多少。只有他们知道你真正关心之后，才会在意你知道多少。

人们对冲突持负面观点并非空穴来风、无中生有——我们很多人都曾有独裁和好斗的老板。这样的领袖就好像撞倒栏杆的跨栏运动员，不仅把自己

many of us have worked under extremely aggressive and authoritarian leadership. Leaders like this resemble runners who knock down every hurdle, tripping themselves and disrupting everyone in their wake. Every fall is blamed on the hurdle, and they never learn to manage the obstacles. Every conflict becomes a fight to prove that "I am right" and "you are wrong." The need to be right at all times reveals an immature and insecure leader. This type of leadership creates a culture of conflict and confrontation where fear and guilt control behavior. This leader has not learned to manage and develop people.

Great leaders are not afraid of conflict within the group. Conflict is a natural part of a growing team or organization. It doesn't have to be negative and can be directed to become a positive force that will improve the overall team. Some researchers hold an interactionist view of conflict. They believe that conflict is necessary for an organization to be effective. They argue that peaceful, harmonious, tranquil, and cooperative organizations are prone to become apathetic and unable to respond to the needs of a fast-changing society. The interactionist encourages leaders to maintain a functional level of conflict in order to keep the team viable, self-critical, and creative.

Therefore, the leader functions to maintain an optimal conflict level in the organization. Leaders should allow a healthy level of conflict while avoiding excessive and aggressive levels. Figure 15.1 illustrates the challenges facing leaders.

Figure 15.1 [6]

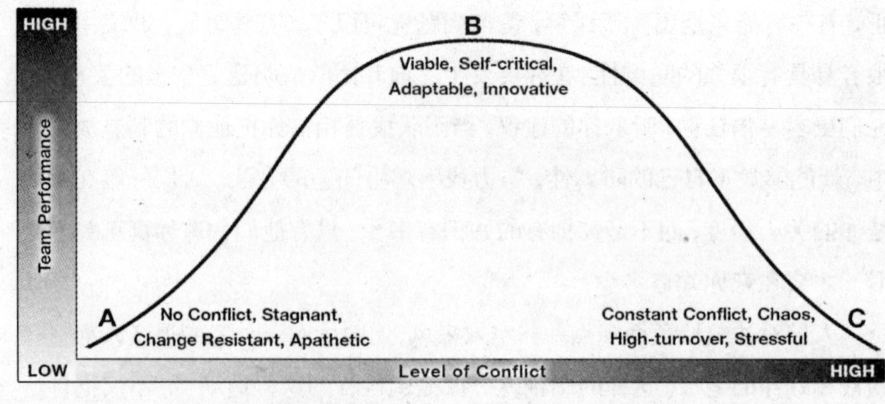

绊倒了，而且还让很多人陷于混乱。他们把每次失败都归咎于栏杆，永远都无法学会怎样处理障碍。每次冲突都变成了一次战斗，为了证明“我是对的”、“你是错的”。这情景让我们看到了一个不成熟和没有安全感的领袖。这样的领导力创造出冲突和对抗的氛围，让恐惧和罪咎控制自己的行为。这样的领袖还没有学会如何管理和栽培他人。

卓越的领袖并不惧怕团队中的冲突。冲突是成长中的团队或机构都要经历的。冲突不见得一定是消极的，它可以被引导成积极的力量，能够改善整个团队。一些研究者认为冲突有交互作用，相信冲突是高效能机构的必要组成部分。他们认为，宁静、和谐、协调和合作的团队倾向于变得无动于衷，无法回应快速改变的社会。交互作用鼓励领袖维持冲突的良好性能，保持团队的活力，帮助团队严格律己、充满创造性。

因此，领袖要在机构中维系理想的冲突状态。领袖要避免极端和过度的状态，让冲突处在健康程度。图表 15.1 说明了领袖面对的挑战。

图表 15.1[6]

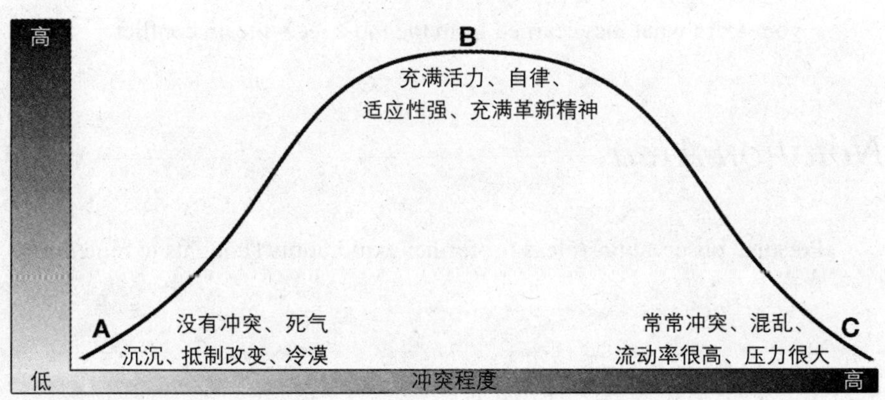

When facing a difficult situation filled with conflict, I remind myself that if leading were easy, everyone would be able to do it. Conflict creates situations that require increased skill and experience, thus creating a worthy challenge to overcome. I recently watched a Chinese kung fu movie in which the only interest the master pursued was finding a worthy opponent. He considered everything else in life meaningless. Don't fear conflict, but see it as an opportunity to test your ability to lead. Conflict will also allow your team to learn more about itself and grow in the areas of communication and cooperation. Those who learn how to overcome and manage conflict are the ones who lead the way to success.

Application

- Seek to build relationships with team members especially those likely to create conflict.
- Evaluate your team's overall conflict level. Are you operating at the optimal conflict level?
- Write out a plan of how you will deal with your fear of conflict so that you will see it as an opportunity to learn.
- Each conflict is an opportunity to learn and teach; therefore, discuss with your team what they learned from the most recent team conflict.

Notation Area

Personal observations/Ideas for further exploration/Thoughts to remember

当我面对冲突的艰难环境时，就提醒自己，假如带领很简单的话，每个人都能够做到了。冲突带来新的挑战，需要增加自己的技巧和经历，因此也创造出更有价值的克服挑战的机会。我最近看了一部中国功夫的电影，影片中大师所关注的是找到配和自己交手的对手，生活中其他一切都索然无味。不要害怕冲突，而是要把它作为测试自己带领能力的机会。冲突也会让你的团队更多了解自己，在沟通和协作方面成长。只有能够克服和处理冲突的人，才能带领团队走向成功。

应用

◆ 和团队成员保持健康人际关系，特别是那些喜欢惹麻烦的人。

◆ 评估团队的总体冲突水平。你们处在理想的冲突状态吗？

◆ 写下一个计划，说明你要怎样处理冲突中的恐惧，帮助你把它变成学习的机会。

◆ 每个冲突都是学习和教导的机会。因此，和团队讨论这个主题，了解他们从最近的团队冲突中学习到了什么。

笔记

个人体会／要进一步探讨的想法／要铭记在心的理念

视其所以，观其所由，察其所安，人焉廋哉？人焉廋哉？

——孔子

Look at the means which a man employs, consider his motives, observe his pleasure. A man simply cannot conceal himself.

——Confucius

分道扬镳

Dividing the Road

第十六天 分道扬镳
——冲突成为激励

Day 16: Conflict Management as a Stimulant

所有的冲突都有起因。要想解决冲突，就要了解其源头。

All conflicts have a cause. To manage a conflict, discover its source.

Look at the means which a man employs, consider his motives, observe his pleasure. A man simply cannot conceal himself.

——*Confucius*

Yuan Zhi was governor of Luoyang under Emperor Xiaowen of the northern Wei Dynasty. One day Yuan Zhi was traveling by carriage on a narrow road when he came upon Li Biao, the Imperial Censor. According to law, common people had to give way to officials, and lower officials were to give way to higher-ranking officials. However, in this situation neither party was willing to give way. They started quarreling, and without any solution in sight, they took the matter before the emperor. Li Biao argued that he was an official of the imperial court while Yuan Zhi was only a local official and should yield the right of way. Yuan Zhi countered that he was appointed governor of the capital city and all the citizens are listed in his census register. Emperor Xiaowen, finding it hard to judge between the two, ordered that the road be divided down the middle so that each could travel on their own path. Thus, he solved the conflict without judging between the two.[1]

Just as new hurdlers learn techniques to jump a hurdle effectively, so leaders must learn how to manage conflict. In some cases, more than one conflict may arise at the same time. Wisely selecting which conflicts to handle requires discernment because not every conflict is worth the time or energy to resolve. Petty conflicts will work themselves out in time if left alone. Other conflicts may not be within your power to resolve. Still other conflicts are better dealt with at a later time when the parties involved have had time to cool off. Prioritizing based on importance is key in effectively handling conflict.

Another key is to evaluate those involved in the conflict. Determine what potential agendas they may have. What levels of maturity are you dealing with? What are the personalities, temperaments, and values of the parties involved? If

视其所以，观其所由，察其所安，人焉廋哉？人焉廋哉？

——孔子

译文：了解一个人，要看他言行的动机，观察他所采取的方法，考察他安心于做什么。这样，此人怎能隐瞒得了呢？此人怎能隐瞒得了呢？

北魏孝文帝的时候，洛阳令元志与御史中尉李彪在路上相遇。根据法律，百姓要给官员让路，官职卑微的人要给要员让路。双方都认为自己的官职比对方的高而互不相让，结果就造成了交通阻塞。两人趾高气扬地来找孝文帝评理。李彪争辩道，自己是皇帝身边的人，而元志只是一个地方官员，应该让出路的右边。元志反驳道，自己被任命首都城市的地方官，所有的人员都记在自己的册上。孝文帝很难在两者中间决断，于是下令应该分道扬镳，各走各道——把路面沿着中间分开，每个人都能够走在自己那侧的路上。因此，他解决了冲突，却并没有在两者之间进行评判。[1]

跨栏选手要学习如何快速有效地跨越障碍。同样，领袖也要学会如何处理冲突。有时候，同时会出现不止一个冲突。要有智慧，选择处理哪个冲突区，这需要很好的分辨能力，因为并不是每个冲突都值得花时间和精力去解决。假如不加理睬的话，一些微小的冲突会随着时间自然消失；有的冲突可能超越了你解决的能力；有些冲突则应该先放一下，留待以后处理，让双方有时间先冷静一下。根据重要性选择优先处理的事情，这是有效处理冲突的关键。

另外一个关键就是评估一下参与冲突的人。了解他们有哪些可能性方案。你在面对什么成熟度的人？双方的个性、性情和价值观是什么？如果你能够从他们的角度看待冲突，再来解决冲突就会容易多了。不要太快下结

you can view the conflict through their eyes, you will have a much easier time handling the situation. Don't be too quick to judge. Take the time to really listen and hear both sides. As the saying goes: Don't judge a man until you walk a mile in his shoes.

All conflicts have a cause. To manage a conflict, discover its source. Researchers have found the causes of conflict are usually the result of differences in communication, style, or personality. Poor communication most often results in some level of conflict. Style differences can cause people to agree on the goal, yet disagree about how to reach that goal. Personality differences simultaneously strengthen and challenge any group.

A leader needs to know the options when dealing with conflict. Some may argue that win/win agreements are always best. This is simply not true. There are situations when time constraints and the maturity levels make a win/win solution impossible. Leaders should consider five approaches when faced with conflict. These approaches are shown in Chart 16.1.

Chart 16.1 [2]

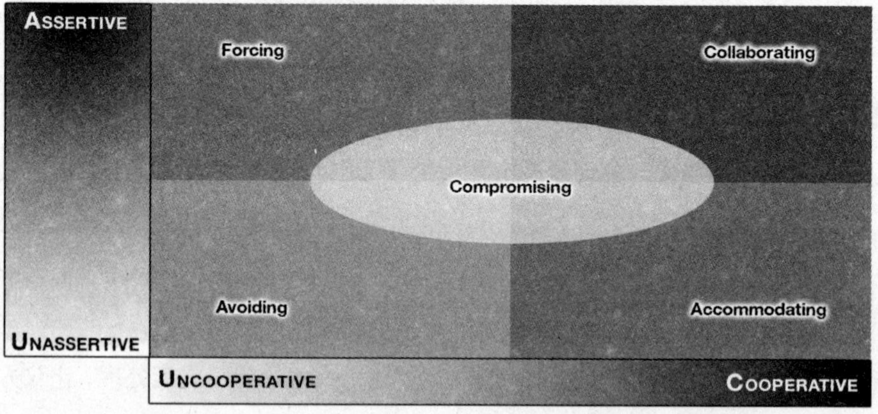

Each of the five approaches to conflict in Chart 16.1 has its own advantages. For example, avoidance is most appropriate for trivial conflicts. Forcing a solution works best when a quick resolution is needed and team member buy-in is not critical. Compromise is often the fastest way to resolve a conflict. Accommodating implies placing others' desires before your own. This is possible when doing

论，需要花时间聆听双方的看法。还是那句老话：要站在别人的角度看问题。

所有的冲突都有起因。要想解决冲突，就要了解其源头。研究者发现，冲突的原因一般都由于沟通、风格或个性差异所致。沟通不畅常常会导致某种程度的冲突。风格的差异让人们虽然认同共同的目标，却在到达目标的方式上产生分歧。个性差异既能够巩固团队，也会给团队带来挑战。

领袖需要知道自己的选择，需要选择自己在何时处理冲突。有的人认为双赢的模式总是最好的，实际上并非完全如此。有的时候，因为时间紧迫而且团队的成熟程度有限，双赢的解决方案不太可能。面对冲突的时候，领袖应该考虑五个步骤。图表 16.1 列出了这些方法：

图表 16.1[2]

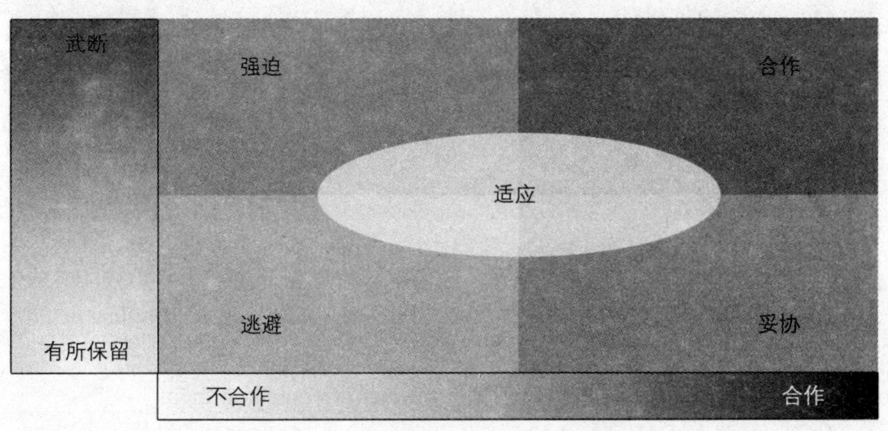

图表 16.1 中五个步骤的每个方面都有自己的优势。例如，逃避对于小冲突来说是最恰当的。当需要迅速解决冲突，团队成员是否买账也并不那么重要时，强迫就是最有效的方法。妥协常常是解决冲突最快的方式。适应意味着把他人的愿望放在自己的想法之前。在没有妥协团队目标的前提下，这也是个可以采用的方法。合作代表着经典的双赢解决方案。当时间压力不太紧急，双方都愿意妥协的时候，双赢就可能出现。[3]

so does not compromise team goals. Collaborating represents a classic win/win solution. Win/win solutions most likely occur when time pressure is minimal and both parties are willing to compromise a little.[3]

A question few leaders ever ask is: Do we need more conflict in our team? Table 16.2 lists questions to help you determine if you need more conflict in your team. Answer the following questions. If you answer yes to even one question, it may indicate your team could use more conflict.

Chart 16.2 [4]

Conflict Questionaire

1. Do the members of your team always agree with you and let you have your way?
2. Are your teammates afraid to admit when they don't know something?
3. Has the pursuit of harmony caused your team to lose sight of your common vision and long-term goals?
4. Is peace within the team the top priority?
5. When making decisions, is a lot of time devoted to not offending people?
6. Is it rare for new ideas to be generated from within the team?
7. Does your team resist most changes?
8. Is it rare to have turnover of team members?

Many studies have examined how to resolve conflict effectively, but few have considered how to stimulate it. Some suggestions on how to stimulate healthy conflict include:

- Set higher goals with greater commitment to reaching them.
- Never be satisfied with the status quo.
- Introduce more competitive reward structures.
- Change the organization's culture.

Experienced leaders expect conflict and use it for organizational growth. However, stimulating conflict with no goal in mind is unwise and will likely end in disaster. On the other hand, stimulating conflict with set goals in mind is purposeful and wise. To illustrate this, picture an eagle teaching its eaglets to fly. The parent eagle with its massive wings hovers over the nest. The beating of its wings

领袖很少提出这样的问题：我们的团队需要更多的冲突吗？图表16.2列出一些问题，帮助你确定自己的团队是否需要更多的冲突。请回答以下问题。即使你只对其中一个问题作出肯定的回答，可能仍然代表你的团队需要面对更多的冲突。

图表16.2[4]

冲突问卷调查表

1. 团队成员总是认同你的观点，让你达成自己的愿望吗?
2. 你的团队成员害怕承认自己对某些事情一无所知吗?
3. 为了追求和谐，你的团队失去了共同的愿景和长期目标吗?
4. 和谐是团队的首要优先次序吗?
5. 作决定的时候，是否把很多时间都用在避免得罪人上?
6. 你的团队内部很少出现新的想法吗?
7. 你的团队抵制大部分改变吗?
8. 团队几乎很少出现人员流动吗?

许多研究都试图了解如何有效地解决冲突，但是很少有人真正如何把冲突变成激励。有的人建议采纳健康的冲突，把它变成激励，这些方法包括：

- 设立较高的目标，下决心达到目标。
- 不要满足于现状。
- 引入更有竞争力的奖励机制。
- 改变机构文化。

有经验的领袖期待冲突发生，把它变成机构成长的机会。然而，引发冲突，心中却没有任何目标，是一个不明智的举动，很可能出现灾难性结果。另一方面，引发冲突时已经胸有成竹，知道自己设定的目标，这样做既明智又有方向。我们来看个例子，想象一下雄鹰教雏鹰学习飞翔的情景。雄鹰展

creates turbulence for the baby eagles. The turbulence slowly forces the baby eagles to the edge of the nest. In desperation the baby eaglet beats its young wings furiously, trying to stay in the nest. Eventually the eaglet cannot hold on and falls out of the nest. Still flapping its young wings, it plummets downward. The eaglet rapidly approaches the forest floor despite its desperate flapping. Moments before the eaglet hits the ground, the parent eagle swoops under it, spreads its wings, and softly catches the baby eaglet. The baby is then safely returned to the nest. The parent eagle repeats this process again and again until the eaglet grows stronger and learns to soar.[5]

As a leader you don't need to fear conflict. Conflict can help you and your team mature. A leader's responsibility is to manage conflict so that it remains a positive force, keeping you on the leading edge and soaring above the competition.

Application

- Answer the questions in Table 16.2.
- Which approach to conflict is most natural for you (avoiding, forcing, compromising, accommodating, or collaborating)?
- Think about conflicts you are likely to face in the near future. Which approach will reap the best results?

Notation Area

Personal observations/Ideas for further exploration/Thoughts to remember

开双翅，一直在巢上面盘旋。双翅的拍打带出了气流，慢慢把雏鹰拍推到了巢边。雏鹰在绝望中奋力拍打着自己稚嫩的翅膀，想继续留在巢中。最后，雏鹰无法继续待在巢中，从巢中掉了出来。虽然它仍然努力拍打着翅膀，但是还是像块儿石头一样垂直向下坠落。不管怎样拼死拍打双翅，雏鹰还是要迅速坠落在森林的地面上。在雏鹰即将坠地的一刻，雄鹰俯冲下去，展开自己的翅膀，轻柔地接住了雏鹰。雏鹰又平安返回了鹰巢。雄鹰一次又一次反复，直到雏鹰变得越来越强壮，学会在空中翱翔。[5]

作为领袖，你不需要惧怕冲突。冲突可以帮助你和团队，给你们带来成熟。领袖的职责就是要处理好冲突，让它成为积极的力量，帮助你处在带领的前沿，翱翔于竞争的浪尖上。

应用

◆回答图表 16.2 中的问题。

◆对于你来说，哪种应对冲突的方式（逃避、强迫、妥协、适应或合作）最自然？

◆想想你将来可能面对的冲突。哪种方法会带来最大的收益？

笔记

个人体会／要进一步探讨的想法／要铭记在心的理念

知己知彼，百战不殆；不知彼而知己，一胜一负；不知彼，不知己，每战必殆。

——孙子[1]

Know the enemy and know yourself; in a hundred battles, you will never be defeated. When you are ignorant of the enemy but know yourself, your chances of winning or losing are equal. If ignorant both of the enemy and yourself, you are sure to be defeated in every battle.

——*Sun Tzu*[1]

集体舞

Synchronized Dance

第十七天 百战不殆
——团队文化

Day 17:Team as Culture

平庸的领袖注重每个人都可见的问题。卓越的领袖要了解问题背后的原因。

Average leaders focus on problems visible to everyone. Great leaders seek to understand issues that lie behind a problem.

Know the enemy and know yourself; in a hundred battles, you will never be defeated. When you are ignorant of the enemy but know yourself, your chances of winning or losing are equal. If ignorant both of the enemy and yourself, you are sure to be defeated in every battle.

——*Sun Tzu* [1]

A leader must see, hear, and understand the people they are called to lead. Every leader approaches situations with their individual style and unique personality. A leader's personality may be described as warm, relaxed, friendly, and flexible or cold, formal, and rigid. But personalities aren't restricted to individuals. Each team exhibits a unique personality as well. We call a team's or organization's personality its culture. Just as tribal cultures have rules and taboos that dictate how members act toward each other and outsiders, teams also have cultures that govern their members' behavior.

My very simple definition of organizational culture is "shared values, assumptions, and beliefs developed over time by experiences within an organization that is the primary cause of people's behavior." The term "culture" was for many years reserved for anthropologists and sociologists. Today, however, it has become the buzzword in leadership and management circles. Anyone who has an interest in leadership or management will run into the concept of "organizational culture" or "corporate culture." Many widely recognize this concept as one of the foundational building blocks of organizational life. Companies such as Avis or Motorola have achieved much of their success because of their ability to train and retain strong leadership. They devote much of their energy at the corporate leadership level to promoting and cultivating organizational culture.

To really understand the power of corporate culture, we need to understand some key principles.

Principle 1 : A culture is a powerful invisible force that creates visible results.

知己知彼，百战不殆；不知彼而知己，一胜一负；不知彼，不知己，每战必殆。

——孙子[1]

译文：了解自己又了解别人，百战都不会有危险；不了解敌人但是了解自己，可能胜利也可能失败；不了解敌人也不了解自己，那就是每战都必定有危险。

领袖必须看到、听到并且理解自己是被呼召要承担带领职责的人。每位领袖在面对不同环境时，都有自己独特的风格和个性。领袖的个性各有千秋，可能温和、放松、友好，或者冷漠、正式和僵化。但个性并不只局限于个人，每个团队也展现出独特的个性。我们把团队或机构的个性称作"文化"。部落的文化包括规章制度和禁忌，决定其成员怎样彼此相处以及对待外人，同样，团队的文化也管理着其成员的行为。

我对机构文化最简单的定义就是："机构文化，是随着时间在机构中积累出来的共享的价值观、设想和信念，这也是人们行为的主要原因。""文化"这个用语多年来只被人类学者和社会学家专用。然而，今天，这已经成为领袖和管理人士的常用语。每一个对领导力和管理感兴趣的人都会遇到"机构文化"和"企业文化"这样的概念。很多人都把这种概念作为机构生活的基本奠基石之一。安飞士或摩托罗拉这样的公司具备培训和留住好领袖的能力，所以取得了很大的成功。他们注重集团领导力层面，倡导并培养企业文化。

要想真正理解企业文化的力量，我们需要理解一些主要原则。

原则1：文化是一种强大的无形力量，能够创造很多可见的结果。文化可以被比作飓风——虽然肉眼不可见，但是其强大的后果却让每个人都确认它的存在。同样，领袖和团队成员既可以在一种文化中成长壮大，也可以在

Culture can be compared to hurricane winds: It is invisible to the eye, but the powerful results convince everyone of its existence. In the same way, leaders and team members alike may flourish in one culture and totally fail in another. The culture of a team can work for or against your success.

Principle 2 : Leaders must develop and direct the development of the team culture. Many factors work against a strong synergistic culture. Leaders must constantly be watching the internal and external influences that affect the culture. New team members and changing demands on time and resources all have effects on culture and can cause team members to forget core values. A strong leader will communicate with the team in a way that keeps the culture strong and moral high.

Principle 3 : Leadership is needed to bring about healthy changes in a culture. In some cases, nonleaders attempt to change cultural norms. Team members become ambitious and decide to change the way things are done. Without proper communication with the leadership, these situations often resemble guerrilla warfare. Well-meaning team members will soon find themselves in factions, gossip, and slander. Healthy cultural change will happen in relationship leadership.

Principle 4 : Your culture will make or break you. Many people have flourished in one culture and completely failed in another. As a leader you may find yourself leading a culture that does not fit your style. You can either change yourself or begin systematically changing the culture. In some cases, differences are great enough that the healthiest choice is for you to leave and start again with a different team. When searching for a new team leader for a successful team, it is essential to look for one who matches the team's values. This is not the case for under-performing or dysfunctional teams. These teams need change, and a new leader with different values may be just what is needed. When joining a team, seek one in which your values match. If you find yourself having major cultural and value differences with a new team, you likely have little chance of success. Your options are basically to perish or parachute.

Principle 5 : Successful leaders are in touch with their cultures. They seek to understand the needs of their team and develop the culture for optimal success. Such leaders are not satisfied with superficial understanding of why things succeed or fail. They focus on values and cultural elements that will foster continued growth and success.[2]

Understanding your culture will result in greater insight. Average leaders focus on problems visible to everyone. Great leaders seek to understand issues that

另一种文化中一败涂地。团队文化可以为你所用，也可以成为摧毁力，破坏你的成功。

原则2：领袖必须培养、引导和发展团队文化。许多因素都不利于培养稳固的和产生效力的文化。领袖必须善于观察，注意到影响文化的外在和内在的影响力。新的团队成员以及在时间上和资源上的改变都对团队有影响力，导致团队成员忘记自己的核心价值观。坚强的领袖知道如何和团队沟通，让企业文化变得更强，士气更高。

原则3：领袖需要在文化中带来健康的改变。有的时候，跟随者会试图改变文化惯例。团队成员雄心勃勃地要改变做事的模式。假如和领袖之间没有进行恰当的沟通，这就有点像游击战。好心好意的团队成员马上就发现自己处于派系斗争、闲言碎语和彼此诽谤之中。在关系型领导力中，才会产生健康的文化改变。

原则4：文化能够塑造你，也能够毁掉你。很多人在某种文化中健康成长，在另一种文化中却一败涂地。作为领袖，你可能发现在带领一种文化上与自己风格迥然不同的团队。你可以改变自己，或者开始有系统地改变文化。某些情况下，彼此的差异过大，很难弥合，最健康的选择就是你离开现有的团队，在另一个团队中重新开始。为一个成功团队寻找领袖的时候，关键一点就是要寻找与团队价值观一致的人。对于表现欠佳或不健康的团队，这种方法则并不适用。这样的团队需要改变，具备不同价值观的新领袖可能才是它真正的需要。在加入团队的时候，也要找一个价值观和自己相匹配的团队。假如你发现自己和新团队之间出现了重大的文化和价值观的差异，很可能你成功的几率也就很小了。你所剩的选择也就只有死亡或是逃亡。

原则5：成功的领袖与自己的文化联系紧密。他们理解团队的需要，培养成功所需的氛围。这样的领袖并不满足于肤浅的解释，说明事物成败的原因。他们注重价值观和文化因素，因为这样能够制造一种氛围，带来持续的增长和成功。[2]

加深对文化的理解能够给人带来洞察力和智慧。平庸的领袖注重每个人

lie behind a problem. Commit to becoming a great leader by growing in your understanding of culture.

Application

- Start the process of identifying the core values in your team. Do you have some team members who just don't seem to fit in?

- Begin to help your team understand your culture's core values.

- Identify at least one aspect of your culture that, if changed, would improve your team's chances for a successful future.

- Become the world expert on your team's culture. If possible, enlist help from outside observers. They can often see areas that you have come to take for granted.

Notation Area

Personal observations/Ideas for further exploration/Thoughts to remember

都可以看见的问题。卓越的领袖要洞察问题背后的原因，让自己立志成为卓越的领袖，在对文化的理解上成长。

应用

◆开始在团队中分辨核心价值观。你们的团队中有看起来格格不入的人吗？

◆开始帮助团队理解团队文化的核心价值。

◆确定文化需要改变的至少一个方面，假如改变的话，能够增加团队未来成功的机会。

◆在团队文化上成为世界级专家。假如可能的话，请团队以外的人帮助。他们常常能够看到你已经习以为常的东西。

笔记

个人体会／要进一步探讨的想法／要铭记在心的理念

己所不欲，勿施于人。

——孔子

Do not do to others what you do not want done to yourself.

——Confucius

义帝被罢黜

Dethroning of Emperor Yi

第十八天 项羽废义帝
——创造文化

Day 18: Creating a Culture

领袖是文化的缔造者、看守者和栽培者。

机构的危机为领袖创造了一个关键的时机，能够让新的文化诞生。

Leaders are the primary creators, keepers, and cultivators of culture.

An organization's crisis creates a key time for leaders to generate culture.

Do not do to others what you do not want done to yourself.

——Confucius

In the fourth month and first year of the Han Dynasty (206 BC), the battle-weary kings returned to their own countries. Xiang Yu, a general of Chu, also returned with his army and decided to dethrone Emperor Yi. He caused the emperor's ministers to leave and secretly convinced the king of Hengshan and the king of Linjiang to attack and kill the emperor.[1] Xiang Yu demonstrated no loyalty to the emperor, yet later complained about the kings and barons who constantly rebelled against him during his reign as Overlord of Chu. He set an example of rebellion that followed him during his own reign. He never saw his shortcomings nor learned from them, and this remained his greatest fault. He never blamed himself, even casting his final defeat on bad luck.[2]

Xiang Yu failed to realize his rebellion against Emperor Yi created a culture of rebellion. Leaders are the primary creators, keepers, and cultivators of culture. The founder and/or leader of a group creates the foundation of a culture, just as the DNA in each person determines what he or she will look like. The founder sets the future by projecting an image of what the organization should be. The small size of most new organizations allows the founder to instill his or her vision into all the members. Early successes and failures also become fundamental in the culture, becoming stories that are passed on and function similar to myths and legends in tribal cultures. The strength and persona of the leader, combined with the trials and triumphs of the organization in its early years, will be embedded into the organization's cultural foundation. Leaders play an important role in embedding cultural values. Primary embedding mechanisms are directly influenced by the leader's personal involvement. Secondary cultural mechanisms are often created

己所不欲，勿施于人。

——孔子

译文：推己及人，自己所不愿意承受的，不要去加在别人头上。

汉朝初年（公元前206年）的第四个月，连年打仗疲惫不堪的王侯们返回了自己的国家。楚国的将军项羽也带着军队返回，他决定废黜义帝。他撵走了皇帝的宰相，秘密说服衡山王和临江王攻击并且杀害了皇帝。[1] 在项羽做楚霸王的统治时期，他抱怨王侯们常常反叛自己，却忘记了自己曾宣誓要效忠皇帝但最终背叛的行径。他自己在反叛上先作了榜样，在他统治时期，各诸侯也纷纷效法。他从来看不到自己的缺点，也没有从中吸取教训，这成为他最大的弱点。他从未自省担当自己的过错，反而把自己最终的失败归咎于运气不好。[2]

项羽没有意识到，自己反叛义帝造就了反叛的文化。领袖是文化的缔造者、看守者和栽培者。团队的创始人和领袖创建文化的根基，就像人体的DNA决定一个人的独特性一样，领袖设计了机构的形象，为机构奠定了未来的走向。大部分新机构起步时都不很大，这就让创始人把自己的愿景传递给所有的成员。每次的成败都成为文化的根基，成为代代相传的故事，这和部落文化中的神话和传奇故事的作用相似。领袖的优点和个性加上机构早期经历的考验与胜利，都会深深地根植下来，成为机构的文化根基。领袖在培植文化价值观上占据重要角色。首要栽培机制直接受到领袖个人参与的影响。次要的文化机制一般由领袖创立，但是不需要领袖个人的亲力亲为。首要栽培机制包括：

by leaders, but they do not require the leader's physical presence. Primary embedding mechanisms include:

1. Leadership reactions and decisions made during crisis
2. Items or activities that leaders control, regulate, and measure
3. Mentoring, role modeling, and orientations
4. Basis for giving promotions, bonuses, and awards
5. Criteria for recruiting, hiring, and firing members
6. Criteria for distribution of resources

Secondary articulation and reinforcement mechanisms include:

1. Team rites and rituals
2. Systems, procedures, structure, and organization
3. Circulated stories about leaders and founders
4. Physical space, building, and work areas
5. Written mission statements, core values, or creeds[3]

An organization's crisis creates a key time for leaders to generate culture. How he or she acts in the midst of crisis will establish new norms, values, and modes of operating. Crisis especially assists the creation of culture because of the increased learning that results from heightened emotions and intensity, imprinting the event in a person's mind more strongly than in a normal situation.

Tom Watson Jr., the former CEO of IBM, exemplified this principle. When a young executive made some bad decisions that cost Watson's company several million dollars, he summoned the executive to his office. The young executive entered the office and said, "I suppose after that set of mistakes you want to fire me." Watson replied, "Not at all, young man. We have just spent a couple of million dollars educating you."[4] Today, IBM's culture is much different from what Watson created because other crises have changed it over time. But the bottom line is that leaders are the key element in the creation of a culture. It is the leader who will create a culture and determine what builds or tears down its members. The following points will foster a culture full of energy, teamwork, and productivity.

- Take time to hear what people are feeling. It is always wise to regularly listen to the concerns of your team.
- Trust others with important assignments. Release control and allow room for mistakes; it's the only way to see your team mature.

1.领袖在危机时的反应和决定；

2.领袖掌控、调节和衡量事物或行动；

3.导师、榜样和确定方向；

4.提升、奖金和红利的标准；

5.招募、雇用和解雇员工的标准；

6.资源分配的标准。

次要的联系和强化的机制包括：

1.团队仪式和庆典组织；

2.系统、程序、结构和组织；

3.流传至今的领袖和创始人的故事；

4.空间距离、建筑物和工作场所；

5.书面的使命声明、核心价值观或信条。[3]

机构的危机为领袖创造了一个关键的时机，能够诞生新的文化。领袖在危机中的行为能建立新的标准、价值观和操作模式。危机尤其能协助创建文化，因为危机时的情感升华以及整个事件，比正常情况下以更深的印象和强度印入了人们的心灵。

IBM的前执行总裁汤姆·沃森(Tom Watson Jr.)在这个原则上作了典范。一个年轻的主管作了一系列错误的决定，让沃森的公司损失了几百万美元。他要这位主管来办公室见他。年轻的主管一进办公室就说："我犯了这些错误，你一定想把我开除了。"沃森回答道："不，年轻人，我们最近刚花了200万美元对你进行培训。"[4]今天，IBM的文化和沃森所创建的机构大相径庭了，因为长期以来其他的危机已经改变了这一切。但是底线在于领袖是创建文化的主要因素。只有领袖才能创建文化，并且决定什么能够扶持或伤害团队成员。以下的几点内容能够培育充满活力、团队合作和积极有效的文化。

- 花时间聆听人们的感受。常常聆听团队的声音，这是一个明智的决定。

- Lead with compelling vision. Give your team a destination worthy of a quest.
- Praise others at every opportunity. A genuine compliment can make a person's day or even his or her month. Be an encourager.
- Keep the vision clear and visible. Talk about it, write about it, and model the vision in as many creative ways as humanly possible.
- Create a learning atmosphere. Set the example by learning something new every day and look for opportunities to share new ideas.
- Celebrate even small victories. Everybody loves to celebrate. Life is too short to miss out on celebrations that recognize success.[5]

How does a culture develop? The formation of any group goes through stages of forming, storming, norming, and performing. The forming stage involves deciding who will be on your team and getting to know one another at a surface level. The storming starts when expectations are not clear or compatible. When this happens, people start questioning goals, procedures, and team leadership. Norming is a benefit that comes from the storm and is enjoyed by those who did not jump ship when the waters turned rough. Those who work through the storm learn how to effectively work together despite differences. People at this stage grow to know each other at a much deeper level. Leaders are more likely to be accepted for who they are, weaknesses and all. The reward for working through these stages is that your teamwork will reach the performing stage and produce visible results. Purposes are clarified and individuals' skills are used to benefit the team. Most healthy teams transition through the four stages. It should be noted that on a much smaller scale, new people who join an established team transition through these stages as well. Each of these stages is shown in Figure 18-1. Chart 18-2 can help you determine the current stage of your group.

- 在重要的任务上信任他人。放开控制权，允许人们有犯错的空间。这是团队走向成熟的唯一方法。
- 带领时的愿景具有很强的吸引力。给你的团队一个值得追求的目的。
- 寻找每一个机会赞美他人。一句真诚的赞美可以让一个人的一天甚至整个月都变得明亮起来。请成为一个鼓励者。
- 让愿景清晰和可衡量。以多种创造性方式和自己能达到的方式讨论，写下你们的愿景，并且在这件事上作典范，表现出你为未来所作的努力。
- 创造学习的氛围。每天学习新事物，寻找分享新想法的机会，给大家做榜样。
- 为每一个小的胜利而庆贺。每个人都喜欢庆祝活动。人生如此短暂，请不要失去庆贺成功的任何机会。[5]

文化怎样形成？任何团队都会经历形成阶段、暴风雨阶段、规范阶段和表现阶段。形成阶段需要决定谁会留在你的团队中，这段时间大家从表面上彼此产生了肤浅的了解。暴风雨阶段出现在期望值不清晰或彼此关系不协调的时候。当这个阶段出现的时候，人们开始对目标、程序和团队领袖出现质疑。规范阶段得益于暴风雨期，只有那些水高浪大的时候没有跳船的人才能够享受这一阶段。共同经历风雨的人学会了怎样有效解决差异，共同协作。这个阶段，人们在彼此的了解上成长，对彼此的了解程度更深入。领袖也更被人接纳，连弱点等等也一起被接纳。走过这些阶段带来了奖赏，你们的团队能够达到表现的阶段，产生更多的可见的结果。团队的目的变得更清晰，个人的技巧也用于建立团队，使团队得益处。大部分健康的团队都会经历这四个阶段。我们还需要注意到，从较小的范围来看，新人进入一个已经完善的团队时，也会经历这四个阶段。这一过程的每个阶段都表现在图表 18.1 中。图表 18.2 可以帮助你确定目前你的团队处在什么阶段。

Figure 18.1 [6]

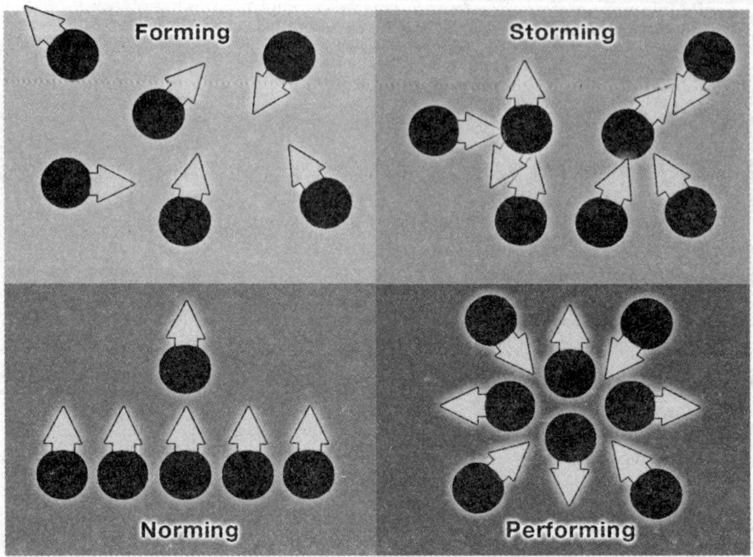

Figure 18.2 [7]

Group Formation & Growth Life Cycles

Stage	Primary Questions	Secondary Questions	Issues in Focus	Primary Tasks
Forming	WHO will be part of the group? WHO is this person next to me?	WHERE will we meet? WHEN will we meet?	Recruitment Assimilation New Members	Entry & Start-up Building Relationships
Storming	WHY do we do things this way? WHY are you like this? WHY did you do that?	WHO will stick with it through this tough time? HOW will we work through this?	Heart Issues Style & Procedures Priorities	Communication Confrontation Troubleshooting
Norming	HOW do we live and work together?	WHO are you beneath the surface?	Fellowship Roles Leadership	Getting Acquainted Personal Growth Life Sharing
Performing	WHAT are we called to be/do?	WHO are we called to reach? How can we be effective? Why were we put here?	Productivity Progress Growth	Using Skills & Gifts Reaching Target Market Unleashing People

图表 18.1[6]

机构组织和成长

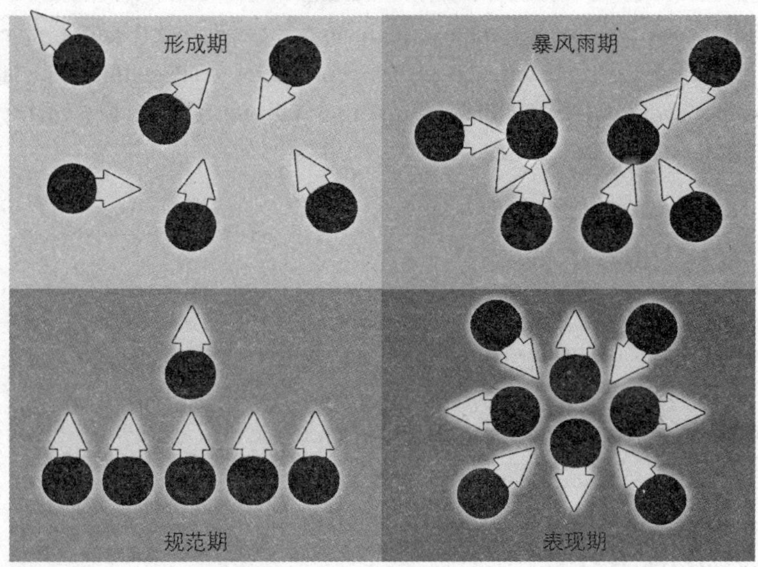

图表 18.2[7]

团队组成和成长过程循环圈

阶段	首要问题	次要问题	焦点问题	首要任务
形成期	谁会成为团队成员？ 谁会成为我的伙伴？	我们共同的目标是什么？ 我们何时能达到这个目标？	招募 吸纳 新成员	开始着手 建立关系
暴风雨期	我们为什么要这样做事情？ 你为什么喜欢这样？ 你为什么要这么做？	在这样的艰难时刻，谁能坚持下来？ 我们怎样才能克服这一切？	心灵的问题 风格、过程 优先次序	沟通 对质 解决问题
规范期	我们怎样才能共同生活和工作？	外表之下的你是谁？	友谊 角色 领导力	彼此熟悉 个人成长 生命分享
表现期	我们被呼召要成为什么样的人？ 要做什么事情？	我们被呼召要影响谁？ 我们怎样才能更有效？ 我们为什么被放在这个位置上？	成效进步成长	使用技巧、才华 获得锁定的市场 让人获得自由

These formation stages (forming, storming, norming, and performing) facilitate the birth of cultural foundations. During each stage of a group's life cycle, team members ask questions, focus on certain issues, and begin tasks. Understanding these stages helps a leader anticipate conflict during the different cycles of the group's development as well as the opportunities to lay cultural foundations. You as the leader will create the culture of your group. You decide what type of cultural foundation will be laid.

Application

◆At what stage of development is your current team?

◆How can you help your team transition to the next stage?

Notation Area

Personal observations/Ideas for further exploration/Thoughts to remember

这些组成阶段（形成阶段、暴风雨阶段、规范阶段和表现阶段）推动了文化根基的诞生。在团队生活循环圈的每个阶段，团队成员都会询问问题，把焦点放在某些特定的问题上，并且着手开始完成自己的任务。理解这些阶段，可以帮助领袖在团队发展的不同循环圈中以及机会中参与冲突，打下文化根基。作为领袖，你会为自己的团队创建文化，要决定打下什么样的文化根基。

应用

◆你现在的团队处在哪个发展阶段？

◆你怎样帮助团队过渡到下一个阶段？

笔记

个人体会／要进一步探讨的想法／要铭记在心的理念

临之以庄，则敬；孝慈，则忠；举善而教不能，则民劝。

——孔子

Rule over them with dignity and they will be reverent; treat them with kindness and they will do their best; praise the good and instruct those who are backward and they will be imbued with enthusiasm.

—— *Confucius* [1]

善良

Kindness

第十九天 赢得民心
——善用权威

Day 19:Leaders Use or Abuse Power

卓越的领袖了解权威并且驾驭权威为团队所用。

Effective leaders are aware of power and harness it to best serve the team.

Rule over them with dignity and they will be reverent; treat them with kindness and they will do their best; praise the good and instruct those who are backward and they will be imbued with enthusiasm.

——*Confucius* [1]

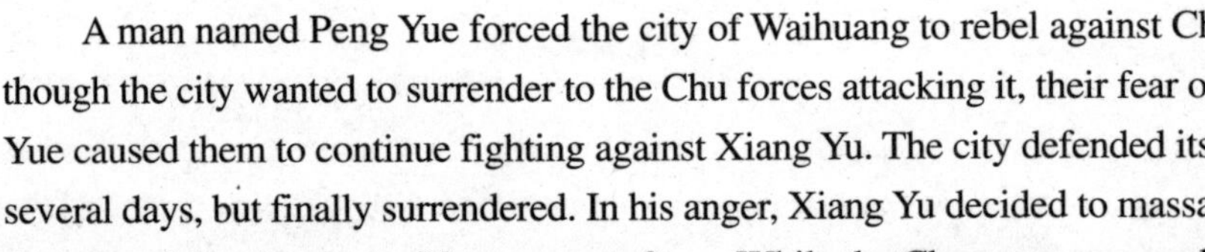

A man named Peng Yue forced the city of Waihuang to rebel against Chu. Although the city wanted to surrender to the Chu forces attacking it, their fear of Peng Yue caused them to continue fighting against Xiang Yu. The city defended itself for several days, but finally surrendered. In his anger, Xiang Yu decided to massacre all the men of the city above fifteen years of age. While the Chu army prepared to execute this plan, the thirteen-year-old son of a magistrate went to Xiang Yu and said: "Peng Yue forced Waihuang to rebel, and the city was afraid. It meant to surrender but was waiting for Your Highness to arrive. Now that you are here, you want to massacre our men. How can you win over the people like this? There are more than a dozen cities further east in Liang, but now they will all be afraid to surrender to you." [2] Xiang Yu listened to the boy and pardoned the men. When the other rebellious cities east of Suiyang heard this, they also quickly surrendered.

When powerful leaders show kindness and mercy, they naturally attract followers. All leaders need to learn how to influence others. That is why power always has been a central topic when studying leadership. In spite of the good that people with great influence can do, abuse of authority has caused many to associate it with evil. Many view power as a negative or prideful goal to pursue, often associating it with selfish ambition and vanity. Sayings such as "absolute power corrupts absolutely" perpetuate this negative image. As a result, books have been written on how to lead without power. This sounds good; however, it is impractical. The person who tries to lead without authority is actually using power, but giving it a different name. As a leader, you must learn about power so you can use it

临之以庄，则敬；孝慈，则忠；举善而教不能，则民劝。

——孔子[1]

译文：你用庄重的态度对待百姓，他们就会尊敬你。对父母孝顺，对子女慈祥，百姓就会尽忠于你；你选用善良的人，又教育能力差的人，百姓就会互相勉励，加倍努力了。

彭越迫使外黄城反叛楚军。虽然城里人心惶惶，都想投靠前来攻击的楚军，但是对彭越的惧怕让他们不得不继续举兵抵挡项羽。整个城市被围困了几天，最后还是投降了。项羽在盛怒之下，想要把城中15岁以上的男丁全部杀掉。楚军在等候执行命令的时候，当地地方官13岁的儿子前去找项羽，对他说："彭越劫掠外黄，迫使我们起兵反叛，满城惊慌。全城的人都在等待将军的到来，好解救大家。现在您来了，却要杀尽我们的男丁。您这样怎能赢得民心呢？梁地向东走还有十多个城市，现在他们都会感到惧怕，不敢向你投降。"[2]项羽听取了男孩儿的意见，赦免了那些人。向东直至睢阳的其他反叛城市听到消息后，都纷纷迅速归降。

当领袖表现出善良和怜悯的一面时，自然会吸引很多跟随者。所有的领袖都需要学习了解如何影响他人。这也是为什么在学习领导力时，权威总是一个核心话题。虽然这些人具有很大的影响力，能够为别人做很多好事，但是滥用职权也会让很多人把它与邪恶挂钩。很多人把权威视为消极的或高人一等的目标去追求，常常把它和自私的野心和空虚放在一起。"集权一定会导致腐败。"这句话就是很好的写照，活画了这消极的一幕。因此，就有很多书籍描写怎样在没有权威的情况下带领。听起来虽然很好，但是却不太切合实际。没有权威下带领的人实际上还是在无形中使用了权威，只不过说法不同罢了。作为领袖，

instead of abusing it. If people were honest, most would admit they desire power. You may argue this, but seldom will you find someone who once gained superiority and willingly gave it up. Responsibility and authority may be easier to release, but power tends to have an addictive effect on people. The popular trilogy *Lord of the Rings* highlights the result of extreme power in the hands of man. Few could handle its influence and remain pure.

Authority and power are often confused. A leadership role automatically grants authority, but power is earned. Authority involves the legitimate right to organize and make decisions, while power refers to the individual's capacity to influence decisions. Power is intangible, multifaceted, and elusive. When a powerful person walks into a room, others can almost sense their dominance. In this chapter you will learn ways to exercise power. You also will learn about five different power bases and the interaction between them.

Power comprises a part of every organization or team. Leaders utilize different forms of power depending on the circumstances. Three common forms of power are vertical, horizontal, and circular. Circular power works well when the team is made up of mature, well-qualified individuals. The leaders serve as a central figure facilitating and coordinating the work of each team member. Circular power has become popular within the U.S. corporate world in recent years. The leader is knowledgeable enough about each team member's work to advise and encourage. The team's strength is developed by diversity and synergy. High levels of trust and effective communication are essential when using circular power to lead a team.

Vertical power is best seen in a hierarchical organizational chart. Decisions are made at the top and information is passed down. Vertical power is most appropriate when the team needs direct guidance and supervision in order to thrive. Leaders using this form of power serve as authority figures. Horizontal power is often present when many teams work together. Leaders relate with other leaders and share information and resources. Power is shared among peers. Horizontal power is most effective when cooperation is high and internal competition is low. Leaders exercising horizontal power keep the overall goal in focus rather than individual success.

Effective leaders are aware of power and harness it to best serve the team. Here in figure 19.1 is a small Power Test[3] to see how much you know about powerful people.

你必须了解权威，这样你能够善用它，而不是滥用它。假如人们诚实的话，大部分会承认自己渴望获得权威。你可以持不同看法，但是，凡是位居高位的人都不愿意放弃自己的位置。放开责任和权力可能稍微容易一些，但是人对权威好像会上瘾一样。畅销书三部曲《指环王》生动地刻画了极权落在人类手中的结果。几乎没有人能够驾驭其影响力，并且保持自身的纯洁。

权威和权力常常被混为一谈。领袖这一角色会自然拥有权力，但需要赢得权威。权力包括组织决定的合法权利；权威是指一个人影响整个决定的能力。权威无形、多方面而且很难下定义。有权威的人走入一个房间的时候，他人能够感受到他们的与众不同。本章中你要学习操练权威。你也会学习五个不同的权威基础，以及它们之间的交互作用。

权威是每个机构或团队的组成部分。领袖根据不同的环境，使用不同形式的权威。权威的三个普遍形式为垂直的、水平的和圆形的。

当团队组成人员成熟和稳定时，圆形权威的效果最好。领袖成为中心人物，推动并且协调每位团队成员的工作。圆形权威近几年在美国的企业界开始流行。领袖的资讯四通八达，了解每位团队成员的工作，并且给予忠告和鼓励。团队中的差异和协调合作成为它最大的优势。当使用圆形权威带领时，高度信任和有效的沟通是其中的核心要素。

垂直权威在等级森严的机构中最常见。决定由最上面一层作出，之后被传递下去。当团队需要直接的引导和监督时，垂直权威最为恰当，可以帮助团队变得更加兴旺。使用这种形式的领袖被看作是权威人士。

当很多团队成员共同协作时，水平权威最常见。领袖和其他团队成员彼此交流，分享信息和资源，也可以在同伴之间相互分享权威。当合作程度很高，内心的竞争欲望很低的时候，水平权威是最有效的。操练水平权威能够把焦点放在全局目标上，而不是注重个人的成功。

卓越的领袖了解权威并且驾驭权威为团队所用。在图表19.1中是个小小的权威测试[3]，看看你对权威人士有多少认识。

Power Test

Answer true or false

___1. Women are just as likely to be driven by a need for power as men.

___2. Power people share few common characteristics.

___3. Power people tend to be attracted to certain occupations more than they are attracted to others.

___4. Power people make super traveling companions because they're so cool and well organized.

___5. Spouses of power people always have a rough time, and their marriage is full of fighting.

___6. Creativity is a common trait in power people and is responsible for their success.

___7. Power and sex are unrelated.

___8. Power people don't usually care about the cars they drive because they're preoccupied with other matters.

Answers: F, F, T, F, F, F, F, F.
If you answered six to eight questions correctly, you are above average in knowledge of this topic.

As a leader you have no choice but to learn about power. It is not a necessary evil but rather a great skill. Power has the ability to bless others and corrects unjust situations. Remember that powerful leaders have the ability to empower others. The best leaders hold power loosely as if it were an object lying in the palm of their open hand. It is never to be used for selfish gain but for the good of others.

权威测试

回答对错

1. 女性和男性一样，很容易被权威诱惑。
2. 权威人士彼此之间的共同点很少。
3. 权威人士更倾向于被某类职业所吸引。
4. 权威人士是很好的旅游伴侣，因为他们很酷，而且能够把一切都打点得井井有条。
5. 权威人士的配偶日子过得很不容易，而且他们的婚姻充满了火药味。
6. 创造性是权威人士的普遍特征，这也是他们成功的重要因素。
7. 权力和性没有任何关系。
8. 权威人士不会太在意自己开什么样的车，因为他们心中装的都是各种事情。

答案：错，错，对，错，错，错，错，错。

假如你答对了6个到8个，那么你在这个领域的知识已经超乎正常水平。

作为领袖，除了了解权力以外你别无选择。与其说它注定会带来邪恶，不如说它是一种重要技巧。权力赋予人能力祝福他人，也能够纠正不公平的境遇。记住，卓越的领袖也具备授权的能力。最好的领袖以平常心看待权力，好像它是一样东西，静静地放在自己张开的手掌中。它的存在不应该被用来达到自私的目的，而是为了他人的益处。

Application

◆ What type of power is most appropriate for your situation?

◆ How can you increase your influence for the good of your team?

◆ What temptations come with power that you need to avoid carefully?

Notation Area

Personal observations/Ideas for further exploration/Thoughts to remember

应用

◆对于你所处的环境来说，什么类型的权威最恰当？

◆为了团队的益处，你打算怎样增加你的影响力？

◆你需要避免哪些和权威并生的诱惑？

笔记

个人体会／要进一步探讨的想法／要铭记在心的理念

故善用兵者，避其锐气，击其惰归，此治气者也。以治待乱，以静待哗，此治心者也。

——孙子[1]

Those skilled in war avoid the enemy when his spirit is keen and attack him when he is sluggish and his soldiers are homesick. This is control of the morale factor. In good order, they await a disorderly enemy; in serenity, a clamorous one. This is control of the mental factor.

——*Sun Tzu*[1]

蓄势待发

Strength Waits

第二十天 以治待乱，以静待哗
——了解自己心灵和情感的极限

Day 20: Knowing Your Mental and Emotional Challenges

当领袖真正了解自己的优势和弱势的时候，他们就更有可能也更能够明智地、谦卑地回应他人。

When leaders truly know their strengths and weaknesses, they are more likely and able to respond wisely and with humility.

Those skilled in war avoid the enemy when his spirit is keen and attack him when he is sluggish and his soldiers are homesick. This is control of the morale factor. In good order, they await a disorderly enemy; in serenity, a clamorous one. This is control of the mental factor.

—— *Sun Tzu*[1]

Emotional and mental strength are fundamental components to a successful team. Leaders need to know their own strengths and master their emotions. After many years of battle, both Chu and Han were weary of fighting. Xiang Yu proposed to Liu Bang, "Because of us, the empire has been in tumult for years. Let us settle the issue by a fight between the two of us. Why make the people suffer with us?"

Liu Bang declined with a smile. "I prefer to fight with my wits, not with brute force."[2] Following this encounter, Xiang Yu commissioned his champions to challenge the men of Han in single combat. Liu Bang, however, didn't accept the challenge. Instead, he commanded his best horseman and archer to shoot and kill each Chu general that emerged to fight. In this way, Liu Bang recognized Xiang Yu's distraction and chose to conduct the battle based on his army's strength.

Some time later, Xiang Yu stationed himself at Suiyang, separate from the majority of his army who were fighting the Han army at Cheng Gao. The Han army, believing they had the strategic advantage, challenged and mocked the Chu forces, hoping to draw them out. After almost a week of insults, the high marshal Cao Jiu lost his temper and led his men across the Si River to attack. When half of the Chu forces had crossed the river, the Han soldiers attacked and routed them. Xiang Yu lost most of his army during the battle because his generals were not able to control their own emotions.

Many will entice you with opportunities that seem too good to ignore. However, successful organizations and leaders know and stick to their strengths, minimizing distractions. Because Liu Bang knew his strength did not lie in physical might but in strategy, he did not allow Xiang Yu to tempt him into a battle of physical combat.

故善用兵者，避其锐气，击其惰归，此治气者也。以治待乱，以静待哗，此治心者也。

——孙子[1]

译文：所以善用兵的人，要避开敌人的锐气，等待敌人士气衰竭时再去打击它，周王室掌握军队士气的方法。以自己的严整对付敌人的混乱，以自己的镇静对付敌人的轻躁，这是掌握军队心理的方法。

情感和心灵的力量是成功团队的基本组成部分。领袖需要了解自己的力量，掌控自己的情感。多年的战争后，楚汉都对战争感到非常厌倦。项羽请求刘邦："因为你我二人，整个国家陷入了多年的战乱。不如我们俩大战一场来解决我们之间的问题，为什么要让黎民百姓跟着我们一起受苦呢？"

刘邦一笑婉拒了："我喜欢斗智，而不是斗勇。"[2]这次遭遇之后，项羽命令自己的将军们去和汉军将军单挑。然而，刘邦却没有接受挑战。相反，他给自己最好的骑兵和射手下命令，每次当楚将出来挑战的时候，就把他射死或杀死。这样，刘邦让项羽分心，选择让军队进行力量上的较量。

后来，项羽驻军在睢阳，大军在成皋抵御汉军，他与大部队分隔。汉军认为自己占据了战略优势，挑战并且嘲笑楚军，想把他们引出来打仗。一周的凌辱之后，楚军的元帅曹咎大怒，率军横渡汜水攻击汉军。当楚军的一半人马横渡汜水之后，汉军突袭，打得他们措手不及，几乎全军覆没。而这仅仅是因为项羽的将军无法控制情感。

你会面对很多诱惑，似乎机会太好了，根本无法放弃。然而，成功的机构和领袖知道并且抓住自己的优势不放，把分心的事情缩小到最小。刘邦因为知道自己的优势不在身体上的力量，而是在战略，所以他没有让项羽诱惑自己，去进行力量上的较量。

当领袖真正了解自己的优势和弱势的时候，他们就更有可能明智地、谦卑

When leaders truly know their strengths and weaknesses, they are more likely and able to respond wisely and with humility. Leaders' pride can cause them to overlook their own failings and lead them to ruin. Controlling emotions, as well as cognitively (or rationally) recognizing strengths and weaknesses, leads to growth in leadership.

Emotionally immature or prideful leaders are natural abusers of power. Their basic motivation is selfishness. These types of leaders are power hungry, using others in order to acquire more influence and serve their own desires. They're primarily concerned with status, control, and success. Confucius says, "To attack a task from the wrong end can do nothing but harm."[3] If your goal entails a selfish end, you will create a destructive path pursuing its realization. Power used for selfish gain causes you to hurt others. However, pursuing power in order to serve a cause or meet the needs of others has the potential to do great good. Power in itself is not wrong, but mixing it with the character weakness and immaturity of its user can create an explosive combination. As a leader, you will need to use power in different forms during your lifetime, and you should be aware of the pros and the cons of each type of power.

The image of the warrior riding out to battle with the words strength, humility, and honor across his breastplate portrays the proper way to wear power. The warrior exhibits mental strength because he knows he can handle the battles before him. He demonstrates humility in the knowledge that he is as fallible as every other human being. His honor from past achievements and accomplishments equips him with a positive view of the future and of his ability to win the victory: anything less would be false humility. This is how a leader can move forward with power.

I love the line in the movie *First Knight* when Guinevere says of King Author, "He wears his power so lightly." I remember feeling this way toward a professor at University of Notre Dame. In the middle of my graduate studies, I learned Professor Georges Enderle, endowed chair in international business ethics at one of the top ranked U.S. business schools in terms of business ethics was familiar with China. . He often lectured in China and even had some of his books on ethics translated into Chinese. I visited him one day, and despite his high position at the university, I perceived him as a very humble leader. During the year following our first meeting, he encouraged me in numerous ways by directing me toward articles important for my own studies. Leaders like Professor Enderle model humility while holding positions of influence.

地回应他人。领袖的骄傲会让他们忽略自己的缺点，导致他们的毁灭。控制情感以及在认知上（理性上）承认自己的优势和弱点，会带来领导力的成长。

在情感上不成熟或骄傲的领袖很自然就会滥用职权。他们的根本动机都很自私。这类的领袖对权力如饥似渴，为了获得更大的影响力，利用他人满足自己的欲望。他们更注重自己的地位、控制力和成功。孔子说："攻乎异端，斯害也已。"[3]（译文：攻击那些与自己不相同的思想言论，只能带来害处。）如果你达到目标只是为了一己私利，你就在成就一条毁灭之路。假如权力被用来获得自私利益，那么你也会伤害他人。然而，假如追求权力是为了服务于一个更高的目标或满足他人的需要，就有潜力完成大善。权力本身并不错，但是加上驾驭之人品格上的弱点和不成熟就能够引起爆炸性的结果。作为领袖，你需要在一生中使用不同形式的权威，也应该清楚每种权威的利弊。

勇士骑着战马进入战场，胸前佩戴的铠甲上展现出力量、谦逊和荣誉，这就是正确驾驭权力的真实写照。勇士表现出心灵中的力量，因为他知道自己有能力控制眼前的战役。他表现出谦逊，因为他知道自己和每个人一样有着缺点和问题。他过去的成就和造诣造就了他，让他对未来拥有积极的看法，也拥有赢得胜利的才华——只要有一点点偏差都是虚伪的谦逊。这就是领袖驾驭权力的方式。

我喜欢电影《亚瑟王》（*First Knight*）中的台词，当中圭尼维娅这样说起亚瑟王："他视权力为无物。"我记得自己对圣母大学的一位教授也有过类似的感受。我在学习硕士课程的时候，乔治·安德利（George Enderle）教授让我受益匪浅。他是美国一流商业伦理系的系主任，很熟悉中国。他常常在中国演讲授课，甚至他的一些伦理方面的书籍也被翻译成中文。一天，我去拜访他，他虽然在学校里有很高的职位，我仍然把他看作是一个谦逊的领袖。我们第一次见面之后的那一年，他多方鼓励我，引导我阅读对自己的研究很重要的文章。像安德利教授这样的领袖，在自己的影响力圈子中仍然保持谦逊的心态。

A leader has the privilege of empowering other leaders. When you do this, you bestow your blessing and encouragement to step out and take risks. Many leaders have done this for me in my own life. Some of these men and women were professors, university presidents, organization leaders, businessmen, and religious leaders. As a leader we can invest in other leaders just as others have invested in us. Seldom can we repay those who have helped us, but we can continue to pass the blessing on to others.

Application

- ◆Assess your current situation and discontinue behavior that serves yourself more than the team.
- ◆Look for other team members with leadership potential and empower them with leadership opportunities.
- ◆Seek out leaders who walk in humility and learn from them.
- ◆Find at least one younger leader in whom you can invest.

Notation Area

Personal observations/Ideas for further exploration/Thoughts to remember

领袖拥有赋权给其他领袖的特权。当你这么做的时候，你就给予他人祝福，鼓励行动起来，敢于冒险。很多领袖在我的生命中这样对待过我，其中一些人是教授、大学校长、机构领袖、生意人和教会领袖。我们作为领袖，可以在他人的生命中投入，就像别人在我们的生命中投入一样。我们很难回报那些帮助过我们的人，但是我们可以常常把祝福传递给其他人。

应用

◆评估你目前的情况，看看你在何时在更多地服务于自己，而不是服务于团队，请放弃这样的行为。

◆寻找其他具备领导潜力的团队成员，栽培他们，给他们领导的机会，授权给他们。

◆找到为人谦逊的领袖，向他们学习。

◆至少找一位比自己年轻的领袖，在他身上投入时间和精力。

笔记

个人体会／要进一步探讨的想法／要铭记在心的理念

举贤用能，国泰民安。

——诸葛亮[1]

Seek the worthy and employ the talented.

——*Zhuge Liang*[1]

寻找

Seeking

第二十一天 举贤用能
——培养团队的优势

Day 21:Develop Your Team's Strengths

领袖需要常常评估团队技巧并且创造培训机会，预备团队面对未来的成长。

Leaders should regularly assess their team skills and create training that will position the team for future growth.

Seek the worthy and employ the talented.

——*Zhuge Liang* [1]

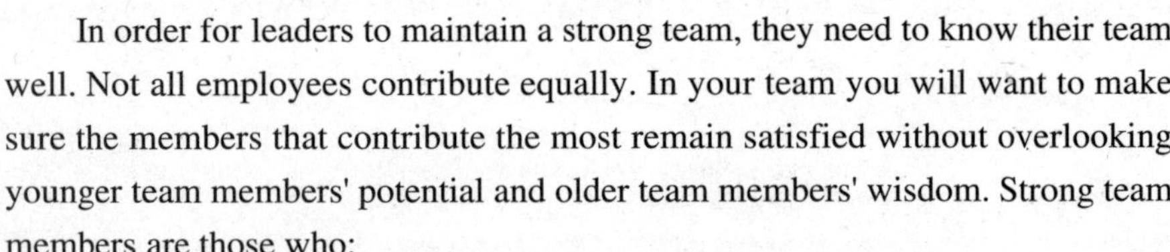

In order for leaders to maintain a strong team, they need to know their team well. Not all employees contribute equally. In your team you will want to make sure the members that contribute the most remain satisfied without overlooking younger team members' potential and older team members' wisdom. Strong team members are those who:

- Provide formal or informal leadership to others
- Consistently create excellent results
- Contribute practical and valuable new ideas
- Require little to no supervision to accomplish their tasks
- Facilitate the work of others
- Have unique knowledge or skills that would be costly and time-consuming to replace[2]

Training and career development in general are great ways to minimize turnover. The National Center on the Educational Quality of the Workforce surveyed three thousand businesses with more than twenty employees and found productivity increased 8.6 percent for businesses with training programs to increase employees' reading and math comprehension by one grade level.

Motorola is known for providing extensive corporate training. However, their managers discovered that return on educational investment depended on the management's encouragement of its implementation. When managers failed to reinforce training, the company didn't profit from the educational opportunities. When management embraced and reinforced training, some plants saw a $33 re-

举贤用能，国泰民安。

——诸葛亮[1]

领袖假如想保持团队的稳定性，就需要深入了解团队。并非所有团队成员的贡献都一样。在你的团队中，你一方面需要保证贡献最多的团队成员能够感到满足，另一方面又不能忽略年轻成员的潜力和年老成员的智慧。稳定的团队成员具备以下特点：

- 在正式或非正式情况下带领他人；
- 持续创造佳绩；
- 提供实际有效的新想法；
- 完成任务时很少需要甚至不需要任何监督；
- 推动他人的工作；
- 拥有独特的技巧和知识，很难有人代替；假如代替的话，代价昂贵而且费时费力。[2]

培训和职业发展一般说来可以把流动率减少到最小，这都是最好的方法。国家劳动力教育质量中心对三千多家企业的二丨多位员工进行调查，发现在那些具备培训项目的企业中，员工的阅读和数学理解每增加一个等级，生产力就增加8.6%。

摩托罗拉因为在企业中提供大量培训而著称。然而，他们的经理们发现一点，培训投资的回报根据管理层对推行培训的鼓励程度而定。当经理们没

turn on every dollar spent. However, the financial benefit of training may not always be measurable.

Training is also a great way to develop employees for more challenging jobs within an organization. Organizations with a reputation for training and good career development can attract a great deal of talented people. You want your people to always feel challenged with new responsibilities within their reach. Leaders should regularly assess their team skills and create training that will position the team for future growth. Leaders should remember these three points when designing career development for their team:

- Develop a career ladder for each team member.
- Identify team members with the greatest potential and assess where they are weak or inexperienced. Assign them tasks and projects that will strengthen their weak areas.
- Involve your whole team in mentoring.[3]

Arranging mentoring within your team is one way to build relationships. Relationships remain the greatest key to attracting and retaining strong team members. History is full of sacrifices made for friendships. Soldiers jump on grenades to save comrades. People dart into flaming buildings to rescue those trapped inside. Wounded soldiers crawl back to the front lines to support friends. What are the motivations for such heroic acts? It's not rewards, for few are given. It is seldom the love for the army or even the cause. Most often, sacrifice springs from the bonds of friendship and love. This type of relationship often develops within a team that shares common experiences. The military calls it "small group cohesion." Loyalty to companies has all but disappeared these days, but loyalty to colleagues is stronger than ever. Team leaders can significantly reduce turnover by encouraging small group cohesion. This can be done through the creation of things such as golf leagues, organizational sports teams, and group activities that involve the whole family.

强调培训的时候，公司并没有因为那些教育机会而受益。当管理层坚信并且强调培训的时候，有的工厂在培训上每投资1美元，能够看到33美元的回报。然而，培训的经济利益有的时候是无法衡量的。

培训也是在机构中栽培员工的绝佳方式，帮助他们面对更富于挑战的工作。拥有培训和良好职业发展声誉的机构能够吸引很多有才华的人。你希望自己的员工在力所能及的事情上常常受到挑战，勇于承担责任。领袖需要常常评估团队技巧并且创造培训机会，预备团队面对未来的成长。领袖在为团队设计发展规划时，应该记住这三点：

- 为每个团队成员创造被提拔的机会；
- 发现有巨大潜力的团队成员，评估他们的弱点和经验不足的地方。给他们分配一些任务和计划，强化他们的弱项；
- 让团队所有成员都成为他人的导师。[3]

在团队中安排导师是建立关系的一种方式。关系仍然是吸引并且留住好员工的最关键的方法。历史上有很多为友谊而牺牲的例子：士兵们为了营救自己的伙伴扑向手榴弹；人们冲进着火的房子，为了援救里面被围困的人；为支持自己的朋友，受伤的士兵爬回前线。这些英雄行为的动机是什么？并不是为了酬劳，因为很少有报酬。也不是因为对部队的爱甚至是理想。这样的关系常常出现在经历相似的团队中。在军事中，把它称作“小组凝聚力”。对公司的忠诚现在已经消失殆尽了，但是对同事的忠诚却比过去有过之而无不及。团队领袖可以鼓励小组凝聚力，从而大大地减少流动率。可以通过一些团队活动来做到这一点，高尔夫社团、机构运动队和让全家都参与的小组活动都是好方法。

Application

- ◆ Ask team members what they feel their strengths and career interests are.
- ◆ Assess how well you are applying the above three points.
- ◆ Assess the small group cohesion level of your team.
- ◆ Implement at least one new activity or event to help your team bond during the normal workday. New activities outside of work should be paid for and exciting.

Notation Area

Personal observations/Ideas for further exploration/Thoughts to remember

应用

◆ 询问团队成员，他们认为自己的优势和职业兴趣是什么。

◆ 评估你在应用以上三点时情况如何。

◆ 评估你们团队的小组凝聚力。

◆ 在正常的工作日中至少推动一项新活动或新事件，帮助团队建立凝聚力。如果新活动在工作时间进行，薪水应当照领。

笔记

个人体会／要进一步探讨的想法／要铭记在心的理念

卒未亲附而罚之，则不服，不服则难用也。卒已亲附而罚不行，则不可用也。故令之以文，齐之以武，是谓必取。

——孙子[1]

If troops are punished before the leader secures their loyalty, they will be disobedient. If not obedient, it is difficult to employ them. If troops have become attached to you but discipline cannot be enforced, you cannot employ them. Thus, command them with civility but keep them under control by iron discipline, and it may be said that victory is certain.

——Sun Tzu[1]

举案齐眉

Mutual Respect

第二十二天 举案齐眉
——心怀善念带领

Day 22: Lead Them with Kindness

我们不应该让自己的恐惧和事务阻止我们给他人带来小小的善举。

We should never let our fear or business stop us from doing a kind deed to another human being.

If troops are punished before the leader secures their loyalty, they will be disobedient. If not obedient, it is difficult to employ them. If troops have become attached to you but discipline cannot be enforced, you cannot employ them. Thus, command them with civility but keep them under control by iron discipline, and it may be said that victory is certain.

——*Sun Tzu* [1]

Treat others the way you want them to treat you.

——*Jesus Christ*

A leader needs to walk a narrow line between taking care of the needs of the team and accomplishing team goals. Focus only on the needs of individuals and your team can turn inward. Focus only on the goal and ignore the needs of team members and you risk causing the team to become dysfunctional. A balance between kindness and productivity should be reached. In terms of time, small acts of kindness usually take very little time or effort. They can occur in the midst of a very productive day. If we look, we can find many opportunities to touch others' lives with kindness.

In my early twenties, I worked with children in the poorest neighborhoods of Flint, Michigan and lived on the second floor of a men's homeless shelter. In those days I focused on trying to make a difference in the many broken lives I saw every week. As part of my job I gave food and clothing to poor families and organized special activities for their children. My bank account didn't benefit much from this job, but my heart grew as I served the poor.

When I received my modest paycheck every other week, I walked down the street to a walk-up bank window where I cashed my check. Because the bank was located in a rough neighborhood, three employees sat safely locked behind a thick metal door and bulletproof glass. The same people worked in the bank each week,

卒未亲附而罚之，则不服，不服则难用也。卒已亲附而罚不行，则不可用也。故令之以文，齐之以武，是谓必取。

——孙子[1]

译文：士卒还没有亲附就执行惩罚，他们就不服，这样就很难使用。士卒已经亲附，如果纪律仍不执行，也不能用来作战。所以要用怀柔的手段去管束他们，这样就必定能取胜。

你希望别人怎样对待你，也要怎样对待别人。

——耶稣

领袖需要把握好尺度，既照顾团队的需求，同时又成就团队的目标。只注重团队中个体的需要，你的团队只会向内发展。只注重目标，忽略团队成员的需要，你就是在冒险，团队可能会变得紊乱。应该努力维持好仁爱和效率之间的平衡。讲到时间方面，实际上小小的善行所需要的时间和精力都不算很多，可以穿插在高效率的日程安排之中。假如我们留意的话，可以找到很多机会，用关爱之心触及他人的生命。

我二十几岁的时候，在密歇根州弗林特（Flint,Michigan）最贫穷的社区中服务儿童。我当时住在一个人开办的收容所二楼的宿舍。那时候，我决心要在每周所见的破碎的生命中带来改变。我工作的一部分职责就是给贫穷的家庭送去食物和衣物，也为他们的孩子们组织特别的活动。我的银行账户并没有因为这份工作而受益，但是当我服务贫穷人士时，我的心胸变得更宽阔了。

我每隔一周拿到自己微薄的薪水，每次都会步行去沿街的一个银行窗口兑换支票。银行坐落在一个不太安全的社区中，三个工作人员都安全地坐在

and during the course of the year I learned a little about them through short conversations. At one point the mother of one of the women became sick, and I offered to pray for her. Her mother recovered, which did much to increase my credibility and build relationship. I continued to show concern for any topic they felt free to share with me.

One Friday I walked up to cash my check as usual, and they asked me to go to the side door. I thought their request strange, but I experienced even more shock when they buzzed the door to release the locks and ushered me into their tightly fortified cubical. After the door closed behind me, I noticed a homemade birthday cake lit with candles in my honor. They had discovered my birthday from my driver's license. Obviously my small acts of kindness blessed them, and I know I will never forget their act of kindness toward me.

We should never let our fear or business stop us from doing a kind deed to another human being. Nelson Mandela, the great African leader, is a world example of standing up for what is right. He once said, "Our deepest fear is not that we are inadequate. Our deepest fear is that we are powerful beyond measure. It is our light, not our darkness, that frightens us most. We ask ourselves, 'Who am I to be brilliant, gorgeous, talented, and famous?' Actually, who are you not to be? You are a child of God. Your playing small does not serve the world. There is nothing enlightened about shrinking so that people won't feel insecure around you. We are born to make manifest the glory of God that is within us. It's not just in some of us; it's in all of us. And when we let our own light shine, we unconsciously give other people permission to do the same. As we are liberated from our own fear, our presence automatically liberates others."

厚厚的铁门后面，面前还装着防弹玻璃。每周都是那几个人在那里工作，所以在那一年中我和他们进行过一些短短的交流，对他们有了一些了解。后来，其中一位女士的母亲得病，我提出为她祷告。她的母亲后来康复了，这就大大增加了我的可信度，加深了我们彼此之间的关系。他们只要愿意和我分享任何事情，我都会不断向他们表示我对他们的关心。

一个星期五，和往常一样，我去银行兑换支票。他们邀请我走到侧门那里，我觉得这个要求很奇怪。他们“嗡”的一声打开了安全门，把我引入了严密封锁的小屋。我这时甚至都感到震惊了。门在我身后关闭后，我注意到一个自制的蛋糕，上面插着蜡烛，是给我的。他们从驾驶执照上发现了我的生日。很明显，我小小的善举祝福了他们，我也知道自己永远也不会忘记他们对待我的善行。

我们不应该让自己的恐惧和事务阻止我们给他人带来小小的善举。纳尔逊·曼德拉（Nelson Mandela）这位伟大的非洲领袖因为坚持正义而举世闻名。他曾说：“我们最大的恐惧不是自己无能为力，而是我们的能力大到无法估量。最让我们感到惧怕的是我们的光明面，而不是黑暗面。我们问自己：‘我到底是谁，怎么可能才华横溢、耀眼夺目、成为名人？’实际上，你到底是谁？你是上帝的孩子。作为小人物，你并不能更好地服务于世界。你为了不让周围的人感到没有安全感，让自己变得渺小，这实际上并没有什么好处。我们生下来就是为了彰显我们里面上帝的荣耀。这一切并不仅仅存在于少数人心中，而是在我们所有人的心中。当我们让心中光芒照亮出来，我们在不自觉之中帮助了别人，让他们也能够和我们一样。当我们获得自由，脱离了自己的恐惧时，我们的存在也会自然产生动力，让他人获得自由。”

Application

◆ In the midst of your busy day, pass on at least one kind word or deed. It will only take a few minutes but will likely make someone else's day.

◆ Assess how well you are balancing kindness and producing product.

Notation Area

Personal observations/Ideas for further exploration/Thoughts to remember

应用

◆在你繁忙的日程中，至少传递一句善言或做一件善行。可能只花你几分钟的时间，却能够点亮他人的一天。

◆评估你怎样平衡仁爱和生产力。

笔记

个人体会／要进一步探讨的想法／要铭记在心的理念

道之以政，齐之以刑，民免而无耻；道之以德，齐之以礼，有耻且格。

——孔子[1]

Guide them by edicts, keep them in line with punishment, and the common people will stay out of trouble but will have no sense of shame. Guide them by virtue, keep them in line with the rite, and they will, besides having a sense of shame, reform themselves.

——*Confucius*[1]

绝对服从

Shameless Obedience

第二十三天 道之以德，齐之以礼——领袖的行为

Day 23:Leaders' Behavior

为了获得一生的成功，你需要强化领导力才华，永远都不能停止学习。

In order to be successful for a lifetime, you should never stop learning and enhancing your leadership ability.

Guide them by edicts, keep them in line with punishment, and the common people will stay out of trouble but will have no sense of shame. Guide them by virtue, keep them in line with the rite, and they will, besides having a sense of shame, reform themselves.

——*Confucius* [1]

Effective leaders guide their teams with both skill and positive behavior. Behavioral theories seek to identify characteristics that differentiate effective from ineffective leadership. Researchers have identified a number of behavior patterns, but have not been able to prove that one leadership style is consistently better than another. Leadership researchers Robert Tannenbaum and Warren H. Schmidt propose that leaders should look at three primary variables:

- Personal comfort level as it relates to different leadership behaviors
- Knowledge of their own leadership style
- Team makeup in relationship to tasks to be completed

Comfort level can be improved by (1) studying leadership, (2) watching other leaders with diverse but effective styles, and (3) via personal experience. Discovering and developing your personal leadership style becomes easier with increased leadership experience. Leaders need to assess their team's willingness to assume responsibility. It stands to reason that even effective leaders can do very little if their team is not willing to take on responsibility.

Some have suggested that subordinate-centered styles of leading produce more long-term positive influence on motivation, decision quality, teamwork, morale, and individual development. However, this style of leadership takes a great deal of time and a relatively mature group of followers. Applying this style of leadership may or may not be possible as a result of followers' maturity level and time pressures. Successful leaders adjust their personal leadership behavior to facilitate

道之以政，齐之以刑，民免而无耻；道之以德，齐之以礼，有耻且格。

——孔子[1]

译文：用法制禁令去引导百姓，使用刑法来约束他们，老百姓只是求得免于犯罪受惩罚，却失去了廉耻之心；用道德教化引导百姓，使用礼制去统一百姓的言行，百姓不仅会有羞耻之心，而且也就守规矩了。

卓越的领袖凭着技巧和积极的行为带领团队。行为理论一直致力于分辨有效领导力和无效领导力的特点。研究者们已经辨别出很多不同的习惯行为模式，但是还未能证实是否某种领袖模式优越于另外一种领袖模式。领导力研究者罗伯特·坦南鲍姆和沃伦·H·史密特（Robert Tannenbaum and Warren H. Schmidt）认为领袖应该着眼于三个基本变量：

- 对不同领导力行为感受到的个人放松程度；
- 对自己的领导力风格的了解；
- 要完成任务时的团队组成情况。

可以通过以下方面改善个人放松程度：(1)研究领导力；(2)观察其他领袖的带领（他们虽然风格各异，但是给人留下深刻印象）；(3)通过个人经历。随着领导力经历的增加，发掘并且培育自己的个人领导力风格就变得越来越容易。领袖需要评估团队承担责任的踊跃程度。显而易见，即使领袖再卓尔不群，假如团队不愿意承担责任，他也会一事无成。

有的人认为，以员工为中心的领导风格能够在动力、高质量的决定、团队协作、士气和个人发展上产生长期积极效果。然而，这样的领袖风格需要花费很多时间，而且团队需要相对比较成熟。由于团队成员的成熟程度和时

the team and meet the needs of the task to be accomplished. Leadership behavior has a direct impact on one's success. Figure 23.1 shows the spectrum of behaviors a leader may use.

Figure 23.1 [2]

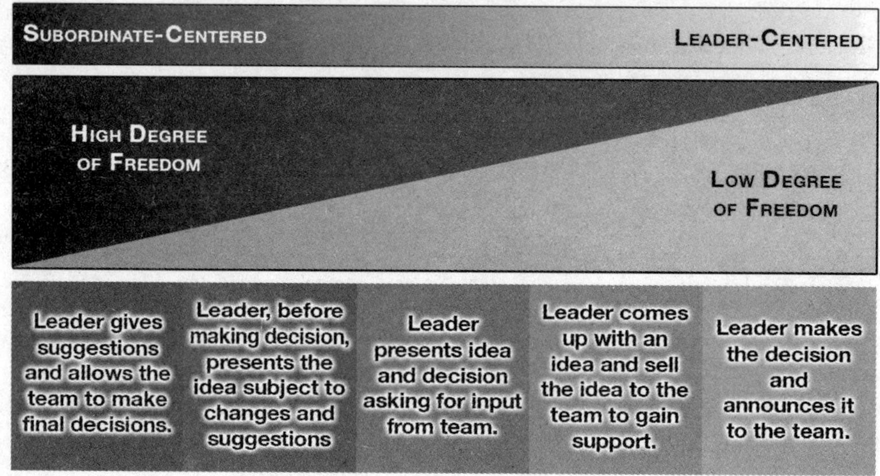

Leaders can adapt different behaviors depending on personal talents, experience, and style. Behavioral theories associated with leadership have helped in dispelling the myth that only few charismatic personality types can lead. By studying your own personal gifts, you can adopt behaviors that will help you be an effective leader. You may naturally be a strong visionary leader if you are most comfortable casting vision and leading the charge to accomplish new challenges. If this is the case, you may benefit from spending time with more subordinate-centered leaders. In order to be successful for a lifetime, you should never stop learning and enhancing your leadership ability. The world needs leaders who are as unerring as the North Star, who will serve before being served, and who want to see those they lead become greater than themselves.

间压力等因素的影响，应用这样的领导力风格可能成功，也可能不成功。成功的领袖调整自己的行为来推动团队，满足完成任务所需要的一切。领导力行为对于一个人的成败有着直接的影响。图表23.1说明了一个领导力行为的范畴。

图表23.1[2]

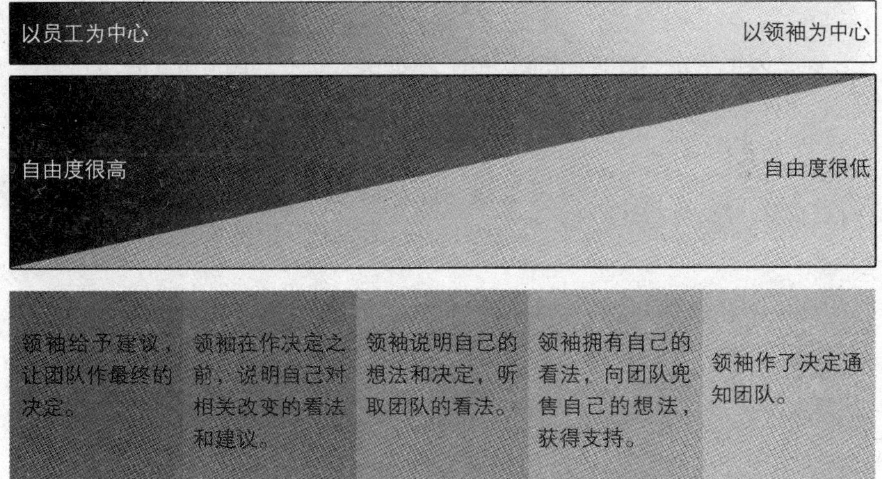

领袖可以根据个人的才华、经历和风格，采取不同的领导力行为。和领导力相关的行为理论破灭了只有具备领袖魅力的人才能带领的神话。了解了自己的个人恩赐之后，你可以采用适合你、可以帮助你成为卓越领袖的领导力行为。假如你能够熟练地传递愿景，鼓励和带领大家，成就新的挑战，你就能够自然而然地成为一个梦想家领袖。真是这样的话，如果你能向一些以员工为中心的领袖多学习，就能够获益匪浅。为了获得一生的成功，你需要强化自己的领导力才华，永远都不能停止学习。世界需要像北极星一样准确的领袖：他们不是要受人服侍，而是要服侍他人；他们想要看到自己所带领的人变得比自己更伟大。

Application

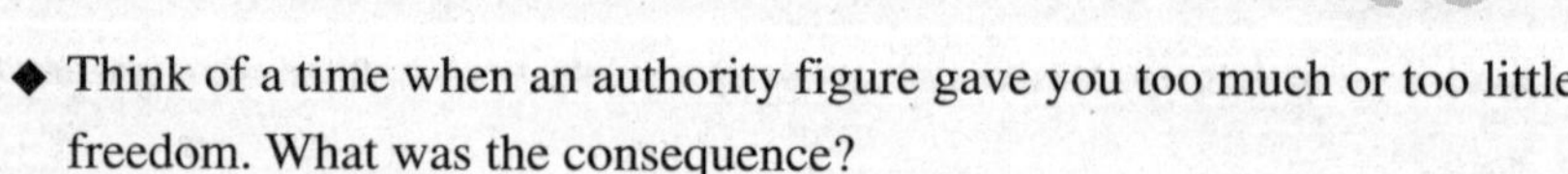

- ◆ Think of a time when an authority figure gave you too much or too little freedom. What was the consequence?

- ◆ What behavior style do you find most natural?

- ◆ Decide which leadership style best fits your current leadership situations.

- ◆ Based on the skills and maturity level of your team, do you need to give more or less freedom?

Notation Area

Personal observations/Ideas for further exploration/Thoughts to remember

....

....

....

....

应用

- 回想某一个时刻，想想是否某个领袖人物曾经给过你太多或太少的自由，后果是什么？

- 你发现自己可以熟练驾驭哪种行为风格？

- 请确定你目前的带领环境适合怎样的领导风格。

- 了解团队的技巧水平和成熟度，看看你需要给予团队更多自由还是更少的自由？

笔记

个人体会／要进一步探讨的想法／要铭记在心的理念

因形而错胜于众，众不能知。

——孙子[1]

In accordance with the situation, plans are laid for victory, but the multitude does not comprehend this.

——*Sun Tzu*[1]

兵形象水

Flowing Water

第二十四天 因敌变化而取胜
——领袖对环境的洞察力

Day 24:Situation-Sensitive Leading Is Strong Leadership

成功的带领需要花时间了解跟随者的成熟度。

Successful leading requires taking the time to understand your followers' maturity level.

In accordance with the situation, plans are laid for victory, but the multitude does not comprehend this.

—— *Sun Tzu* [1]

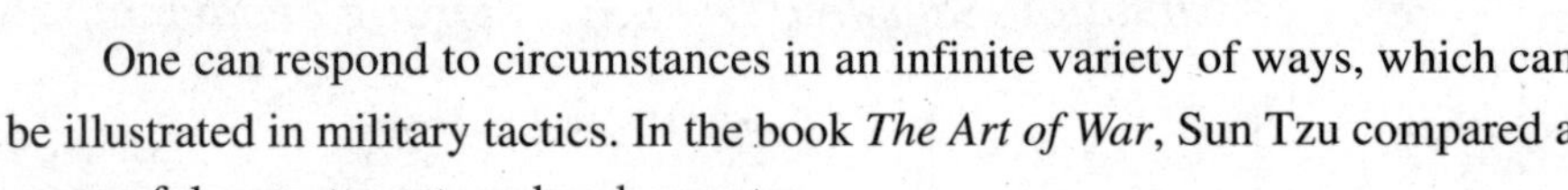

One can respond to circumstances in an infinite variety of ways, which can be illustrated in military tactics. In the book *The Art of War*, Sun Tzu compared a successful army to water when he wrote:

An army may use water as an analogy, for just as flowing water avoids the heights and hastens to the lowlands, so an army should avoid the enemy's strength and strike its weakness. As water shapes its flow in accordance with the ground, so an army manages its victory in accordance with the situation of the enemy. And as water has no constant form, warfare elicits no constant conditions. Thus, one who is able to win the victory by modifying his tactics in accordance with the enemy situation may be said to be divine.[2]

The theory of situational leadership was developed by Paul Hersy and Kenneth Blanchard. They focused on selecting the right leadership style based on the level of the followers' maturity. Multinational companies such as BankAmerica, IBM, Mobil Oil, and Xerox have implemented this theory. The ability of situational leadership theories to transcend political and cultural contexts increases its value for international companies. It emphasizes gauging leadership effectiveness based on the needs and response of the followers because, ultimately, the followers are the ones who accept or reject the leader. Regardless of the actions of the leader, effectiveness depends on the actions of followers. According to Hersy and Blanchard, situational leadership theory divides leadership styles into four categories. Each category is then described as high or low. For example, high task leaders focus primarily on the work to be accomplished. High relationship leaders focus a great deal of attention on relationally connecting with team members. The

因形而错胜于众，众不能知。

——孙子[1]

译文：把根据敌情的变化而取得的胜利摆在众人面前，众人还是看不出其中的奥妙。

一个人对环境的应对方式多种多样，我们可以用军事战略来举例说明。孙子在《孙子兵法》中，把成功的军队比作水，他这样写道：

“夫兵形象水，水之形避高而趋下，兵之形避实而击虚，水因地而制流，兵因敌而制胜。故兵无常势，水无常形，能因敌变化而取胜者，谓之神。”[2]（译文：用兵的规律好像水的流动，水的流动避开高处流向低处；作战的规律要避开敌人雄厚的实力，而攻击其弱点。水因地势的高低而制约流向，作战则根据敌人的变化而夺取胜利。战争没有固定的态势，水流没有不变的形态。能根据敌情的变化而取得胜利的，就叫做用兵如神。）

保罗·赫塞（Paul Hersy）和肯尼思·布兰查德（Kenneth Blanchard）提出了情景领导模式理论。根据跟随者的成熟度，让他们选择正确的领导力风格。美国银行、IBM、美孚石油和施乐复印机等跨国公司推行了该理论。情景领导力理论具备超越政治和文化背景的能力，因此就增加了它对跨国大公司的魅力。它强调根据跟随者的需要和回应，评估领导力的有效程度，因为，跟随者是最终接受或拒绝领袖的人。不论领袖的行为如何，有效程度要根据跟随者的行为而定。赫塞和布兰查德的情景领导力理论把领导力风格分成四类，每种类型都有高低之分。例如，高任务领袖主要注重完成任务。高关系领袖注重建立与团队成员的交往联络。四种类型包括：

- 告诉型（高任务／低关系）：领袖确定角色，告诉人们做什么、怎么

four categories encompass:

- Telling (high task/low relationship): the leader defines roles and tells people what, how, when, and where to do various tasks.
- Selling (high task/high relationship): the leader provides both directive behavior and supportive behavior.
- Participating (low task/high relationship): the leader and follower share in decision making; the main role of the leader is facilitating and communicating.
- Delegating (low task/low relationship): the leader provides little direction or support.

Let's assume you, as the team leader, were just told you have half the scheduled time to finish the project your team is working on. The final product must be sent from China to London by Saturday evening. Today is Wednesday, so you only have four days to finish what would normally be finished after eight full working days. Using the above four different approaches of telling, selling, participating, and delegating to communicate the emergency may sound something like this:

1. Telling: "Everyone listen up. We need to mail this shipment out by Saturday, and you all will have to work double shifts to get it done."
2. Selling: "I have just been informed that this project needs to be in London by Saturday night. I know this seems impossible, but I need everyone who can to work double shifts. I will be working double shifts the next four days myself. I apologize for the inconvenience, but this has to happen."
3. Participating: "I have just been informed that this project needs to be in London by Saturday. I need everyone's help in figuring out how we are going to accomplish this. We will have a meeting of the whole team in one hour. Come with the best solutions you can provide."
4. Delegating: " I have just been informed that this project needs to be in London by Saturday night. You all know what part of this project you are responsible for. I put Eddy in charge of getting everyone's work in the mail. Get it done."

The effectiveness and appropriateness of the above styles depend greatly on your team's maturity and skill level. The final component in Hersy and Blanchard's theory includes defining four stages of your team's readiness, as shown in Figure 24.1. This figure integrates the various components into a situational leadership model.

做、何时做和何地做。

- 兜售型（高任务／高关系）：领袖提供指导性行为和支持型行为。
- 参与型（低任务／高关系）：领袖和跟随者共同作决定；领袖的主要角色是推动和沟通。
- 委任型（低任务／低关系）：领袖提供的方向感或支持很少。

我们来作一个假设：你作为团队领袖刚刚得知，你们完成手头任务的时间比预期时间少了一半儿。最后的成品必须在星期六晚上从中国送到伦敦。今天是星期三，所以你只有四天完成一般情况下八个工作日的工作量。我们看看如何使用以上四个不同的方法（告诉型、兜售型、参与性和委任型）来沟通以下此类紧急情况：

1.告诉型："大家都听好了。我们要在星期六把这批货运出去，大家都需要两班倒把活儿干完了。"
2.兜售型："我刚刚得到通知，这批货需要在星期六晚上到达伦敦。我知道这听起来好像不太可能，但是我希望每个人都能够两班倒。我自己在以后的四天中会两班倒工作。很抱歉给大家带来不方便，但是只能如此了。"
3.参与型："我刚刚得到通知，这批货需要在周六之前送到伦敦。我希望大家都参与，看看我们该怎么完成这项任务。我们整个团队要开一个小时的会，请大家提出自己的最佳解决方案。"
4.委任型："我刚刚得到通知，这批货需要在周六晚上送到伦敦。你们都知道自己所负的责任是什么部分。我让埃迪发邮件通知大家每个人的工作任务，争取把它完成。"

以上风格的有效和恰当程度主要根据你们团队的成熟度和技巧水平而定。保罗·赫塞和肯尼思·布兰查德理论的最后组成部分如图表24.1所示，其中包括评价团队预备程度的四个阶段。这个图表综合了构成情景领导模式理论的多种因素。

Figure 24.1 [3]

Hersy and Blanchard's Situational Leadership Model

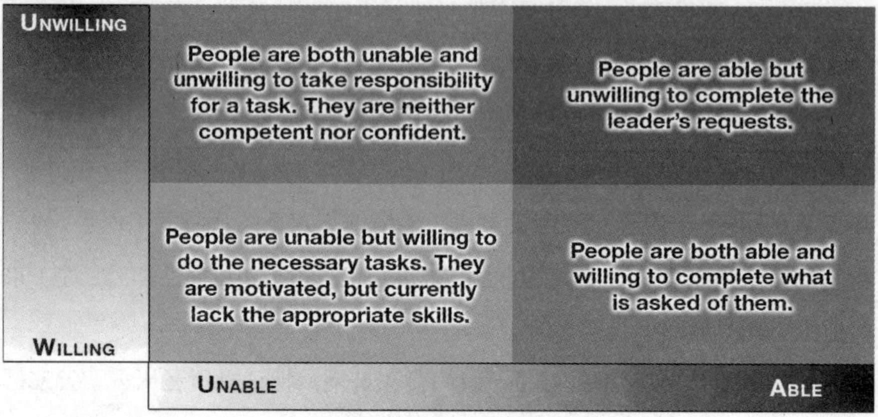

Successful leading requires taking the time to understand your followers' maturity level. Maturity relates to experience, training, ability, interpersonal skills, and emotional stability. In an ideal situation, the team is constantly maturing. Whenever possible, tasks should be assigned that stretch and test their abilities. You want to stretch your team without breaking them. While studying for my doctorate, I had a professor who said his goal was to push us to reach our full potential or, as he put it, "push you to the edge of a cliff-not so far that you fall off, but far enough to scare you to death and challenge you to grow." We seldom enjoyed the stress his classes produced, but we grew and benefited from being challenged. We also were motivated because we knew he believed in our ability to succeed.

In every team, relationship is highly important. This is true even for a highly mature team. The effective leader accepts the dual task of getting the job done while also helping team members grow. Too much emphasis on growth can create a risk level that could be negative for the organization. Leaders need to keep the organization's vision and goals in mind when delegating tasks. If an assignment is critical to the organization's success, a leader should minimize the risks by placing the best people on it. Such assignments may not challenge them, but are crucial to the success of the overall team. Less critical assignments are ideal for challenging team members to develop and strengthen abilities.

图表 24.1[3]

赫塞和布兰查德环境领导力模式

	没能力	有能力
不情愿	人们没有能力也不情愿承担责任。他们即无法胜任也没有信心。	人们有能力，但是不情愿去完成领袖的要求。
情愿	人们没有相应的能力，但是愿意完成相应的责任。他们有动力，但是目前缺少恰当的技巧。	人们既具备能力，也愿意完成领袖对自己的要求。

成功的领袖需要花时间了解跟随者的成熟度。成熟关乎一个人的经历、培训、才干、人际技巧和情感的稳定性。在理想的环境中，团队的成熟度保持稳定的水平。在必要的情况下，应该把责任分配给团队中每一个成员，测试并且发挥他们的能力。你需要既能够提高团队的能力，又松弛有度，不至于让他们垮掉。在我读博士学位的时候，一位教授说他的目标是推动我们，让我们能够发挥所有的潜能。用他的话来说就是："把你们推到悬崖边上——既不会太远，让你们掉下去，但是又足够让你们感到害怕，甚至快要吓死了。这样的挑战可以让你们成长。"我们并不太喜欢他的课带来的压力，但是我们成长了，也因为接受挑战而受益匪浅。我们也受到激励，因为我们知道，他相信我们有成功的能力。

在每个团队中，关系都高度重要。即使在成熟度很高的团队中，情况也一样。卓越的领袖面对双重任务：一方面要完成任务，另一方面要帮助团队成员成长。过分强调成长会冒一定的风险，可能会给机构带来消极后果。在分配任务的时候，你应该把机构的愿景和目标谨记在心。假如某项任务对机构的成败至关重要，领袖应该尽量减少风险程度，委任最恰当的人才。这样的任务可能给他们带来的挑战并不大，但是对整个团队的成功却无可替代。不那么重要的任务对于需要挑战的团队成员很理想，可以帮助他们培养和加强能力。

Application

- Are the members of your team challenged or bored with the difficulty level of their daily tasks? Don't just assume you know. Ask them.

- Attempt to increase the responsibility of every member of your team.

- Stay relationally connected, and encourage even those who fail. Let them know you believe in their ability as you lead them to the edge of the cliff.

Notation Area

Personal observations/Ideas for further exploration/Thoughts to remember

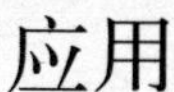

应用

◆日常工作的难易程度让团队成员感到厌倦还是受到挑战？不要以为自己知道答案，询问一下他们。

◆尽力增加团队中每个成员的责任。

◆和大家保持关系，甚至要鼓励那些失败的人。当你带领他们走在最前沿的时候，让他们知道你信任他们的能力。

笔记

个人体会／要进一步探讨的想法／要铭记在心的理念

友者也，友其德也。

——孟子

Friendship with a man is friendship with his character.

——*Mencius*

管鲍之交

Friendship of Guang and Baoshu

第二十五天 管鲍之交
——赞美团队，共奔卓越

Day 25:Praising Your Team to Greatness

团队成员的态度和你帮助他们成功和成熟的能力有直接联系。

The attitude of your team members will be directly related to your ability to help them succeed and mature.

Friendship with a man is friendship with his character.

——Mencius

Guan Zhong and Baoshu Ya lived during the Spring and Autumn Period (770-477 BC). They grew up together in the state of Qi as close friends, always looking out for each other. As young men they engaged in trade, and from time to time Guan Zhong would take more than his share of the profits. Baoshu Ya didn't mind because he knew Guan Zhong's family was poor and needed the help. Guan Zhong also sought official positions in government, but failed time and time again. Baoshu Ya attributed each failed attempt to bad luck and always thought the best of his friend.

Years later they both secured positions in government. Baoshu Ya served Prince Xiaobo and Guan Zhong served Prince Jiu. As fate would have it, the princes fought each other for the Qi throne. Prince Xiaobo defeated his brother and secured the throne for himself, which meant success for Baoshu Ya. Prince Jiu, however, was slain and Guan Zhong was imprisoned. Baoshu Ya's loyalty and belief in his friend's ability caused him to risk his own position by recommending Guan Zhong to be appointed as an official. He told the king that with Guan Zhong's advice the kingdom would soon surpass the other kingdoms in the land. The king listened to his advice and appointed Guan Zhong to a position higher than that of Baoshu Ya. With Guang Zhong as prime minister, the state of Qi became the strongest and most prosperous kingdom.[1]

When speaking of his friend, Guan Zhong often commented that his mother gave him life, but it was his friend Baoshu Ya that truly knew him. The phrase "like the friendship of Guan and Bao" has come to stand for a deep friendship.[2] Baoshu Ya served as a powerful example of what can happen when you believe

友者也，友其德也。

——孟子

译文：交朋友，是因为他的品德而去结交他，不能有任何倚仗的因素。

管仲和鲍叔牙生活在春秋时期（公元前770－公元前477年）。他们是亲密的朋友，一起在齐国长大，一直彼此照顾。他们年轻的时候一起经商，管仲从利润中所拿的份额总比他应得的多。鲍叔牙并不介意，因为他知道管仲的家境贫穷，需要资助。管仲想要谋个一官半职，却屡试屡败。鲍叔牙把失败都归咎于时运不好，总是从最好的方面去看自己的朋友。

多年后，他们都开始辅佐自己的主公。鲍叔牙辅佐公子小白，管仲辅佐公子纠。后来命运使然，王子们为了争夺齐国的王位彼此不和。公子小白打败了公子纠，夺得了王位，这也就意味着鲍叔牙成功了。于是公子纠被杀头，管仲被囚禁。鲍叔牙对朋友很忠诚，而且坚信朋友的能力，他冒着自己失去职位的危险，大力推荐管仲。他告诉齐王，有了管仲的辅佐，齐国能够很快超越其他王国，成为霸主。齐王听取了他的建议，对管仲委以重任，比鲍叔牙的职位还高。管仲成了齐相，齐国成为各诸侯国的霸主。[1]

当管仲谈到自己朋友的时候，总是交口赞誉。他说是父母给了自己生命，但是朋友鲍叔牙却是自己真正的知音。“管鲍之交”这个词用来形容深厚的友谊。[2] 鲍叔牙就是一个很好的榜样，从他身上我们可以看出，当我们相信他人的能力时，最后能够成就什么。

团队成员的态度和你帮助他们成功和成熟的能力有直接联系。道格拉斯·麦格雷戈（Douglas McGregor）根据马斯洛的需要层次图，提供了两种方式来

the best about someone else.

The attitude of your team members will be directly related to your ability to help them succeed and mature. Douglas McGregor, working from Maslow's hierarchy of need, offered two ways to view people. He has labeled these two distinct views Theory X and Theory Y. Theory X assumes people are primarily motivated by lower level, basic needs. Therefore, someone who holds a Theory X view of people assumes they lack ambition, are passive, and prefer to be led. They also assume people dislike responsibility, are self-interested, and seek to avoid work. Leaders that view team members as Xs assume they are not motivated, and therefore devote energy to rewarding, punishing, and overseeing behavior.

In contrast, if a leader views his team as Ys, he assumes they are motivated by higher-order needs in Maslow's system. The team is viewed as ambitious, seeking greater responsibility, and being active. They also desire self-direction and can be counted on to perform their jobs. A Y leader believes people should be trusted and involved in decision making, so they seek to establish an atmosphere of trust and supportiveness. Figure 25.1 contrasts the assumptions defined by Theory X and Theory Y:

Figure 25.1 [3]

Team Dynamics

Theory X assumes employees are:	Theory Y assumes employees are:
Passive	Active
Lacking ambition	Ambitious
Averse to responsibility	Desirous of responsibility
Willing to be led	Interested in self-control
Self-interested	Supportive of the organization
Averse to work	Willing to work

No one would likely argue that all people in their team fall exclusively under the stereotype of Theory X or Y. The implication of either theory will vary from time to time based on the situation and job to be performed. The important thing is that the leader understands his or her assumptions of the team's makeup will affect the team's overall results and satisfaction. Effective leaders choose the appropriate theory, or combination thereof, to suit the situation.

看待人。他把这两种截然不同的看法称作X理论和Y理论。X理论假设人的主要动力是较低层次的需要，也就是基本需要。因此，持X理论的人认为人本身缺少雄心、被动，而且愿意被带领。他们认为人不喜欢责任，只关心自己的利益，想逃避工作。领袖如果把团队成员看作是X型，实际上认为他们没有动力，因此把自己的精力花在奖励、惩罚和监督团队的行为上。

对比说来，假如领袖把自己的团队看作是Y型，他就会认为他们的动力是马斯洛体系中更高层次的需求。团队成员被当作雄心勃勃的人，他们会寻求更大的责任，积极进取。他们渴望寻求自己的人生方向，在完成任务时值得信赖。一个持有Y理论的领袖认为应该信任他人，让他们参与作决定的过程，所以要建立信任和支持的氛围。图表25.1对X理论和Y理论进行了对比。

图表25.1[3]

团队动力

X理论假定员工：	Y理论假定员工：
消极	积极
厌恶责任	渴望获得责任
愿意被带领	自律能力很强
只对自己的利益感兴趣	支持机构工作
厌恶工作	愿意工作

没有人能够说自己团队的所有人完全处于X理论或Y理论中。根据环境和执行职责的不同，任何一种理论都会不时产生相应的变化。重点在于领袖理解自己观念的重要性，他或她对团队成员的假设会影响整个团队的效率和满意度。卓越的领袖选择恰当的理论，或结合不同理论，适应环境的发展。

1995年，我负责帮助一群美国大学生，让他们在中国度过一个学期。这些学生都很好，其中一个团队对我的祝福尤为特别。他们的成熟程度虽然不同，但是组织起来却很和谐健康，具备很多活力。他们是一群Y理论组合。

In 1995, I was in charge of a group of American university students spending an academic semester in China. I was blessed with one of those perfect groups that had a healthy mix of maturity with a lot of exciting energy. They were a Theory Y group. I often described them as "a party on wheels." They found fun and had a good time in most every situation. The experience was so successful that I hosted a group the following year. Within the first week I realized this group was not a party on wheels and needed a lot more support. They had more characteristics of Theory X than Theory Y. Unfortunately, I was not mature enough to hide my disappointment and adjust my leadership style to match the group. I found myself critical of the group and regularly dealing with interpersonal relationship problems.

In the midst of the situation, I learned some great lessons about human behavior. For example, when criticizing people, they are likely to respond in two different ways. They either will accept your criticism and change (this most often happens when the person feels very loved and supported by the person who criticized them), or they will reject the criticism and find fault in the one who brought it. The latter result is most often the case. We all have a great ability to self-protect our physical and emotional well-being. By finding fault in the other person, we are able to reject the criticism and remain as we are. I finished that program and realized I knew less about leadership than I thought. Experience has a great way of humbling us and teaching us how much we still need to learn and grow.

Another phenomenon that relates to Theory X and Y is that of self-fulfilling prophecy. Robert Rosenthal of Harvard University and a colleague of his conducted research on the power of expectation. One of his studies involved elementary students and their teachers. In this study a group of teachers were told at the beginning of the school year that some of their students scored exceptionally high on an academic aptitude test. The teachers were informed the high scoring groups of students were likely to bloom academically during the year. The students in the high performing group were actually randomly selected. In spite of this, the pupils that the teachers believed would bloom academically actually did bloom. Test results at the end of the year showed the expected bloomers outscored their classmates. The only difference between the students was the teachers' expectation.[4]

The teachers' belief in the students' ability basically created a self-fulfilling prophecy. Rosenthal and Jacobson's study was titled "Pygmalion in the Classroom." They concluded that the teachers' expectation and behavior based on the infor-

我常常把他们称作“车轮上的一群人”。他们几乎随时随地都能找到好玩儿的事情，常常感到非常开心。那次经历给我留下了深刻的印象，所以第二年我又招待了一群人。第一周的时候，我就发现这群人并不是车轮上的一群人，他们需要更多支持。他们具备更多的X理论人群的特点，而不是Y理论。不幸的是，我当时不够成熟，没有办法隐藏自己的失望情绪，调整自己的领导风格适应团队的需要。我发现自己常常在心中挑剔团队，而且不得不处理人际关系问题。

在这种情形中，我对人类行为有了更深刻的了解。例如，当你批评他人的时候，人们一般有两种回应：接受批评改变自己（当感受到批评人的关爱和支持的时候，一般会出现这样的情况），或者拒绝批评，并且挑衅批评自己的人，挑对方的毛病。一般后者更常见。我们都有保护自己身体和情绪利益的倾向，所以当我们挑别人毛病的时候，就能够抵制批评，保持自己的本性，不需要改变自己。在项目结束的时候，我意识到自己对领导力的理解程度远比自己所想象的差很多。这些经历让我们不得不谦卑，也让我们看到自己学习和成长的空间还很大。

另一个与X理论和Y理论相关的现象就是预言的自我实现。哈佛大学的罗伯特·罗森塔尔（Robert Rosenthal）和一位同事对期待产生的力量进行了研究。其中一个试验把小学生和他们的老师作为测试对象。在这次研究中，老师们在学年一开始被告知，一些学生在学业能力倾向测试中出类拔萃。研究者告诉老师们，这些高分学生会在这一年中在学业上取得特别的成就。实际上，这些高成就组的学生也是随机抽取的，并无特别之处。尽管如此，那些被老师认为会在学业上取得卓越成就的学生的确表现不凡。学年结束后的考试结果说明，那些被期待要取得特别成绩的学生的确远远超过了他们的同学。学生们之间唯一的区别就在于老师的期待。[4]

老师对学生能力的信任创造了自我实现的预言。罗森塔尔和雅各布森的研究被称作“教室中的皮革马利翁效应”（Pygmalion in the Classroom）。他们得出了结论，老师根据学年开始时所获得的资讯产生了期待和相应的行

mation given at the beginning of the year caused some students to bloom while others did not. An additional study titled "Pygmalion Goes to Boot Camp" also studied self-fulfilling prophecy. This study randomly assigned some Israeli army soldiers as "high command potential." The soldiers were placed in different units where their instructors were informed of their alleged potential. The soldiers who were designated as "high command potential" did display superior performance in comparison with the others.[5]

These studies show that as a leader, the expectations you project to your team members will play a significant role in their success. They can rise to your high expectation or match their behavior to meet your low expectation. If your team members are lazy, irresponsible, and unmotivated, you may want to examine your own attitude first. You may be projecting your low expectation to them. You are responsible to release the potential within those you are called to lead.

Application

- Are there any situations where you may be projecting low expectations on others?
- How can you intentionally think better of others and expect more?
- Keep a written record of the improved behavior you observe in others during the next two weeks.

Notation Area

Personal observations/Ideas for further exploration/Thoughts to remember

为，导致一些学生表现出众，而另外一些则不然。另外一个“皮革马利翁效应进入军营”（Pygmalion Goes to Boot Camp）的实验也对自我实现的预言进行了研究。这项试验随机选择了一些以色列士兵作为“被最高指挥部认为很有潜力的人”。士兵被编入不同班里，他们的教官被告知这些人具有所谓的潜能。被指定为“最高指挥部认为很有潜能的人”和其他人相比的确具备更出色的表现。[5]

这些研究表明，作为领袖，你对团队成员的期待对他们的成功起至关重要的作用。他们或者奋起直追达到你的期待，或者降低标准和你的低标准匹配。假如你的团队成员很懒惰、不负责任、缺乏动力，你可能需要先检查自己的态度。你可能在心中给他们设定的标准很低，并且投射了出来。作为领袖，你有责任释放跟随者的潜力。

应用

◆你是否在某些情况下会对他人产生很低的期待？

◆你怎样才能有意地较高评价他人，具备较高的期待？

◆在以后的两周内，把你在他人身上观察到的改善了的行为记录下来。

笔记

个人体会／要进一步探讨的想法／要铭记在心的理念

语言只是沟通的一小部分，一个明智的领袖知道如何诠释团队成员所说的话，更重要的是理解他们要说的真实意思。

Words are a small part of communication, and a wise leader will learn how to interpret not just what team members say, but more importantly what they intend to say.

非语言沟通

More than Words

第二十六天　魏武子的遗言
——沟通

Day 26: Communication

卓越领袖创建稳固团队最快的方式之一就是促进彼此的沟通。

One of the fastest ways effective leaders create a strong team is to facilitate their communication.

Words are a small part of communication, and a wise leader will learn how to interpret not just what team members say, but more importantly what they intend to say.

Wei Ke was the son of Wei Wuzi, an official of the state of Jin during the Spring and Autumn Period (770-221 BC). Wuzi became ill and instructed his son to take care of his favorite concubine after his death. He asked him to find her a good husband who would take care of her. Just before he died, when his body and mind had all but wasted away, he instructed Wei Ke to kill his concubine and place her beside him in the grave so they would be united in the afterlife. Wei Ke didn't kill the concubine, however, but married her off as his father had first suggested. When questioned about his actions, he responded, "When a person's mind and body are sick and close to death, they do not always speak their true feelings. When my father was in his right mind, he communicated to me his will. The true desire of my father's will I have carried out."

Later Wei Ke and the Jin army went to battle against Du Hui, commander of the Qin army. As the battle formations closed in on each other, an old man was seen knotting clumps of grass in the middle of the battlefield. In the confusion of battle, Du Hui's horse stumbled because of the bundles, causing him to be captured. That night in a dream, Wei Ke saw the old man who had tied the bundles of grass. He said, "Your father's concubine was my daughter. I have repaid you for the kindness you showed to my daughter."[1]

This story serves as an excellent example of the importance of clearly understanding a person's intended message. Often when people speak out of anger, stress, frustration, or fatigue, they do not communicate effectively. Words are a small part of communication, and a wise leader will learn how to interpret not just what team members say, but more importantly what they intend to say.

语言只是沟通的一小部分，一个明智的领袖知道如何诠释团队成员所说的话，更重要的是理解他们要说的真实意思。

春秋战国时期（公元前770年－公元前221年）晋国的大夫魏颗的父亲魏武子病重，他告诉儿子，要他在自己死后照顾自己的宠妾，给她找一个爱护她和照顾她的丈夫。在他病危弥留之际，他又要魏颗杀死自己的妾，给自己陪葬。然而，魏颗在父亲死后，没有把她杀死，反而遵照父亲一开始的要求把她嫁了出去。有人问起的时候，他这样回答："当一个人病重的时候，头脑也不清醒。他所说的并非是自己真实的感受。父亲头脑清醒的时候告诉我的才是真实的意思。我执行的是父亲真实的愿望。"

后来魏颗率领晋军对抗秦国将领杜回。在战役的紧要关头，一个老人在战场中间用草编成环。在混乱之中，杜回的马被草环绊倒，杜回被捕。那一夜，魏颗在梦中看到了编草环的那位老人。老人说："你父亲的妾是我的女儿。因为你救了她的命，我特来报恩。"[1]

这是一个绝佳的故事，说明清楚理解一个人真实意思的重要性。当人们在愤怒、压力、挫败或疲劳的时候，他们不能有效沟通。语言只是沟通的一小部分，一个明智的领袖知道如何诠释团队成员所说的话，更重要的是理解他们要说的真实意思。

在成年人中很少出现清晰的沟通。这一切都是由于我们生活中出现的紊乱经历。世界知名的管理大师彼得·杜拉克（Peter Drucker）认为，60%的管理问题是由于沟通问题导致的。[2]领袖需要说话和聆听的基本技巧。一般

Clear communication rarely happens among adults. This accounts for much of the dysfunction experienced in our lives. Peter Drucker, a world-renowned management educator, claims that communication is to blame for 60 percent of management problems.[2] Leaders need to master the basic skills of speaking and listening to others. Groups of people in general-whether a family, company, school, or social club-cannot thrive without clear communication.

One of the fastest ways effective leaders create a strong team is to facilitate their communication. Without communication, you merely lead a collection of individuals instead of a team. In high school I had the privilege of playing on a winning football team. Our school was known as the powerhouse of the area, defeating all the local teams and regularly qualifying for state finals. The key to our school's consistent success was a coach named Walt Braun. Coach Braun had the ability to inspire us to perform our best. When someone once asked him why he didn't allow his players to listen to music in the locker rooms, he replied, "Communication." The players needed to know each other and that involved talking to each other. Communication off the field improves relationships, and communication on the field is essential to create a winning team.

As a leader you need to be a communicator. This does not, however, imply that you should talk all the time. "The more words, the less meaning" is a wise saying to remember. Most human communication is nonverbal. Your team may listen to the words that come out of your mouth, but they will hear much more. They will pick up on your mood, body language, and expressions. If your relationship with a particular team member is strong, they are likely to interpret your communication as positive; if it is strained, they will hold everything in suspicion. All of your communication will be filtered through their expectations, needs, and perceptions. If you are having trouble understanding this, think of the last time you were told "it was not what you said but how you said it that upset me." Or, "It was not what you said but what you didn't say." Because of this, leaders need to choose their words carefully in order to maximize communication. Some words are more important than others. For example, consider these words and their interpretation:

I — discourages teamwork, productivity, and relationship

We—encourages relationships, increases productivity, and fosters teamwork

Some words that strengthen a team and build relationships include:

说来，不论是在家庭中，还是在公司、学校或社交的俱乐部之中，如果没有清晰的沟通，很多人无法建立健康的关系。

卓越领袖创建稳固团队最快的方式之一就是促进彼此的沟通。假如没有沟通的话，你只是在带领一群单独的个体，而不是一个团队。在高中的时候，我有幸参加了一个常胜的橄榄球队。我们的学校在这个领域像是个发源地，打败当地所有的团队，常常有资格参与州里的比赛。我们学校常胜的关键是拥有一位名叫沃尔特·布劳恩（Walt Braun）的教练。布劳恩教练有能力鼓舞我们，让我们达到最佳水平。当有人询问为什么他不允许队员在更衣室听音乐，他回答道："沟通。"队员需要彼此了解，在一起交流。赛场之外的沟通可以改善关系，赛场之中的沟通是创建成功团队的核心。

作为领袖，你需要成为沟通者，然而，这并不意味着你要把所有的话说尽。"话越多，越没有意义。"这句话值得我们牢记在心。人们之间的大部分沟通都是非语言的。你的团队可能听到你嘴里说出来的话语，但是他们感受到的更多。他们会捕捉到你的情绪、肢体语言和表情。假如你和团队成员的关系稳定，他们很可能会积极诠释你的沟通；假如关系紧张，他们会对一切产生怀疑。你所有的沟通都会经过他们的期待、需要和感受的过滤。假如你很难理解这一点，想想上一次别人告诉你什么："不是你说的话，而是你的说法让我觉得不舒服。"或者，"不是你说的，而是你没有说的东西让我感觉不舒服。"因为这些原因，领袖需要认真选择自己的话语，最大程度发挥沟通的作用。有些话语要比另外一些更重要。例如，想想下面这些话语以及它们的诠释：

我——阻碍团队协作、生产力和关系

我们——鼓励关系，增进生产力以及团队协作

可以强化和建立团队关系的话语包括：

谢谢你——表达欣赏

我饶恕你——重建、释放罪咎感，建立彼此的交往

Thank you-expresses appreciation

I forgive you-restores, releases guilt, builds community

Tell me your idea-shows respect

You did a good job-motivates and encourages

I believe you can do it-empowers

Tell me more about yourself-builds friendship

Communication is more prolific and more difficult today than ever before. We live in an age when technology makes communication possible with any person at any time or place. However, with increased technology has come increased noise. The noise makes it difficult to send a clear message. People are constantly bombarded with information, so much so that we suffer from information overload. Most of your mail is not worth the time it takes to open. Many phone calls are just telemarketers to be screened out. E-mail has more junk mail than anything else. TV has more channels but less content and little worth watching. The irony is that we have the greatest capacity to communicate, but are failing to do so.[3] What can leaders do to get their message across in this frenzy of noise? My advice is to keep your message simple and clear. "Think like a wise man, but communicate in the language of the people."[4]

Information-stimulated societies are full of individuals desiring real relationships. They long for people they can trust. Trust is an essential ingredient for clear communication. One challenge to clear communication is people often hear what they expect to hear, regardless of what is said. If they don't trust you, it doesn't matter what you say because they will question your motives and doubt your words. Therefore, building relationships and earning trust should be a primary goal when seeking to build effective communication within a team. Effective communication, as both a skill and an art, needs to be practiced to improve. A disciplined study of effective listening unlocks the floodgate of information and relationships.

告诉我你的想法——表示尊重

你干得很好——激励和鼓励

我相信你能够做到——授权

告诉我你的生活——建立友谊

今天的沟通比以往更多、更困难。我们生活的年代中，技术让任何人在任何时候、任何地点都可以顺利进行沟通。然而，随着技术的增加，也同时增加了噪音。噪音让清晰沟通变得更加艰难。人们被信息轰炸，甚至让我们载荷了过多的信息。你的很多邮件都不值得花时间阅读。很多电话都是需要被拦阻的电信商业广告。E-mail中的垃圾邮件比任何东西都多。电视的频道很多，但大多数电视节目都根本不值得一看。其中最大的讽刺在于：我们沟通的能力比任何时候都强，却没有这么做。[3]领袖怎样才能在这繁杂的噪音中传递自己的信息呢？我的建议是：让你的信息简单明了。“思考要睿智，要用别人能够理解的语言沟通。”[4]

被信息刺激的社会充满了渴望真正友谊的人。他们渴望找到自己可以信任的人。信任是清晰沟通的核心要素。要想清晰沟通，其中面对的挑战在于无论说的内容是什么，人们常常听到自己想听的话。假如他们不信任你，你说什么都没用，因为他们会质疑你的动机，怀疑你所说的话。因此，在团队中建设有效的沟通时，建立关系和赢得信任都应该是基本目标。有效的沟通既是一项技巧也是一门技术，需要常常操练才能够改善。对有效聆听进行系统研究可以开启信息和友谊的大门。

Application

- Identify two people with whom you have had a misunderstanding as a result of poor communication. Ask them for advice on how you could communicate more clearly.

- Remember these three basic principles when communicating:
- Next time you need to communicate to your team, think about keeping it simple. How can you work on keeping your messages simple and clear?
- Seek opportunities in order to establish trust with team members. What opportunity can you use this week to build trust?
- Clear communication doesn't come naturally, it must be nurtured. How can you commit to becoming a strong communicator?

Notation Area

Personal observations/Ideas for further exploration/Thoughts to remember

应用

◆可能你会因为沟通问题和他人之间产生误解，请想出两个人来，询问他们你怎样才能更好地沟通。

◆在沟通的时候，记住以下三个基本原则：

◆下次沟通的时候，记住要简捷。怎样保持信息的简捷和清晰？

◆寻找机会和团队建立信任感。你本周可以使用哪些机会建立信任感？

◆简捷的沟通并不能自然而然地形成，必须经过训练。你怎样坚持不懈地培养自己这方面的才华，成为良好的沟通者？

笔记

个人体会／要进一步探讨的想法／要铭记在心的理念

子贡问政。子曰：“足食，足兵，足信之矣。”子贡曰：“必不得已而去，于斯三者何先？”曰：“去兵。”子贡曰：“必不得已而去，于斯尔者何先？”曰：“去食。自古皆有死，民无信不立。”

——孔子

Three things are need for government: sufficient food, sufficient military equipment, and the trust of the people.” Tsze-Kung asked Confucius, “If one had to dispense with one of those three, which should be given up first?” “The military equipment, “ said the Master. Tsze-Kung again asked, “If on had to dispense with one of the two remaining, which should be given up?” The Master answered, “Give up the food. From of old, death has always been the lot of men; but if the people have no faith in their rulers, they cannot stand.

——*Confucius*

失去信任

Broken Trust

第二十七天 挑拨离间
——失去信赖

Day 27:Trust

谦卑是让人们放松和建立信任关系的关键。

Humility is key to putting people at ease and building trust.

Three things are need for government: sufficient food, sufficient military equipment, and the trust of the people." Tsze-Kung asked Confucius, "If one had to dispense with one of those three, which should be given up first?" "The military equipment, " said the Master. Tsze-Kung again asked, "If on had to dispense with one of the two remaining, which should be given up?" The Master answered, "Give up the food. From of old, death has always been the lot of men; but if the people have no faith in their rulers, they cannot stand.

——*Confucius*

In the third year of the Han Dynasty, Xiang Yu continually attacked the Han troops and cut off their supplies, causing a food shortage. As a result Liu Bang, leader of the Han, chose to call a truce and discontinued their expansion. Xiang Yu wanted to agree, but the counsel of Fan Zeng convinced him otherwise. When Liu Bang learned that Fan Zeng had opposed his plan for peace, he exploded with anger. Liu Bang knew he had to remove Fan Zeng's influence from Xiang Yu, so he devised a plan.

When Xiang Yu sent envoys to Liu Bang, Liu Bang ordered a great banquet. However, he acted surprised when he learned the envoys were from Xiang Yu and canceled the feast. Instead, he presented the envoys with a simple meal. When the envoys questioned this change, Liu Bang answered, "We expected envoys from Lord Fan Zeng, but you come to us from Xiang Yu." When the envoys returned and reported this to Xiang Yu, he suspected that Fan Zeng secretly partnered with Liu Bang. As a result Xiang Yu slowly removed Fan Zeng from power. Fan Zeng soon left Xiang Yu, and Liu Bang's plan to breed mistrust had succeeded.[1]

子贡问政。子曰："足食，足兵，足信之矣。"子贡曰："必不得已而去，于斯三者何先？"曰："去兵。"子贡曰："必不得已而去，于斯尔者何先？"曰："去食。自古皆有死，民无信不立。"

——孔子

译文：子贡问怎样治理国家。孔子说："粮食充足，军备充足，老百姓信任统治者。"子贡说："如果不得不去掉一项，那么在三项中先去掉哪一项呢？"孔子说："去掉军备。"子贡说："如果不得不再去掉一项，那么这两项中去掉哪一项呢？"孔子说："去掉粮食。自古以来人总是要死的，如果老百姓对统治者不信任，那么国家就不存在了。"

汉国成立的第三年，项羽常常攻击汉军，切断他们的粮食供应。结果汉王刘邦选择休战，停止扩张。项羽想要同意对方的建议，但是谋士范增则进言让他改变了主意。刘邦知道范增反对自己求和的建议后大发脾气。刘邦知道自己需要从项羽的身边减少范增的影响力，所以他设计了一个计划。

当项羽的使节来见刘邦的时候，刘邦命令摆设盛宴。然而，当他得知使节是从项羽那里来的，就命令撤去了盛宴，给使节摆上了简单的饭菜。当使节质疑这样的改变时，刘邦回答道："我们设盛宴等候的是亚父范增的使节，但你是项羽派来的，只能用简单的饭菜。"使节返回向项羽汇报以后，项羽怀疑范增和刘邦暗中来往。后来项羽慢慢冷淡范增，削去了他的权力。范增后来离开了项羽，刘邦的反间计成功了，让他们之间产生了不信任。[1]

刘邦知道得胜的唯一方法就是破坏范增和项羽之间的关系。达到目标的

Liu Bang knew the only way to win was to destroy the relationship between Fan Zeng and Xiang Yu. The best way to accomplish his goal was to destroy their trust. Once the seed of distrust was planted in Xiang Yu's mind, the relationship between Fan Zeng and Xiang Yu was destroyed.

The same principle applies in your teams. Without an atmosphere of trust, relationships will never develop and communication will be disjointed at best. Leaders begin building trust by being approachable. The American Olympic gymnast Mary Lou Retton once said, "You know when somebody is standing in the corner and saying, 'Hey, I don't want to be talked to.'" Retton's advice on how to avoid giving this impression is simple: "Being down-to-earth and humble is extremely important. I just try to put people at ease. Everybody's the same. I think everybody is on a certain level, whether you are the CEO of a company or a salesman. It's just a different job."[2]

Humility is key to putting people at ease and building trust. This is especially important when working in cross-cultural situations. I have seen humble people commit major cultural blunders, but no one seemed insulted. On the other hand, I have observed proud individuals offend others while outwardly doing everything correctly. Humility naturally makes people feel comfortable and opens the doors for honest, effective communication.

When people communicate actively and openly, trust naturally increases. Trust, in turn, fosters ownership and ownership increases commitment. A successful team is made up of committed people, and it is the team leader's role to foster an atmosphere that builds this commitment.[3] The ability to communicate will separate average leaders from great leaders. The team that makes people feel special is the team that will bring success to their business.

Harvard business school professor John A. Quelch reported on a survey conducted at Harvard. He found graduates were technically competent but lacking in written and oral communication skills. To be successful, understanding the latest technology is important. However, success primarily depends on the quality of human relations more than technical competence. In almost every business and organization, people are the most valuable assets, and people work well when they are involved in trusting relationships.[4] You can build trust with your team members by being:

- Honest. Open and honest leaders are easy to trust and follow.
- Humble. Humility draws people in and lowers walls of defensiveness.

最佳方式就是破坏他们的信任。一旦在项羽的心中埋下不信任的种子，项羽和范增之间的关系就被破坏了。

同样的原则也可以应用在你的团队中。缺少了信任的氛围，就无法培养信任的关系，沟通也会迅速脱节。当领袖平易近人的时候，就很容易建立彼此的信任。参加过奥林匹克运动会的美国体操运动员玛利·洛·瑞腾（Mary Lou Retton）曾说："你知道有人会站在角落里说：'嗨，我不希望你和我交谈。'"兰顿也说明了如何避免给别人留下这样的印象："实际和谦卑非常重要。我只是想让人们放松。每个人都一样。我认为无论你是公司的执行总裁还是推销员，每个人都处在某个特定的层面上，只是工作不同。"[2]

谦卑是让人们放松和建立信任关系的关键，尤其在跨文化的环境中工作时更是如此。我见过谦卑的人犯下了文化上的大错，但似乎没有人感到不舒服。另一方面，我也见过一些骄傲的人，虽然所有的事情都做得无懈可击，却让别人感到被冒犯。谦卑会让人感到放松和自然，打开诚实和有效沟通的大门。

人们积极和坦诚沟通的时候会自然产生信任。信任产生归属感，归属感带来承诺。成功的团队由忠诚的人组成，团队领袖的职责就是培养能够建立忠诚的氛围。[3]沟通的能力能把卓越的领袖和一般的领袖区分开来，让人们感到特别的团队就是成功完成自己任务的团队。

哈佛商学院的约翰·A·魁尔奇教授（John A. Quelch）在哈佛进行的一次调查表明，毕业生在学业上很有竞争力，但是缺少写作和口头沟通的技巧。想要成功，明白最新的科技很重要。然而，成功主要依靠人与人关系的品质，这可能要比技术上的竞争力更重要。在每个公司和机构中，人都是最重要的资源，当人与人之间的关系和谐的时候，他们的工作效率也最好。[4]你可以培养自己以下的品质来和团队成员建立信任：

- 诚实：坦诚和诚实的领袖容易被信任和跟随。
- 谦卑：谦卑把人吸引到自己身边，让他人放下自己的防御。
- 可靠：你的团队成员能够信赖你，按照你所说的去做。

- Dependable. Your team members should be able to rely on you to do what you say.
- Real. Perfection is seldom expected, but genuine honesty about your strengths, weaknesses, failures, and successes will build trust.
- Caring. People trust those whom they feel care for them and have their best interests in mind.

Trust is a foundation on which relationships grow, communication flows, and teamwork flourishes. A house cannot stand for long without a solid foundation, and a team cannot produce successful results without trust.

Application

- Does your team trust you? How and why?
- Write down the following words: honest, humble, dependable, real, caring. Next to each word write one specific action you can do to exhibit these trust-building qualities to your team.

Notation Area

Personal observations/Ideas for further exploration/Thoughts to remember

● 真实：人们并不期待你完美。只要诚实地面对自己的优势和弱势、失败和成功，就能够建立信任。

● 关怀：人们信任关心自己、在心中放着自己最佳利益的人。

信任是培养关系、有效沟通和团队协作和谐的基础。没有稳固的根基，房屋就不能稳定；没有信任，团队就无法拥有成功的结果。

应用

◆你的团队信任你吗？如何信任？为什么？

◆写下如下词语：诚实、谦卑、可靠、真实和关怀。在每个词语的后面写出你可以做的具体行为，在团队中表现出这些建立信赖的品质。

笔记

个人体会／要进一步探讨的想法／要铭记在心的理念

见日月不为明目，闻雷霆不为聪耳。

——孙子[1]

To distinguish between the sun and moon is no test of vision; to hear the thunderclap is no indication of acute hearing.

——*Sun Tzu*[1]

聆听时光

Time to Listen

第二十八天 沟通之始
——聆听

Day 28:Listening

聆听意味着等候，听他人在说什么。

Listening means wanting to hear what the other person has to say.

To distinguish between the sun and moon is no test of vision; to hear the thunderclap is no indication of acute hearing.

—— *Sun Tzu* [1]

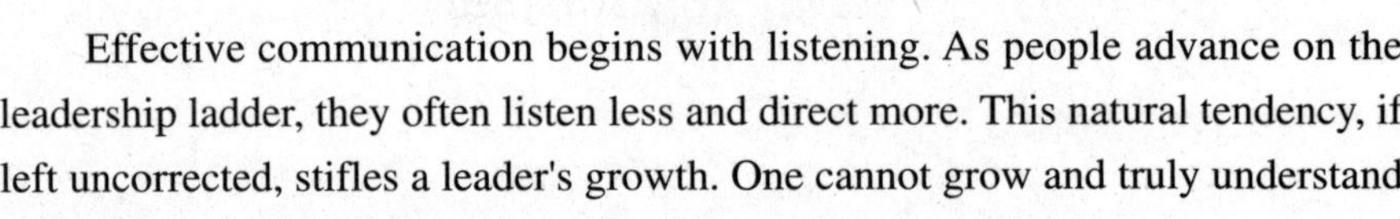

Effective communication begins with listening. As people advance on the leadership ladder, they often listen less and direct more. This natural tendency, if left uncorrected, stifles a leader's growth. One cannot grow and truly understand people and situations without the valuable trait of active listening.

Richard C. Buetow, director of quality at Motorola, Inc., sees listening as his greatest tool. Buetow commented, "I don't sit on top of a mountain and get these visions of what we ought to do. I have to find out from other people. I have to do a lot of listening."[2] At Motorola, effective listening is a must for top executives. They regularly encourage employees to present ideas while a top executive sits and quietly listens. "I've sat and listened to hundreds of teams tell me about all these issues and solutions," says Buetow.[3] Motorola's future has and will continue to depend on their leadership's ability to listen to ideas from the people closest to the situations.

When you truly listen to others, two things are likely to happen: you may learn something and others will respond to you. William Savel, former chairman of Baskin Robbins, the worldwide ice cream and yogurt retailer, worked in Japan in his younger days. Working internationally helped him gain valuable business insights. Savel learned from listening, and his success shows that others have responded positively to his leadership. According to Savel, "The important thing is to listen, to really listen, before you go in and start shooting your mouth off and telling everybody how smart you are. You've got to learn how dumb you are first. You have to go in and get to know the people, interact with them, don't put yourself above anyone else. Get around, talk to everybody, listen very intently, and

见日月不为明目，闻雷霆不为聪耳。

——孙子[1]

译文：看得见日月算不上眼明，听得见雷霆算不上耳聪。

有效的沟通始于聆听。当人们在领袖阶梯上前进的时候，他们的聆听会变少，指导相应变多。假如对这样的自然倾向不加纠正的话，就会让领袖驻足不前。假如缺少了积极聆听这个可靠的品质，一个人就很难成长并且真正理解他人和周围的环境。

摩托罗拉的质量总监理查德·C·保托(Richard C. Buetow)把聆听当作自己最有效的工具。保托这样评论道："我并不是只要坐在山顶上，就能够看到愿景，知道我们下一步要干什么。我需要从人群中发现目标。我需要常常聆听。"[2]在摩托罗拉，有效的聆听是执行主管必须做到的一件事。他们常常鼓励员工说出自己的想法，高级主管坐在那里静静地聆听。保托说："我曾经坐在那里聆听数百个团队告诉我所有的问题和解决方案。"[3]摩托罗拉曾经注重聆听，在未来会继续看重领袖的聆听能力，以便了解当时环境中人们的想法。

当你真正聆听他人的时候，很可能会发生两件事：你会学习到东西，他人会回应你。巴斯金·罗金斯（Baskin Robbins）前主席、世界著名的冰激凌和酸奶零售商威廉姆·塞维尔（William Savel），年轻时曾经在日本工作。国际工作的经验帮助他获得了宝贵的商业洞察力。塞维尔因为聆听而获益匪浅，他的成功说明他人也积极回应他的带领。塞维尔说："在你夸夸其谈，告诉别人你有多聪明之前，重要的一点是要聆听——真正的聆听。你首先要知

don't make up your mind too fast."[4]

Just the other night, my wife and I watched a movie in which an expert matchmaker helps needy guys win the hearts of the women they love. The movie was a comedy, but some of the advice was priceless. He advised one man, "When she is talking to you, don't look at her lips, don't daydream. Listen to what she is saying. That way, when she asks you what you think, you will have something interesting to say." This advice sounds simple, but is often overlooked. If you want others to respond to you, listen to what they have to say. Leading others to agree with your opinion has more to do with listening than talking. It is best to let others express their ideas fully. People find it difficult to listen when they have a lot on their mind to share. Try not to interrupt or express any negative comments while others are sharing ideas. If someone truly feels listened to and respected, they are much more likely to listen to you in return and respect your opinion. "Listen more, talk less" is a great phrase to plant into your brain.

If you really listen to those around you, you will learn. Even if you disagree with others, you may find they will be more open to your opinion because you respected them enough to listen to their viewpoint. Sincere listening conveys respect every time. And when people feel respected, they are less resistant to change and alternative points of view.

Listening means wanting to hear what the other person has to say. You may pride yourself on your ability to thrill your listeners with exciting stories. You may be a gifted writer or possess a powerful voice and dynamic personality. But none of these communication skills influence others more than the skill of listening.

道，自己实际上笨口拙舌。你要去了解他人，和他们交往，不要把自己放在别人前面。到处走走，和每个人交谈，专心聆听，不要太快作决定。”[4]

就在前几天的一个晚上，妻子和我观看了一部电影，讲的是一个超级媒人帮助交往能力很差的男生赢得自己所喜爱的女孩子的心。电影是个喜剧，但是其中一些建议却很有意义。他建议其中一位男士：“当她和你交谈的时候，不要看着她的嘴唇，不要做白日梦。聆听她所说的内容。这样，当她问你有什么看法的时候，你就能够脱口而出，也会很有吸引力。”这个建议听起来很简单，但常常被忽略。假如你希望他人回应你，就要聆听他们在说什么。要想引导他人认同你的意见，聆听要比说话更重要。最好让他人完全表达自己的观点。当一个人心中有很多要分享的内容时，人们发现自己很难聆听。当别人在分享自己的想法时，不要打断对方，或者表达自己消极的看法。如果别人真正感到自己被聆听、被尊重，他们也会回报你，愿意聆听你的话语，尊重你的想法。“多听少说”应该被深深地根植在你的心中。

假如你真正聆听周围人的声音，你就能够学习。即使你不认同他人的看法，你还是会发现，他们会坦诚面对你的意见，因为你尊重他们的意见，聆听他们的看法。真诚的聆听传递的是尊重。当人们感到被尊重的时候，他们就不会过分抵制改变和不同的看法。

聆听意味着等候，要听到他人在说什么。你可能为自己感到骄傲，因为你讲故事绘声绘色，扣人心弦，或者你是一个天赋很高的作者，有哄亮的嗓音和个性魅力。但是这些沟通技巧的影响力在聆听技巧面前都略逊一筹。

Application

- Do you listen to others or do you do most of the talking?

- Next time you have a meeting, go in with a little mouth and big ears. Let your input be:
  What do you think?
  Why do you feel that would work?
  Could you further explain that thought?
  I like your idea; let's build on that.
  What do the rest of you think?

- Your team will go away energized and you will likely gain a great deal of insight.

Notation Area

Personal observations/Ideas for further exploration/Thoughts to remember

应用

◆你常常聆听他人讲话，还是占据了大部分的讲话时间？

◆下次你有会议的时候，多听少说。你要说的是：

你的看法是什么？

你为什么认为这样的方法有效？

你能进一步解释一下这个想法吗？

我喜欢这个想法，我们进一步探讨一下。

其他人的看法是什么？

◆你的团队在离开的时候会感到自己受到激励，你也很可能会获得很多的新想法。

笔记

个人体会／要进一步探讨的想法／要铭记在心的理念

假如我们拒绝秦王用城池交换美玉的提议，我们就不在理；但是假如我们放弃了美玉，却没有得到城池，秦王理亏。从这两种方法看来，最好就是同意对方的提议，让秦王承担不讲理的名声。

——蔺相如

If we refuse Qin's offer of cities in exchange for the jade, that puts us in the wrong; but if we give up the jade and receive no cities, that puts Qin in the wrong. Of these two courses, the better one is to agree and put Qin in the wrong.

——*Lin Xiangru*

和平之玉

Famous Peace of Jade

第二十九天 十五座城换美玉
——风险与责任

Day 29:Risk and Responsibility

成熟的领袖能够把资讯、权柄和相应的责任委托给他人。有的时候，所交托的一切甚至超越了这个人的经历。

Mature leaders are able to entrust others with information, authority, and responsibility that match-and sometimes exceed-a person's experience.

If we refuse Qin's offer of cities in exchange for the jade, that puts us in the wrong; but if we give up the jade and receive no cities, that puts Qin in the wrong. Of these two courses, the better one is to agree and put Qin in the wrong.

—— *Lin Xiangru*

Trusting others closely correlates with your ability to take risks. Mature leaders are able to entrust others with information, authority, and responsibility that match-and sometimes exceed-a person's experience. They are comfortable with the risk that others will be able to perform tasks successfully without constant input. If employees commit mistakes that reflect negatively on the leader's overall performance, a mature leader willingly bears the loss of reputation. Not trusting team members affects the productivity of the team more adversely in the long run than a few mistakes made along the way.

When trusting others, you run the risk of being let down. However, leaders are responsible for choosing the appropriate path with the largest guarantee of success. When faced with a dilemma, the question is "What is the right thing to do?" Your focus should not solely hinge on the desired result.

The following story illustrates this point: King Huiwen of Zhao conquered the city of Yangjin, and in doing so, came into possession of a famous piece of jade. When King Zhao of Qin learned of this, he sent an envoy to King Huiwen offering him fifteen cities in exchange for the jade. King Huiwen did not trust King Zhao to keep his promise, but he feared that refusal would lead to war. The king then summoned a wise man named Lin Xiangru and asked him what he should do. Lin Xiangru advised, "Qin is strong, we are weak. We cannot refuse."

King Huiwen asked, "What if he takes the jade, but will not give me the cities?"

"If we refuse Qin's offer of cities in exchange for the jade, that puts us in the wrong; but if we give up the jade and receive no cities, that puts Qin in the wrong.

假如我们拒绝秦王用城池交换美玉的提议，我们就不在理；但是假如我们放弃了美玉，却没有得到城池，秦王理亏。从这两种方法看来，最好就是同意对方的提议，让秦王承担不讲理的名声。

——蔺相如

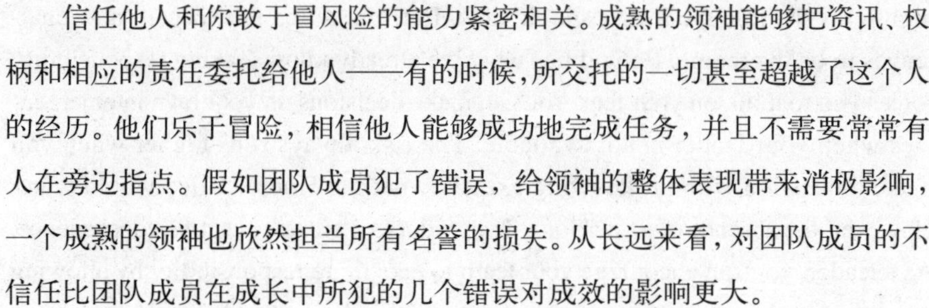

信任他人和你敢于冒风险的能力紧密相关。成熟的领袖能够把资讯、权柄和相应的责任委托给他人——有的时候，所交托的一切甚至超越了这个人的经历。他们乐于冒险，相信他人能够成功地完成任务，并且不需要常常有人在旁边指点。假如团队成员犯了错误，给领袖的整体表现带来消极影响，一个成熟的领袖也欣然担当所有名誉的损失。从长远来看，对团队成员的不信任比团队成员在成长中所犯的几个错误对成效的影响更大。

当你信任他人的时候，你就冒着被他人辜负的风险。然而，领袖有责任选择成功率最高的最恰当的道路。当进退两难的时候，我们面对的问题是："怎么做是正确的？"你的注意力不应该单单盯在自己想得到的结果上。

下面的故事说明了这一点：赵国的惠文帝领兵征服了阳晋城，也获得了当地一块美玉。秦昭王听说后，打发了一位特使来见惠文帝，提出要用15座城换美玉。惠文帝并不相信昭王能够遵守诺言，但是他又担心自己拒绝后，会给对方发兵攻打赵国的理由。惠文帝命令蔺相如晋见，向他询问。蔺相如建议道："秦国强大，我们弱小。我们不能拒绝。"

惠文帝问道："假如他们拿走了我们的和田玉，却不给我们城池，该怎么办？"

"假如我们拒绝秦王用城池交换美玉的提议，我们就不在理；但是假如我们放弃了美玉，却没有得到城池，秦王理亏。从这两种方法看来，最好就

Of these two courses, the better one is to agree and put Qin in the wrong."[1]

Doing the right thing can be an end in itself, regardless of the results. The same can be said for trusting others. If we trust others, they may cheat us from time to time. But not to trust places us in the wrong more often and will hinder your team. A trusting person will have many friends, for they look for the good in others. People love being around those who see the good in them.

Along with trusting others, leaders need to take responsibility. This includes overseeing those things within your capability, as well as accepting work that may be beyond your current experience. Accepting only simple responsibilities at your experience level can ensure consistent results, but you will not grow. Effectively facing the unknown and unexpected challenges causes growth.

The simple but powerful image of the leader walking in front of his team highlights the role the leader should take. In front lie the unexpected new challenges to be overcome. Behind lies what we already know. Taking responsibility forces you to think on your feet. You can make decisions on your own in emergencies when your leader is not available. The risk always runs higher when you make a decision without knowing exactly what the Home Office would want. However, the absence of a decision often produces a greater negative consequence. As a leader, you can encourage your team to take more responsibility by allowing them the freedom to make some wrong decisions. You should discuss the wrong decisions with them, but praise your team members for taking the initiative to make the decision.

The following story highlights an employee who lacked the ability to think creatively in the most obvious situation: Gene Marine, the editor of the *Bellefontaine Examiner*, sent a young sports writer to cover a game. The reporter returned early without a story. When Marine questioned the reporter, he simply replied, "No game."

"No game?" Marine asked. "What happened?"

"The stadium collapsed," responded the reporter.

"Then where is the story on the stadium collapse?"

"That wasn't my assignment, sir," answered the reporter.[2]

A leader who encourages initiating decisions when appropriate will less likely have a reporter return without a story. If you desire your team to operate with a high-risk tolerance, then you as the leader must first set the example.

是同意对方的提议，让秦王承担不讲理的名声。”[1]

不论结果怎样，做正确的事情本身就是结果。信任他人也是一样。假如我们信任他人，他们可能有的时候会欺骗我们。但是不信任让我们处在理亏的位置上，就会阻碍团队的发展。一个信任他人的人拥有很多朋友，因为他们从别人身上找到优点。人们喜欢能看到自己身上优点的人。

领袖不仅要信任他人，同时还需要承担责任——其中包括监督自己能力范围内的事情，也包括接受超越自己目前经历的工作。只接受自己经历范围以内的简单责任能够保证业绩的稳定，但是你失去了成长的机会。积极面对不期而至的和未知的挑战就能够带来成长。

领袖在团队中的形象朴素但有力，突显一位领袖所担当的角色。前面是要去克服的不期而至的新挑战，后面是我们已经知道的一切。承担责任迫使你必须清醒地思考。领袖不在的情况下，你可能会在紧急状态中独立作决定。在你不知道总部确切意思的时候，作决定所冒的风险就很高。在总部不知情的情况下作决定，常常会带来更大的消极后果。作为领袖，你可以给团队更大的自由，允许他们犯错误，鼓励他们承担更大的责任。你可以和他们讨论错误的决定，但是同时称赞团队成员作决定的主动性。

以下的故事说明在大多数情况下员工都缺乏创造性思维：《美女枫丹研究》(*Bellefontaine Examiner*) 的编辑吉恩·马瑞恩派了一个年轻的体育栏目记者报道一次比赛。记者早早地回来了，没带回任何故事。当马瑞恩询问这个记者的时候，他简单地回答：“没有比赛，”

“没有比赛？”马瑞恩问道。“怎么了？”

“体育场塌了。”记者回答道。

“那么体育馆坍塌的故事在哪儿呢？”

“先生，我的任务不是报道这个消息。”记者回答道。[2]

当领袖鼓励跟随者在恰当的时候主动作决定，就不太可能出现记者没有带着故事返回的情况。假如你希望自己的团队具备忍耐力，能够承担高风险，那么你作为领袖就必须先树立这样的榜样。

Application

- ◆ Are you a risk taker?
- ◆ Are you walking in the front?
- ◆ Take on a task or responsibility that is beyond your experience level. Mentally and physically seek to walk in the front and lead your team.
- ◆ Who on your team has the potential to lead in your absence?
- ◆ How can you develop more team members who could have this potential?

Notation Area

Personal observations/Ideas for further exploration/Thoughts to remember

应用

◆你会冒风险吗？

◆你愿意走在前面吗？

◆接受超越自己经历程度的任务或责任，身体力行，让自己走在前面，带领你的团队。

◆在你的团队中，谁有潜力在你不在的时候带领团队？

◆你怎样栽培更多具备这样潜力的团队成员？

笔记

个人体会／要进一步探讨的想法／要铭记在心的理念

投之无所往，死且不北，死焉不得，士人尽力。兵士甚陷则不惧，无所往则固，深入则拘，不得已则斗。

——孙子

Throw the troops into a position from which there is no escape, and even when faced with death they will not flee. For if prepared to die, what can they not achieve?

——*Sun Tzu*

破釜沉舟

Sink the Boats

第三十天　破釜沉舟
——委身

Day 30: Commitment

勇于委身的寻常人能够创造非凡的结果。

Ordinary people with commitment can produce extraordinary results.

Throw the troops into a position from which there is no escape, and even when faced with death they will not flee. For if prepared to die, what can they not achieve?

—— *Sun Tzu*

Following several victories, Xiang Liang, leader of the Chu army, became overconfident and underestimated the power of the Qin army. One of his advisors tried to warn him, saying, "If a general swaggers and his men loaf after a victory, they are sure to be defeated. Now your troops are taking it easy while the Qin army grows stronger every day. I am worried to think what will come of you."[1] But Xiang Liang ignored his counselor. The Qin army did mobilize its troops and attack Xiang Liang, defeating his army and killing him, just as Xiang Liang's advisor predicted.

In spite of Xiang Liang's arrogance and fall, his nephew Xiang Yu continued to gather troops, winning many battles. In one particular battle, many Chu generals built more than ten ramparts to rescue the city of Julu from the Qin. However, none dared to attack. When Xiang Yu arrived, he led his troops across the river to attack the Qin army. To guarantee his troops' commitment to the coming battle, he burned and sank the boats, destroying any possibility for retreat. They also carried only three days' rations and smashed their cooking pots. Xiang Yu made victory the only option if his men wanted to live to fight another battle.

The Qin troops outnumbered Xiang Yu's army ten to one, but the Chu warriors bellowed so fiercely they struck terror into the hearts of the enemy. As the other Chu generals watched from their ramparts, Xiang Yu defeated the Qin army. Following the battle, Xiang Yu summoned the other Chu generals, and they each vowed their allegiance to him. He became their commander-in-chief. Xiang Yu established himself as overlord of Western Chu and fought against the forces of the Han Dynasty for many years.

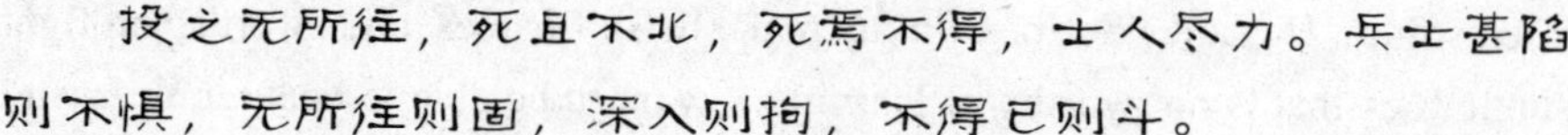

投之无所往，死且不北，死焉不得，士人尽力。兵士甚陷则不惧，无所往则固，深入则拘，不得已则斗。

——孙子

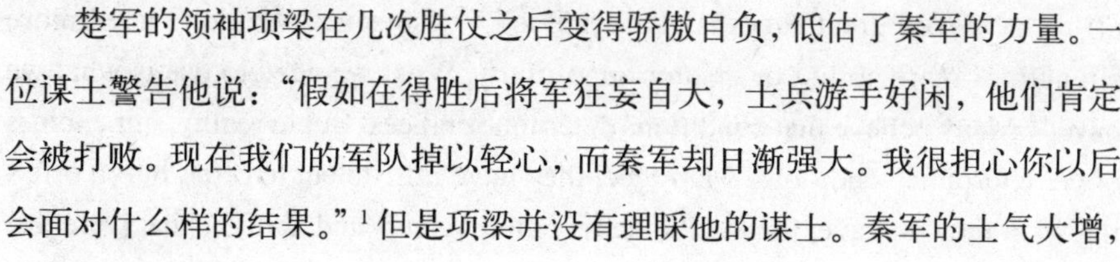

楚军的领袖项梁在几次胜仗之后变得骄傲自负，低估了秦军的力量。一位谋士警告他说：“假如在得胜后将军狂妄自大，士兵游手好闲，他们肯定会被打败。现在我们的军队掉以轻心，而秦军却日渐强大。我很担心你以后会面对什么样的结果。”[1]但是项梁并没有理睬他的谋士。秦军的士气大增，攻击项梁的部队，战胜项梁并且杀死了他，就像项梁的谋士所预测的那样。

虽然项梁傲慢无礼而且落到了那样的下场，他的侄子项羽仍然集合军队，赢得了很多战役。在一场特别的战役中，楚将搭建了十多个营垒，要从秦军手中营救钜鹿，却迟迟不敢发动攻击。当项羽抵达后，他带领军队横跨河流，攻击秦军。为了激励军队一鼓作气的锐气，他把船击沉烧掉，绝了自己的后路。他们只携带三天的口粮，击碎了做饭用的锅。假如士兵还想活着面对下一次战役的话，那么赢得胜利是唯一的选择。

秦军数量远远超过了项羽的军队，是他的十倍，但是楚军勇士的怒吼声让敌军不寒而栗。当其他楚国的将军从自己的堡垒中向外观望的时候，项羽已经战胜秦军。这次战役之后，项羽联合了其他楚将，他们都宣誓效忠项羽。项羽成了军队的元帅，诸侯军队的上将军，率部抵挡汉军多年。

勇于委身的寻常人能够创造非凡的结果。项羽就是一个绝佳的例子。他年轻的时候，对读书并不感兴趣，所以他的叔叔项梁就教导他剑术。他对这个也不感兴趣。他说：“抄写员抄抄名字而已，剑术也只能够对抗一个敌人，

Ordinary people with commitment can produce extraordinary results. Xiang Yu is an excellent example. As a young man he was not satisfied with academic study, so his uncle Xiang Liang taught him to be a swordsman. This also did not interest him. He said, "Scribes simply make lists of names, and swordsmen fight single foes-that is not worthy of learning. I want to be able to beat ten thousand men."[2] Xiang Yu went on to overthrow the emperor and lead a vast army.

Commitment is a matter of personal choice and willpower. Emotions may change as often as the ocean tide, but commitment must remain rock solid. The same can be said about circumstances, but the committed person weathers the bad times and capitalizes on the good. We all think of highly talented people who squandered their gifts from lack of commitment and determination. We also probably know less talented individuals who, due in part to their commitment and effort, achieved great success. Author Basil Walsh said, "We don't need more strength or more ability or greater opportunity. What we need to use is what we have."[3] Many believe that conditions determine choices. But in reality, our choices often determine conditions. Many feel they have little talent to offer, but in offering what they do have, they will discover more talents and abilities that were just waiting for a chance to be used.

Difficulties and problems test commitment. Adversity, however, often strengthens the resolve of those committed. As I mentioned earlier, Coach Walt Braun consistently produced winning football teams and was, on occasion, voted Coach of the Year. I vividly remember how he conditioned our team to handle adverse conditions. Our school's team name was the Marysville Vikings. Any time it rained, snowed, or sleeted, he would smile and ask, "Men, what kind of weather is this?" All fifty of the boys on our team would shout out, "It's Viking weather!" He had us convinced that the worse the weather, the easier it would be for our team to win. Why? Because Vikings thrived in bad weather, and we were the Vikings.

The coach's idea was simple, but it had a great effect on the success of our football team. Simple attitudes of success in the face of adversity can help you achieve positive results. Our team spirit remained consistent regardless of external conditions. While others complain, you will move one step ahead of them into success. Adversity fosters commitment, and commitment fosters hard work. The more effort you invest in something, the harder it will be for you to quit.[4] America's National Football League Hall of Fame coach Vince Lombardi said, "The harder

这一切都不值得学习。我希望能够打败一万精兵。”[2]项羽希望能够带领大军推翻皇帝。

委身是个人选择和意志力的问题。情感就像潮汐一样易变，但是委身却必须像岩石一样稳固。我们也可以用同样的态度看待环境，但是勇于委身的人不仅能够经受风吹雨打，同时能够充分利用风调雨顺的日子。我们都能够回想起周围有这样的人，他们才华横溢却因为缺少委身和决心浪费了自己的天赋。我们也可能认识不如他们聪明的人，由于自己的委身和努力，获得了很大的成就。作家巴兹尔·沃尔什（Basil Walsh）说：“我们所需要的并不是更多力量、更多的才能或者更大的机会，而是利用我们所拥有的一切。”[3]很多人相信环境决定选择，但是在现实生活中，我们的选择常常决定环境。很多人觉得自己没有什么才华，但是当他们提供自己确实拥有的东西时，也会发现更多的才华和才能等待着恰当的时机被发掘出来。

困难和问题能够考验承诺和委身。然而，逆境却能够强化委身的决心。正如我从前所提到的，沃尔特·布劳恩教练带领着一只常胜的橄榄球队，有时候，他被推举为本年度最佳教练。很多事情仍然历历在目，我还记得他调教我们球队如何面对逆境。我们校队的名字是玛莉思维尔海盗队（Marysville Vikings）。每次下雨、下雪或下冰雹的时候，他都会笑着问：“小伙子们，这到底是什么天气？”我们队里的50个男孩儿会大声喊叫道：“是海盗的天气！”他已经让我们相信，天气越糟糕，我们队赢的机会越大。为什么？因为海盗在糟糕的天气里如鱼得水，而我们就是海盗。

教练的想法很简单，但是对我们橄榄球队的成功却产生了很好的效果。在逆境中用简单的态度对待成功可以帮助你赢得积极的结果。不论外在的环境如何，我们的团队精神仍然保持不变。当其他人抱怨的时候，你就可以比他们提前向成功迈进一步。逆境产生委身，委身产生努力的工作。你在一件事情上的投资越大，就越难以放弃。[4]美国国家橄榄球联赛的著名教练文斯·隆巴迪（Vince Lombardi）说：“你越努力，就越不可能屈服。”[5]

什么让你无法勇于委身？荷南·科尔蒂斯（Hernán Cortés），1519年的

you work, the harder it is to surrender."[5]

What keeps you from commitment? Hernán Cortés, a Cuban explorer in 1519, set an example for his men of serious commitment. Cortés sailed from Cuba to the Mexican mainland. His goal was simple: gain riches for his country and fame for himself. He had prepared and worked his whole life for this opportunity. At the age of thirty-four, he set out with his crew. Although they reached the mainland, his men lacked his commitment and began to grumble. Some even talked of mutiny in order to sail home to Cuba. In order to demonstrate his commitment and guarantee theirs, Cortés burned the ship. When difficulties overwhelm us, the old country often tempts us to turn back. Sometimes we need to burn a few ships in our lives in order to guarantee our full commitment.[6]

Sun Tzu said: "Throw the troops into a position from which there is no escape, and even when faced with death they will not flee. For if prepared to die, what can they not achieve? Then officers and men together put forth their utmost efforts. In a desperate situation, they fear nothing; when there is no way out, they stand firm."[7]

一位著名古巴探险家，他在委身方面为自己的手下树立了榜样。科尔蒂斯从古巴出发探索墨西哥大陆。他的目标很简单：为自己的国家赢得财富，为自己赢得名誉。他一生都为了这个机会而准备和努力。在34岁的时候，他和一群人出发了。虽然他们到达了大陆，但是队员却缺少他那样的承诺和委身，变得牢骚满腹。有的人甚至要造反，好返回古巴。为了说明自己的勇气和委身，也为了加强大家的勇气，科尔蒂斯烧毁了船只。当困难冲击我们的时候，我们的老家就会诱惑我们，要我们返回。有时候，我们需要烧毁生活中的这些船只，好保证自己不会三心二意。[6]

孙子说："投之无所往，死且不北，死焉不得，士人尽力。兵士甚陷则不惧，无所往则固，深入则拘，不得已则斗。"[7]（译文：置部队于无路可走的境地，虽死也不会败退。既然死都不怕，官兵就能尽力而战了。士卒深陷危险的境地就不恐惧，无路可走军心就会稳固，深入敌国军队就团结，迫不得已就坚决作战。）

Application

◆ Are you a committed person?

◆ What are your most important goals at work and at home?

◆ Commit time and finances to these goals in order to increase your chances of success.

◆ What boats do you need to burn in order to increase your team's commitment?

Notation Area

Personal observations/Ideas for further exploration/Thoughts to remember

应用

◆你是个勇于委身的人吗？

◆你在工作和家庭中最重要的目标是什么？

◆把时间和财力投入这些目标，好增加你成功的机会。

◆为了增加团队委身的深度，你需要烧毁什么样的船只？

笔记

个人体会／要进一步探讨的想法／要铭记在心的理念

当你回首往事的时候，哪些记忆更让你满意呢？是那些给别人的生活带来快乐的时刻，还是你把他们当作对手胜过或打败的时刻？答案显而易见。

——哈洛德·库希纳

When you come to look back on all that you have done in life, you will get more satisfaction from the pleasure you have brought to other people's lives than you will from the times that you outdid and defeated them.

——*Harold Kushner*

历经时间考验的卓越

True Greatness Tested in Time

第三十一天 大器晚成
——精彩下半场

Day 31:Finishing Well

下半场也是赢家的领袖不仅学会面对现实，同时也相信不可能的事情能够成为可能。

Leaders who finish well learn to face reality while believing in the impossible.

When you come to look back on all that you have done in life, you will get more satisfaction from the pleasure you have brought to other people's lives than you will from the times that you outdid and defeated them.

——*Harold Kushner*

Adults often ask kids, "What do you want to be when you grow up?" Without hesitation, most of them shout out the answer as if they were on a quiz show, "A nurse!" "A doctor!" "A police officer!" "The President!" "A race car driver!"

Once children grow into adults, the question no longer seems relevant. Most of us are too busy with life's daily activities to even ask ourselves, "What do I want to be when I am done growing up?" Many find themselves climbing the ladder of success, only to discover they've climbed a ladder to the wrong building. While prodded by social pressure to work feverishly, forever sacrificing the future for outward appearances of success, many people discover their career choices unfulfilling late in their careers.

What happens to all the young, energetic, idealistic, strong leaders? Why do so many fade away before they reach the climax of their career or-better yet-their potential? In this book I have discussed many aspects of leadership as it relates to teams. I hope to encourage you to finish well and to gain perspective by taking the advice of many who have fallen and many who have succeeded. Those who finish well demonstrate determination, perseverance, and the ability to keep dreaming.

Leaders are determined to get the job done and accomplish the tasks set before them. In order to finish well, be willing to be pushed beyond your comfort zone. As Winston Churchill said, "It is not enough that we do our best; sometimes we have to do what's required." During times when we are pushed outside of our perceived limits, we find we are capable of far more than we ever imagined. Push yourself beyond your comfort zone, but not outside of your giftedness. The first will challenge and cause growth, while the second will bring frustration.

当你回首往事的时候，哪些记忆更让你满意呢？是那些给别人的生活带来快乐的时刻，还是你把他们当作对手胜过或打败的时刻？答案显而易见。

——哈洛德·库希纳

成年人常常问孩子们："你长大后要做什么？"好像参加智力竞赛一样，大部分孩子会毫不犹豫地喊出自己的答案："护士！""医生！""警察！""总统！""赛车选手！"

孩子们一旦长大成人，这个问题似乎就不再重要了。我们大部分人忙于生计，甚至都没有时间问自己："在我长大之后想干什么？"很多人发现自己在攀爬成功的梯子，却爬错了楼。很多人受到社会压力的刺激，疯狂工作，牺牲自己的未来，要获得外表的成功，结果却发现自己的职业选择无法让自己在以后的职业生涯中获得满足。

那些年轻、精力充沛、充满梦想并且坚强的领袖到底怎么了？为什么那么多人在达到职业的顶峰时（或者更好的说法是尚未完全发挥自己的潜能时），就渐渐陨落了呢？这本书中，我们讨论了很多相关团队的领导力层面。我希望也能够鼓励你活出精彩的下半场人生，从很多失败和成功的人身上汲取经验，从全新的视角看待这个问题。那些下半场也保持优秀战绩的人表现出决心、忍耐和坚持梦想的能力。

领袖们有决心完成摆在自己面前的任务。要想拥有精彩的下半场人生，就必须迫使自己离开安逸区。温斯顿·丘吉尔说："我们尽自己最大的可能还远远不够，有时候，我们必须按照当时情形的需要做事。"当我们被迫离开自己熟知的领域时，会发现自己所具备的能力比想象中的更大。迫使自己

A leader must learn to persevere when others give up. They push themselves to continue when they themselves want to quit. Biologist and educator Thomas Huxley stated, "Perhaps the most valuable result of all education is the ability to make yourself do the thing you have to do, when it ought to be done, whether you like it or not."[1]

Last fall my mental strength and perseverance were tested beyond anything I had previously experienced. I learned what it means to "hit the wall." At mile twenty-two of the Beijing marathon with only four miles to go, I slammed against it. My body just shut down. I didn't think about stopping-my legs just stopped. I stood there in the road, surprised and wondering what happened. It was as if my legs disconnected from my brain. It took all my mental and physical focus to start moving them again. Personal goals, however challenging, can be accomplished through perseverance.

Ma Yuan, who lived during the early eastern Han Dynasty, serves as an excellent example of perseverance. He lost his parents when he was a young boy and was raised by his brother Ma Kuang. In spite of his misfortune, he had great ambitions. However, as a youth he did not prove to be the most talented or the brightest. He compared himself to a boy named Zhu Bo who could recite *the Book of Odes* and *the Book of History* at age twelve. In time, Ma Yuan lost hope and asked his brother to send him to the frontier regions where he would live out his life as a shepherd.

In spite of his early lack of success, Ma Kuang saw his brother's potential and encouraged him to persevere. He pointed out that small vessels can be completed in a very short time; however, great vessels take much longer to complete. "Zhu Bo's intelligence is evident to all at a very young age. You, however, are a great vessel taking longer to complete." In this way, his brother encouraged Ma Yuan to work hard and persevere until he reached his goals. Ma Yuan did succeed later in his life and served as prefect of Xincheng and governor of Longxi. At fifty-five, he ascended to the position of General of Fupo and Marquis of Xinxi.[2] For leaders to finish well, perseverance is a must. I remember a saying that hung in our football locker room that said, "Big shots are just little shots that keep on shooting." Be a big shot and keep shooting.

Leaders who finish well learn to face reality while believing in the impossible. They continue dreaming despite circumstances and setbacks. The life of a leader is not easy, and no one guarantees happy endings. It is, however, challenging and

离开安逸区，并不是让我们去自己恩赐所不及的领域。前者能够带来挑战和成长，而后者会让人感到灰心丧气。

当大家都放弃的时候，领袖必须学会忍耐。当他们自己也想放弃的时候，仍然推动自己继续前进。生物学家和教育家托马斯·赫胥黎（Thomas Huxley）说："或许一切教育最宝贵的结果都归结成一种能力：不论自己喜欢与否，在应该的时候，就迫使自己去做该做的事情。"[1]

去年秋天，我的精神力量和忍耐程度都受到了前所未有的考验。我明白了"极限"的真正意思。当我在北京马拉松杯赛中跑到22英里（约35.4公里）的时候，那时还有4英里（约6.4公里）就跑完全程了，我突然停住了。我的身体当时不听使唤了。我并没有想到要停止，但我的腿自然而然就站住了。我站在路中间，感到很惊讶，不知道到底发生了什么。好像自己的双腿和大脑脱节了。我集中自己全部的精神和体力才再次移动双腿。不论挑战多么大的个人目标，都能够靠着忍耐最终成就。

马援是东汉时期的人士，他是忍耐方面的一个好例子。他少年父母双亡，由兄长马况抚养长大。虽然有这样不幸的经历，他却胸怀大志。他年少时并没能像大多数神童那样能倒背如流、过目不忘，表现出超常的聪明才智。一位名叫朱勃的少年在12岁的时候能够把《诗经》和《书经》倒背如流。与他相比，马援自愧不如，相形见绌，对自己失去了希望，让哥哥把自己送往边疆做牧羊人。

虽然马援年少时没有任何成功的迹象，马况却看到了弟弟的潜力，鼓励他坚持下去。他指出，有人是"小器速成"，你是"大器晚成"，要发奋努力。"朱勃的聪明小小年纪就显明出来，但你是大器晚成的人。"这样，哥哥鼓励马援继续努力和忍耐，完成自己的目标。马援后来的确成功了，先后被任命为新成大尹和陇西太守。在55岁的时候，他被提拔为伏波将军和新息侯。[2]领袖如果希望自己拥有精彩的下半场人生，就必须忍耐。我记得在我们橄榄球队更衣室中挂着这么一句话："不积跬步，无以至千里。"从一小步开始迈向你的远大目标，永不放弃。

at times very exciting. As a leader you should hold reality in one hand and a dream in the other. I want to leave you with this:

Remember :

- They will forget to say thank you — you must remember
- They will criticize you when you are not around — you must praise
- Your greatest ideas will create the greatest conflict — use the conflict to perfect your idea
- The battles will grow as your influence increases—learn to love the fight
- Your team will forget your success — but remember your character
- You were created to lead — you will never be truly alive until you do
- You lead not for success, fame, or praise — you lead because you are a leader
- Remember this and you will finish well.

Application

◆ Never stop dreaming.

◆ Finish the race.

Notation Area

Personal observations/Ideas for further exploration/Thoughts to remember

下半场也是赢家的领袖不仅学会面对现实，同时也相信不可能的事情能够成为可能。尽管环境艰辛、困难重重，他们却持续保持自己的梦想。领袖的生活并不容易，没有人能够保证一个快乐的结局。然而，这一切却充满挑战，甚至有些会让人感到振奋不已。作为领袖，你应该一手抓住现实，一手抓住梦想。我希望你记住：

- 他们会忘记说“谢谢”——你必须要记住；
- 当你不在的时候，他们会批评你——你必须赞美；
- 你最大的理想会引发带来最大的冲突——利用冲突完善自己的理想；
- 随着影响力的增加，战斗会愈演愈烈——学会珍视战斗；
- 你的团队会忘记你的成功——但是会记住你的品格；
- 你被造乃是为了要带领——除非你做到了，否则你没有真正活过；
- 你带领并非为了成功、名誉或赞美——你带领因为你是领袖。
- 记住这些，你就会拥有精彩的下半场人生。

应用

◆永远都不要失去梦想。

◆跑完全程。

笔记

个人体会／要进一步探讨的想法／要铭记在心的理念

End Notes

Introduction

1. S. R. Levine and M. A. Crom, *The Leader in You* (New York: Pocket Books, 1993).

Section I: Are You a Team Leader?

Day 1: Leadership Style

1. S. M. Qian, *Selections from Records of the Historian* (Beijing: New World Press, 2002), 189.
2. S. R. Levine and M. A. Crom, *The Leader in You* (New York: Pocket Books, 1993), 18.
3. Qian, *Selections from Records of the Historian*, 115.

Day 2: Traits of Leaders

1. Z. Lingzhong and H. Zenren, *The Stories Behind 100 Chinese Idioms* (Beijing: Beijing Foreign Language Printing House, 1999), 74.
2. Ibid.
3. S. A. Kirkpatrick and E. A. Locke, Leadership: So Traits Really Matter? (*Academy of Management Executive* May, 1991), 48. Also found in S. P. Robbins and M. Coulter, *Management*, 5th ed. (Upper Saddle River, New Jersey: Prentice Hall, 1996), 574.

Section II: Successful Leaders Develop Teams

Day 3: Teamwork

1. S. M. Qian, *Selections from Records of the Historian* (Beijing: New World Press, 2002), 212-213.
2. J. C. Maxwell, *The 17 Essential Qualities of a Team Player* (Nashville: Thomas Nelson Publishers, 2002), 17-18.

Day 4: Attracting and Keeping Talented People

1. S. M. Qian, *Selections from Records of the Historian* (Beijing: New World Press, 2002), 139.
2. Ibid.
3. *Hiring and Keeping the Best People* (Boston: Harvard Business School Press, 2002), 78.
4. Ibid.
5. Ibid.

Day 5: Charisma

1. S. Tzu, *The Art of War* (Beijing: Foreign Language Research Press, 1997), 17.
2. *Merriam-Webster's Collegiate Dictionary*, 10th ed., s.v. "Charisma."
3. J. C. Maxwell, *Be a People Person* (Colorado Springs: Nexgen, 1989), 33-34.

Day 6: Do the Small Stuff

1. S. M. Qian, *Selections from Records of the Historian* (Beijing: New World Press, 2002), 60-61.

Section III: Successful Leaders Lead from Within

Day 7: Enthusiasm to Succeed

1. X. Wang, *The Art of Management: Sixteen Strategies of Zhuge Liang*, trans. Alan Chong (Singapore: Asiapac Books, 1995), 2-11.

Day 8: Enlargers

1. C. Tang, *A Treasury of China's Wisdom* (Beijing: Foreign Language Press, 1996), 158-160.
2. Ibid., 160.
3. S. R. Levine and M. A. Crom, *The Leader in You* (New York: Pocket Books, 1993), 32.
4. J. C. Maxwell, *The 17 Essential Qualities of a Team Player* (Nashville: Thomas Nelson Publishers, 2002), 111.

Day 9: Other-Centeredness

1. S. M. Qian, *Selections from Records of the Historian* (Beijing: New World Press, 2002), 189.
2. S. R. Levine and M. A. Crom, *The Leader in You* (New York: Pocket Books, 1993), 55-56.
3. Ibid., 56.

Day 10: Exceed Expectations

1. S. Tzu, *The Art of War* (Beijing: Foreign Language Research Press, 1997), 42.
2. S. R. Levine and M. A. Crom, *The Leader in You* (New York: Pocket Books, 1993), 72.
3. Ibid.
4. Ibid., 76.

Section IV: Successful Leaders Master Change and Conflict

Day 11: The Leader's Role in Change

1. C. Tang, *A Treasury of China's Wisdom* (Beijing: Foreign Language Press, 1996), 232-233.
2. S. R. Levine and M. A. Crom, *The Leader in You* (New York: Pocket Books, 1993), 2.
3. G. Barna, *Leaders on Leadership* (Ventura, California: Regal, 1997), 189.
4. Levine and Crom, *The Leader in You*, 8.
5. J. C. Maxwell, *The 17 Essential Qualities of a Team Player* (Nashville: Thomas Nelson Publishers, 2002), 9.
6. Ibid.
7. Barna, *Leaders on Leadership*, 201.

Day 12: The Challenges of Change

1. B. Y. Yin, *100 Chinese Idioms and Set Phrases*, trans. Hui Han (Beijing: Sinolingua, 1999), 14.
2. G. Barna, *Leaders on Leadership* (Ventura, California: Regal, 1997), 207-208.

Day 13: The Changing Environment

1. C. Tang, *A Treasury of China's Wisdom* (Beijing: Foreign Language Press, 1996), 164-165.
2. S. P. Robbins and M. Coulter, *Management*, 5th ed. (Upper Saddle River, New Jersey: Prentice Hall, 1996), 424.
3. G. Barna; *Leaders on Leadership* (Ventura, California: Regal, 1997), 187.
4. Ibid., 191.

Day 14: Sources of Change

1. Space Shuttle. http://www.kepu.gov.cn/zlg/htfj/y2.htm
2. S. P. Robbins and M. Coulter, *Management*, 5th ed. (Upper Saddle River, New Jersey: Prentice Hall, 1996), 428.
3. R. P. Vecchio, *Organizational Behavior*, 3d ed. (Orlando: Dryden Press, 1995), 660.
4. Ibid., 660-661.
5. Robbins and Coulter, *Management*, 434.

Day 15: Conflict as a Tool

1. S. Tzu, *The Art of War* (Beijing: Foreign Language Research Press, 1997), 9.
2. G. Barna, *Leaders on Leadership* (Ventura, California: Regal, 1997), 240.

3. S. P. Robbins and M. Coulter, *Management*, 5th ed. (Upper Saddle River, New Jersey: Prentice Hall, 1996), 631.
4. *Merriam-Webster's Collegiate Dictionary*, 10th ed., s.v. "Confict."
5. Barna, *Leaders on Leadership*, 240.
6. Robbins and Coulter, *Management*, 633.

Day 16: Conflict Management as a Stimulant

1. S. Tan, *Best Chinese Idioms*, trans. Tang Bowen, vol. 2 (Hong Kong: Hai Feng, 1998), 49.
2. S. P. Robbins and M. Coulter, *Management*, 5th ed. (Upper Saddle River, New Jersey: Prentice Hall, 1996), 635.
3. Ibid.
4. Ibid., 637.
5. R. Clinton and P. Leavenworth, *Starting Well* (Altadena, California: Barnabas Publishers, 1994), 210-211.

Section V: Successful Leaders See Beyond the Surface

Day 17: Team as Culture

1. S. Tzu, *The Art of War* (Beijing: Foreign Language Research Press, 1997), 14.
2. E. H. Schein, *Organizational Culture and Leadership*, 2d ed. (San Francisco: Jossey-Bass, 1992), 231.

Day 18: Creating a Culture

1. S. M. Qian, *Selections from Records of the Historian* (Beijing: New World Press, 2002), 87-88.
2. Ibid., 109.
3. E. H. Schein, *Organizational Culture and Leadership*, 2d ed. (San Francisco: Jossey-Bass, 1992), 231.
4. G. Barna, *Leaders on Leadership* (Ventura, California: Regal, 1997), 267. Also found in Schein, *Organizational Culture and Leadership*, 238.
5. Barna, *Leaders on Leadership*, 267.
6. S. P. Robbins and M. Coulter, *Management*, 5th ed. (Upper Saddle River, New Jersey: Prentice Hall, 1996), 498.
7. Adapted from D. Fike, Lecture Notes (Hong Kong, 1996)

Day 19: Leaders Use or Abuse Power

1. Confucius, *Confucius, The Analects*, trans. D. C. Lau (New York: Penguin Books, 1979), 65.

2. S. M. Qian, *Selections from Records of the Historian* (Beijing: New World Press, 2002), 100.
3. Adapted from J. Brothers, "What Do You Know about Power People?", *Los Angeles Times, 28 September* 1994. Also found in P. V. Lewis, *Transformational Leadership* (Nashville: Broadman & Holman, 1996), 24.

Day 20: Knowing Your Mental and Emotional Challenges

1. S. Tzu, *The Art of War* (Beijing: Foreign Language Research Press, 1997), 29.
2. Adapted from S. M. Qian, *Selections from Records of the Historian* (Beijing: New World Press, 2002), 98.
3. Confucius, *Confucius, The Analects*, trans. D. C. Lau (New York: Penguin Books, 1979), 65.

Section VI: Successful Leaders Guide Successful Teams

Day 21: Develop Your Team's Strengths

1. X. Wang, *The Art of Management: Sixteen Strategies of Zhuge Liang*, trans. Alan Chong (Singapore: Asiapac Books, 1995), 103.
2. *Hiring and Keeping the Best People* (Boston: Harvard Business School Press, 2002), 91.
3. Ibid.

Day 22: Leading them with Kindness

1. S. Tzu, *The Art of War* (Beijing: Foreign Language Research Press, 1998), 38.

Day 23: Leaders' Behavior

1. Confucius, *Confucius, The Analects*, trans. D. C. Lau (New York: Penguin Books, 1979), 63.
2. S. P. Robbins and M. Coulter, *Management*, 5th ed. (Upper Saddle River, New Jersey: Prentice Hall, 1996), 576.

Day 24: Situation-Sensitive Leading Is Strong Leadership

1. S. Tzu, *The Art of War* (Beijing: Foreign Language Research Press, 1997), 24-25.
2. Ibid.
3. Adapted from S. P. Robbins and M. Coulter, *Management*, 5th ed. (Upper Saddle River, New Jersey: Prentice Hall, 1996), 576.

Day 25: Praising Your Team to Greatness

1. Z. Lingzhong and H. Zenren, *The Stories Behind 100 Chinese Idioms* (Beijing: Beijing Foreign Language Printing House, 1999), 35-36.

2. Ibid.
3. R. P. Vecchio, *Organizational Behavior*, 3d ed. (Orlando: Dryden Press, 1995), 340.
4. Ibid.
5. Ibid., 226-227.

Section VII: Successful Leaders Create Leaders

Day 26: Communication

1. Z. Lingzhong and H. Zenren, *The Stories Behind 100 Chinese Idioms* (Beijing: Beijing Foreign Language Printing House, 1999), 41.
2. J. C. Maxwell, *Be a People Person* (Colorado Springs: Nexgen, 1989), 21.
3. S. R. Levine and M. A. Crom, *The Leader in You* (New York: Pocket Books, 1993), 7.
4. J. C. Maxwell, *Be a People Person* (Colorado Springs: Nexgen, 1989), 28.

Day 27: Trust

1. S. M. Qian, *Selections from Records of the Historian* (Beijing: New World Press, 2002), 93-94.
2. S. R. Levine and M. A. Crom, *The Leader in You* (New York: Pocket Books, 1993), 35.
3. J. C. Maxwell, *The 17 Essential Qualities of a Team Player* (Nashville: Thomas Nelson Publishers, 2002), 35.
4. Levine and Crom, *The Leader in You*, 7.

Day 28: Listening

1. S. Tzu, *The Art of War* (Beijing: Foreign Language Research Press, 1997), 16.
2. S. R. Levine and M. A. Crom, *The Leader in You* (New York: Pocket Books, 1993), 81.
3. Ibid., 89.
4. Ibid., 87.

Day 29: Risk and Responsibility

1. S. M. Qian, *Selections from Records of the Historian* (Beijing: New World Press, 2002), 206.
2. J. C. Maxwell, *The 17 Essential Qualities of a Team Player* (Nashville: Thomas Nelson Publishers, 2002), 51.

Day 30: Commitment

1. S. M. Qian, *Selections from Records of the Historian* (Beijing: New World Press, 2002), 66.
2. Ibid., 58.
3. J. C. Maxwell, *The 17 Essential Qualities of a Team Player* (Nashville: Thomas

Nelson Publishers, 2002), 23-24.
4. Ibid.
5. Ibid., 23.
6. Ibid.
7. S. Tzu, *The Art of War* (Beijing: Foreign Language Research Press, 1997), 48.

Day 31: Finishing Well

1. J. C. Maxwell, *The 17 Essential Qualities of a Team Player* (Nashville: Thomas Nelson Publishers, 2002), 60-61.
2. S. Tan, *Best Chinese Idioms*, trans. Tang Bowen, vol. 2 (Hong Kong: Hai Feng, 1998), 25.

Bibliography

- Barna, G. Leaders on Leadership. Ventura, California: Regal, 1997.
- Confucius. Confucius, The Analects. Translated by D. C. Lau. New York:Penguin Books, 1979.
- Clinton, R. and P. Leavenworth. Starting Well. Altadena, California:Barnabas Publishers, 1994.
- Fike, D. Lecture Notes. (Hong Kong, 1996).
- Hiring and Keeping the Best People. Boston: Harvard Business SchoolPress, 2002.
- Kirkpatrick, S. A. and E. A. Locke (1991). Leadership: So Traits ReallyMatter? Academy of Management Executive (May).
- Levine, S. R. and M. A. Crom. The Leader in You. New York: Pocket Books,1993.
- Lewis, P. V. Transformational Leadership. Nashville: Broadman & Holman,1996.
- Lingzhong, Z. and H. Zenren. The Stories Behind 100 Chinese Idioms.Beijing: Beijing Foreign Language Printing House, 1999.
- Maxwell, J. C. Be a People Person. Colorado Springs: Nexgen, 1989.
- Maxwell, J. C. The 17 Essential Qualities of a Team Player. Nashville:Thomas Nelson Publishers, 2002.
- Qian, S. M. Selections from Records of the Historian. Beijing: New World Press, 2002.
- Robbins, S. P. and M. Coulter. Management. 5th ed. Upper Saddle River,New Jersey: Prentice Hall, 1996.
- Schein, E. H. Organizational Culture and Leadership. 2d ed. San Francisco: Jossey-Bass, 1992.
- Space Shuttle. http://www.kepu.gov.cn/zlg/htfj/y2.htm
- Tan, S. Best Chinese Idioms. Translated by Tang Bowen. Vol. 2. Hong Kong: Hai Feng, 1998.
- Tang, C. A Treasury of China's Wisdom. Beijing: Foreign Language Press, 1996.
- Tzu, S. The Art of War. Beijing: Foreign Language Research Press, 1998.
- Vecchio, R. P. Organizational Behavior. 3d ed. Orlando: Dryden Press, 1995.
- Wang, X. The Art of Management: Sixteen Strategies of Zhuge Liang. Translated by Alan Chong. Singapore: Asiapac Books, 1995.
- Yin, B. Y. 100 Chinese Idioms and Set Phrases. Translated by Hui Han. Beijing: Sinolingua, 1999.

This book articulates values that have helped me advance in my life and career. Success lies in discipline, self-control plus 100% self-exertion.

—— Peter Lin (Mr. China 2002 - 2005, International Master of Sports)

这本书清楚地展示了能帮助我在生命和事业上奋力前行的价值。成功在于自律、节制，加上百分百的付出。

——林沛渠（2002–2005 度中国健美先生，国际运动健将）